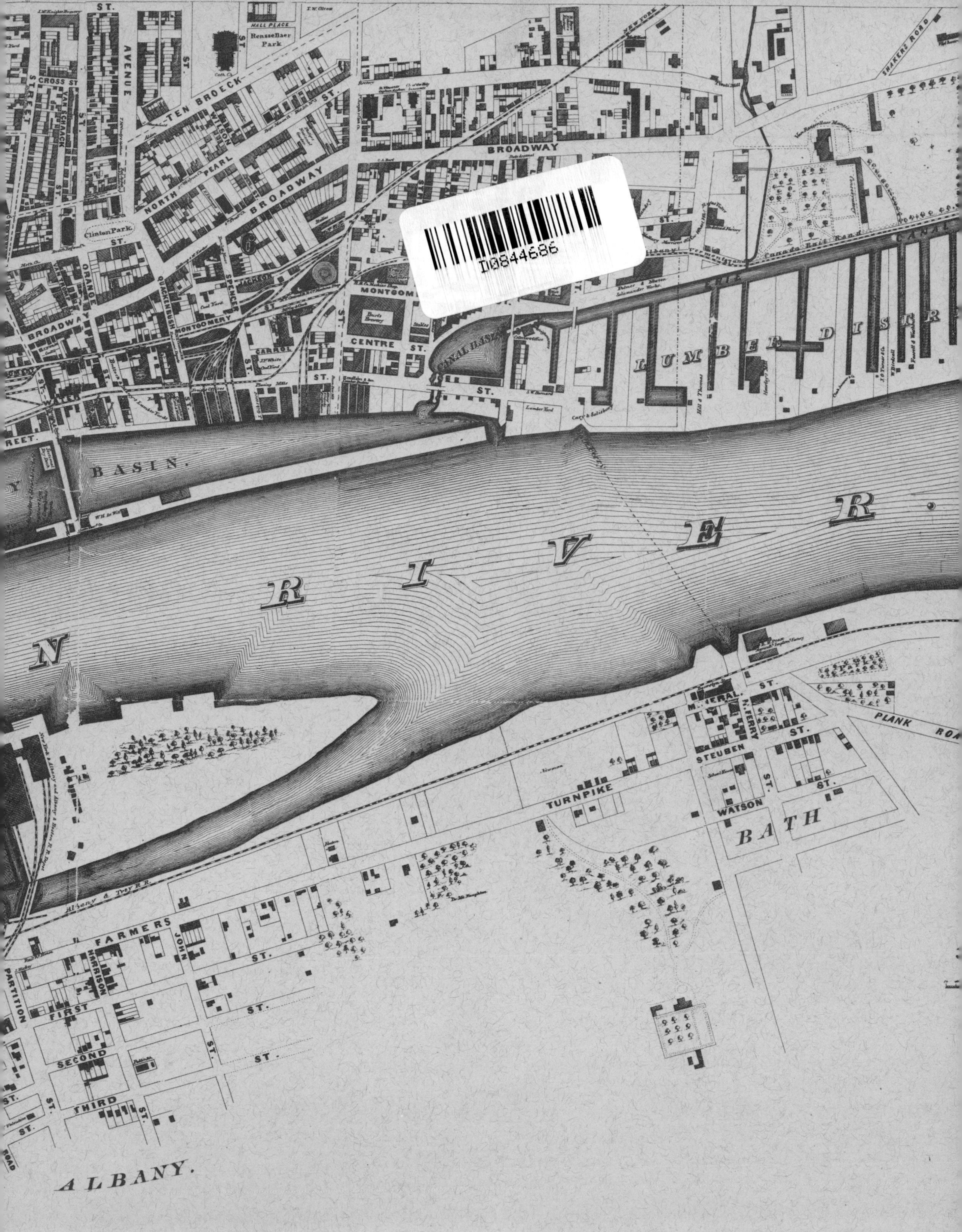

ST.
HALL PLACE
Rensselaer Park
AVENUE
CROSS ST
VAN SCHAICK
STREET
TEN BROECK
WILSON
NORTH PEARL
BROADWAY
Clinton Park
ORANGE
ST.
QUACKENBUSH
SPENCER
MONTGOMERY
BROADWAY
CARROL
MONTGOMERY
CENTRE ST.
CANAL BASIN
BROADWAY
SHAKERS ROAD
CANAL
ERIE
LUMBER DISTR
BASIN.
R I V E R
N
MINERAL
N. FERRY
ST.
STEUBEN
PLANK ROA
TURNPIKE
WATSON
ST.
BATH
Albany & Troy R.R.
FARMERS
JOHN
HARRISON
ST.
PARTITION
FIRST
ST.
SECOND
ST.
THIRD
ST.
ROAD
ALBANY.
D0844686

To Dad, '81
Christmas
w love
Ken + Sue

ALBANY

CAPITAL CITY

ON THE HUDSON

An Illustrated History by John J. McEneny

picture research by Dennis Holzman

special material by Robert W. Arnold III

editorial coordination by Margaret Tropp

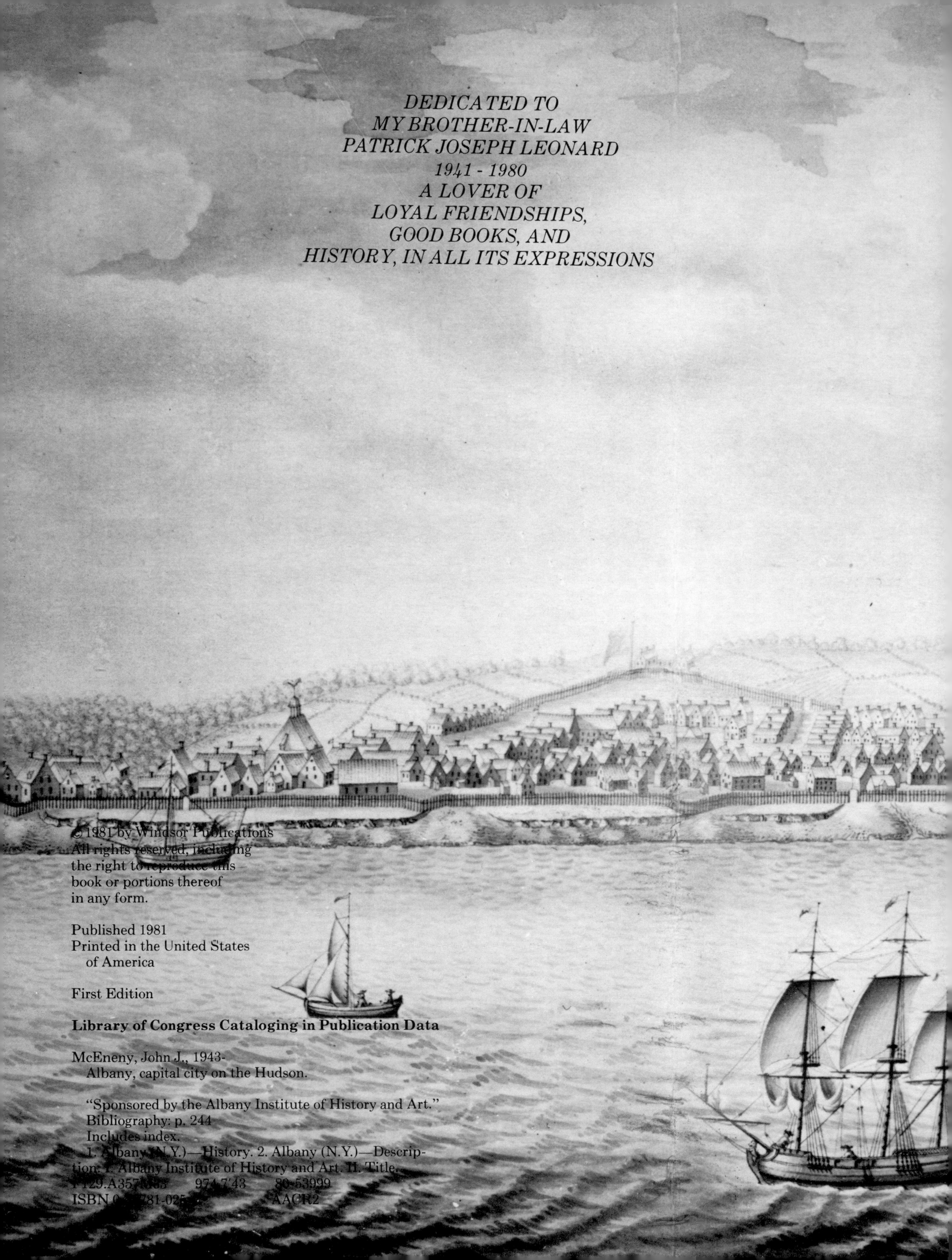

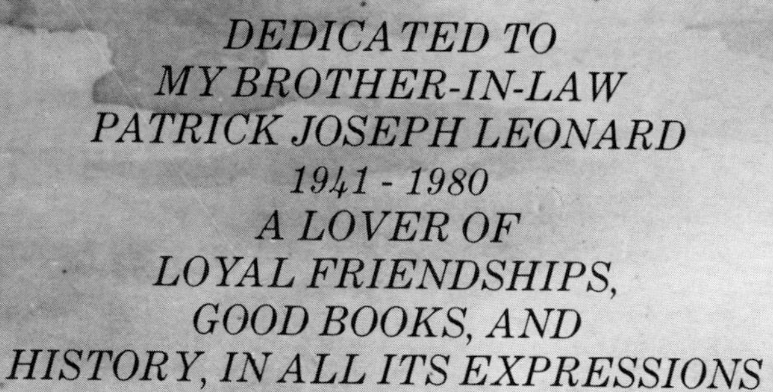

DEDICATED TO
MY BROTHER-IN-LAW
PATRICK JOSEPH LEONARD
1941 - 1980
A LOVER OF
LOYAL FRIENDSHIPS,
GOOD BOOKS, AND
HISTORY, IN ALL ITS EXPRESSIONS

Published 1981
Printed in the United States
of America

First Edition

Library of Congress Cataloging in Publication Data

McEneny, John J., 1943-
Albany, capital city on the Hudson.

"Sponsored by the Albany Institute of History and Art."
Bibliography: p. 244
Includes index.
1. Albany (N.Y.)—History. 2. Albany (N.Y.)—Description. I. Albany Institute of History and Art. II. Title.
F129.A357M33 974.7'43 80-53999
ISBN 0-89781-025-8 AACR2

TABLE OF CONTENTS

In this recently discovered 1763 wash drawing, Albany is shown circa 1715 as a fledgling, stockaded fur trading and military post dominated by Fort Frederick. The blockhouse on the north gate in the stockade is near the site of present-day Orange Street. The cluster of tall buildings just behind the riverbank and north of the blockhouse appears to include today's restored Quackenbush House. Its exact date of construction remains a mystery.

Albany Institute of History and Art

FOREWORD

Albany, as it extends westward from the great river where it was first established as a Dutch fur-trading post 367 years ago, to the dunes and pitch pine of the sand plains on the city's outskirts, is a celebration of contrasts. In many ways Albany is a 19th-century city; yet it is now crowned by Nelson Rockefeller's architectural vision of the 21st century.

Like other settlements that cover America, Albany can be regarded as a patchwork quilt. The varied colors of Albany's distinctive neighborhoods, the diverse cultural textures, and the many shapes of its topography make it wonderfully unique. The myriad fabrics that have been pieced and sewn together through time have mostly proven strong and durable. Some wear and tear, however, have resulted from the city's occupying an important place in the course of history, so that portions have been replaced or restored. Beneath the design is an interlining composed of the lives and dreams of immigrants drawn from many lands, whose labors have firmly stitched in the swatches representing the city's basic industries. Some design elements look arbitrary or haphazard, as in a crazy-quilt. In other places they seem consciously shaped and deliberately placed.

Each passing glance at Albany invites another look, for there are many features which should draw the intrigued attention of both lovers and critics of the city. Here is a special hue, a curious texture, a new addition, or an unnoticed embellishment; perhaps something comes sharply and suddenly into focus, to be scrutinized in a new way by an informed eye that now can translate what once seemed dull, ugly, or commonplace.

Like some treasured, oft-mended patchwork quilt passed on from family forebears, today's Albany transmits a special warmth and value to those who seek to understand its design and handiwork.

Since I approach Albany history in an eclectic way, I have informally and discursively recounted the city's past. After presenting Albany's foundations in the colonial and early federal periods, I gathered together aspects of the city's development and character into units which do not strictly adhere to a chronological format. Therefore, Robert W. Arnold III has created, specially for this book, an initial chapter that serves as a timeline for the rest of the tale of Albany.

John J. McEneny
Albany, New York
August 1981

INTRODUCTION

Although there have been many excellent works published in the last few years on particular facets of Albany's past and present, Albanians for more than a generation have lacked an updated, comprehensive, and readable presentation of their city's history. Through sponsoring this book, the Albany Institute of History and Art has taken the initiative to fill an important need in our community.

When I first heard of the plans for this project, I could think of no one better suited than John McEneny to tell the story of Albany in an absorbing way that would also make it relevant to today's generations. Commissioner McEneny has long been renowned among us for his enthusiastic and thorough knowledge of Albany's past, especially in its connections with the present city and its citizens.

Jack shows both originality and insight in portraying and explaining the unique, diverse, and enduring qualities in his native city. His personal style of narration, coupled with the wide variety of illustrations painstakingly gathered by Dennis Holzman, has guaranteed this book's role for years to come as a valuable and attractive illumination of Albany's evolution and character. Its chronology and bibliography will help to make it a standard reference work.

I congratulate the author and his writing assistants, the picture researcher, the sponsor, and all others who have worked so long and well on this fine book that is sure to increase our appreciation of Albany.

—Erastus Corning 2nd
Mayor of Albany
August 1981

CHAPTER 1

ALBANY THROUGH TIME: A CHRONOLOGICAL NARRATIVE

by Robert W. Arnold III

Wilderness and Tribes: Before the 17th Century

In the Northeastern section of North America, the dominant element was the forest: trees in their millions stretching in almost unbroken ranks from the Atlantic Ocean to the Mississippi River in the interior. These woodlands, and the waterways within them, would shape the cultures of their earliest human inhabitants and affect the lives and livelihoods of the first white settlers from Europe.

ca. A.D. 1000 – A.D. 1300: The place that would become Albany was in the heart of the Eastern Woodlands, nearly at the confluence of this region's two principal navigable rivers, later called the Hudson and the Mohawk. The last great immigration of Algonkian-speaking people had rolled into the area of what is now New York State shortly before 1000 A.D., and for more than three centuries would dominate the region.

Of the widely dispersed Algonkian nations the most dominant in the Albany vicinity was the Mahikan, whose people called the land *Mahikan-aki.* Their principal town was at Schodack, and a satellite community occupied the site of Albany, a place they called *Pempotowwuthut–Muhhcanneuw,* meaning "the fireplace of the Mahikan nation." From Schodack, their sachem (chief) ruled a

Corn harvest at Mount Morris (a diorama)

New York State Archives

dominion reaching from Lake Champlain to the Catskill Creek. On the east bank of the Hudson River Mahikan power extended south to present-day Poughkeepsie. To Schodack and the primordial site of Albany came the Indian traders, diplomats, and chieftains of the surrounding nations. From the first Albany was an intersection of commercial and political traffic.

ca. A.D. 1300 – A.D. 1600: Threatening the Mahikan-aki were Iroquoian-speaking people who around A.D. 1300 began filtering into the area that became New York. Iroquoian nations included the Senecas, their offshoot Cayuagas, the Onondagas, the Mohawks and their cadet branch Oneidas, the Eries, the Hurons, the Susquehannocks, and many others. Wherever they came, the Algonkians were pushed out, killed, or assimilated.

Sometime between 1450 and 1570 the Huron chief Deganawidah came to the Iroquois people of the New York State area to settle the differences among them. He brought a plan for peace based on harmony, law, and justice. Iroquois legend tells that Deganawidah converted Hiawatha (a Mohawk or an Onondaga), who agreed to spread the message among the tribes, resulting finally in formation of the League of the Five Nations.

By 1600 the Five Nations occupied most of central New York west of the Genesee River to Lake Champlain, with the Mohawks and the Oneidas nearest Albany. During the coming European colonization, the Iroquois would assume a position of major influence; they would be the anvil on which the French and the English in North America tried one another for a century. The Iroquois shared a common fate with their ancient Algonkian enemies: both faced a sociological and demographic catastrophe brought on by white colonization.

Exposure to European civilization created a social revolution among the American Indians; the encounter involved two cultures with mutually unintelligible world views. The Indian and the white man had different concepts of property ownership; Indian life was largely communal; European, individualistic and competitive. The whites possessed a written language, were advanced in the organization of business, possessed sophisticated weapons and machinery, and were urban-inclined. Indian time sense was cyclical; European, linear.

New York State Archives

Seneca hunter's lodge (a diorama)

The Voyagers: 1524-1624

1524: White men first saw the Hudson River, that vast drain of the virgin woodlands' interior, when Giovanni de Verrazano, sailing for Francois de Valois, King of France, steered into New York Bay. His ship's small boat was rowed into the upper bay, which Verrazano described as a beautiful lake formed by a larger river. The land was named by Francis I as *La Nouvelle France,* the Hudson *La Grande Rivière.*

1540: Albany tradition maintains that in this year French fur traders in barques sailed upriver as far as Cohoes, to erect a fortified post on an island on the west side of the Hudson just south of the present city of Albany. But before their fort was completed, a freshet carried away its walls and the project was abandoned. (Its outline, however, was visible to Jasper Danckaerts nearly 150 years later.)

Then Deganawidah and Hiawatha together created the laws of the Great Peace, and for each part of the law, they talked the words into wampum so that they could better remember it.

When they had created the Great Law, Deganawidah and Hiawatha, together with chiefs of the Mohawk Nation, brought the Good Message to the Mohawks' less powerful neighbors, the Oneidas, who lived to the west. Gladly did the Oneidas accept the New Mind.

Next Deganawidah and Hiawatha approached the Cayugas, a small nation living between the Onondagas and the Senecas. They were glad of the protection of the Great Peace and quickly took hold of it. Then Deganawidah and Hiawatha persuaded all the Onondaga chiefs except Atotarho to grasp the Good Message. The two leaders together with the chiefs of the four nations, were now able to persuade the warlike Seneca, the nation farthest to the west, to take hold of the Great Peace.

Paul A.W. Wallace. *The White Roots of Peace.* Philadelphia: University of Pennsylvania Press, 1946.

1609: As Holland's long war for independence from Spain slowed to a truce, the Dutch entered their golden age of economic prosperity, religious toleration, and artistic florescence. An English mariner, Henry Hudson, was engaged by the Dutch East India Company to seek La Grande Rivière and press along its channel to India, land of exotic spices and beautiful textiles. The company "shall in the first place equip a small vessel or yacht of about 30 lasts [60 tons] burden with which, well provided with men, provisions, and other necessaries, . . . Hudson shall . . . sail in order to search for a passage by the North. . . ."

Fort Orange Club

Henry Hudson's ship Half Moon

Hudson's *Half Moon* sailed up the great river as far as the Albany area, which was visited in September. Around Albany, where the contact with Indians was friendly, the Dutch would later establish fairly amicable relations with the Indians; but downstream, where the crew's treatment of the natives had been less gentle, the Indians would remember, so that the Dutch relationship with those tribes remained uneasy. A Dutch historian afterwards reporting on Hudson's voyage commented that: "They found this a good place for cod-fishing, as also for traffic in good skins and furs, which were to be got there at a very low price." Clearly, though, Hudson's River did not provide the sought-for Northwest Passage to the Orient.

Only weeks after Hudson's departure, French explorer Samuel de Champlain, moving down from Canada with two Frenchmen and 60 Hurons, had a significant encounter with a band of 200 Iroquois near Ticonderoga. Champlain's treatment of the Iroquois earned the French their enmity, although French priests, traders, and envoys would at times wield considerable influence among the Five Nations.

Trade alone attracted the Dutch to Hudson's River, not the promise of colonizing some Zion in the wilderness. While God, gold, and glory motivated the Spaniards, gold alone did nicely for the Dutch. Veterans of Hudson's voyage soon persuaded Amsterdam merchants to send a vessel to trade for furs with the natives. By 1614 a Dutch map showed "Fort Nassoureen," built by Hendrick Christiaensen on the site of the French post on Castle Island, inside a stockade 50 feet square. In 1618 it too would be wrecked by a freshet, and the transient population of fur traders abandoned it for a new location at the mouth of the Normanskill.

1621: The Lord States-General of the Netherlands (Holland) chartered the Dutch West India Company, granting exclusive 24-year trading privileges on the West African coast and in the West Indies and America, as well as the right to make contacts and alliances with the nations of those places. The Company soon afterwards founded New Netherland in North America; it would jealously guard its territories and cultivate good relations with the fur-selling Indians of the regions it claimed along the Hudson, Connecticut, and Delaware rivers. Since their colony was mainly maritime, its principal settlements would be built on waterways navigable by ship. It established a main office later at New Amsterdam (now New York City).

The Dutch: 1624–1664

1624: Thirty families of French-speaking Walloons, Protestant refugees from the Spanish, sailed from Amsterdam in the *Nieu Nederlandt*. A dozen families were landed to counter a threatened French settlement at Manhattan; instead, they located New Amsterdam at first on Governors Island. The remainder continued upriver to land at the site of Albany and there constructed Fort Orange, named in honor of Maurice, Prince of Orange.

1626: Pieter Minuit, a shrewd and determined man whose coarseness at times offended those he governed, became director of New Netherland for the Dutch West India Company. Minuit purchased Manhattan Island from the Indians. The total European population of the New Netherland colony was about 200 persons.

A crude little settlement grew up around the small fort at Fort Orange. It was recommended that families arrive in New Netherland in spring, so that in their first year they could clear land, build shelters, and grow subsistence crops. In the winter the settler would be able to fell timber, and the next summer acquire livestock and erect houses, barns, and outbuildings.

In the ongoing friction between Algonkian and Iroquois, the war between the local Mahikans and Mohawks led the Mahikans to seek Dutch support. The commander of Fort Orange, Daniel Van Krieckebeck, and six soldiers advanced west against the Mohawks; they fell into an ambush somewhere in the vicinity of what is now Lincoln Park.

1629: The directors of the Dutch West India Company decided that its expense in sending ships and troops

"I, ——-, promise and swear that I shall be true and faithful to the noble Patroon and Co-directors, or those who represent them here, and to the Hon'ble Director, Commissioners and Council, subjecting myself to the Court of the Colonie; and I promise to demean myself as a good and faithful inhabitant or Burgher, without exciting any opposition, tumult or noise; but on the contrary, as a loyal inhabitant, to maintain and support offensively and defensively, against every one, the Right and Jurisdiction of the Colonie. And with reverence and fear of the Lord, and uplifting of both the first fingers of the right hand, I say—SO TRULY HELP ME GOD ALMIGHTY."—Oath taken by the Colonists of Rensselaerswyck to the Patroon.

and building fortifications was cutting too deeply into their profit margin and stopped sending settlers. They adopted a new concept of colonization, the *patroon* system, in which members of the Dutch West India Company who established a settlement of 50 adult tenants in New Netherland could obtain tracts of land 16 miles along one shore of a navigable waterway, or 8 miles on each bank. The patroon was lord of his domain; as in Europe, tenants were not to hunt, fish, trade, or mill lumber or grain without his consent.

The first patroon was an Amsterdam pearl and diamond merchant, Kiliaen Van Rensselaer; he selected land on the west bank of the Hudson River and bought title to it from the Indians. A patroon had to lay out large sums of money in sending out cattle, horses, brewing vats, tools, and millstones and in recruiting artisans and indenturing others. Of the five patroonships granted, only Van Rensselaer's would endure; his property included present-day Albany, Rensselaer, and Columbia counties, all or in part—700,000 acres, altogether.

1640: Failing to populate New Netherland rapidly, the Dutch West India Company modified its criteria for colonization.

New Netherland offered a lucrative fur trade and religious toleration rare in the Counter-Reformation era. Its rich and fertile land was much touted by recruitment literature distributed by the Dutch West India Company and the patroons. Settlers came from throughout Europe under Dutch sponsorship. Although the patroon system is better known, most settlers were independent proprietors who owned their own land. By the time the colony was seized by England in 1664, it was populated by 8,000 Europeans. At this time New Netherland claimed parts of present-day New York, New Jersey, Connecticut, Delaware, and Pennsylvania—claims disputed by England, France, and Spain.

The quick and considerable money to be made in the fur trade steadily diverted the energies of those artisans and farmers who were induced to settle. The effects of European contact were also beginning to be felt by the Indians: the brass kettle replaced traditional ceramic vessels, and

Dutch soldier, 1630

firearms, the bow; steel tools superseded worked flint, bone, or antler. Already the hunting grounds of the Five Nations were drained of beaver (in 1633 alone 30,000 pelts were shipped out), and the Iroquois pressured the Hurons for control of the Great Lakes fur trade.

1642: A French Jesuit missionary, Father Jogues, was taken captive by the Mohawks and tortured. Escaping, he took refuge in Albany. Based on his stay there, Jogues provided an early description of Albany: "There are two things in this settlement . . . first, a miserable little fort called Fort Orange, built of logs, with four or five pieces of Breteuil cannon and as many swivels. . . . Second, a colony sent here by this Rensselaer, who is the Patroon. This colony is composed of about a hundred persons, who reside in some twenty-five or thirty houses . . . solely of boards and thatched, with no mason-work except the chimneys."

1647: Pieter Stuyvesant arrived at New Amsterdam to serve as Governor of New Netherland. Resolute, quick-witted, hot-tempered, and vitriolic, he had an autocratic philosophy of government already becoming obsolete in the more fluid American environment. More successful in external affairs than with New Netherland, Stuyvesant would resist Spanish and English ambitions, capture New Sweden on the Delaware for the Dutch, and establish peace with the Indians, with whom relations had been ghastly under his predecessor, Willem Kieft.

1648: Conflict between Stuyvesant and the director of the Van Rensselaer patroonship, Brant Van Slichtenhorst, developed when Stuyvesant ordered the demolition of all buildings within cannon shot of Fort Orange. After Van Slichtenhorst refused to execute the command, troops were sent to arrest him. The colonists quickly took sides.

1652: As the tension in the upper Hudson Valley area became explosive, Stuyvesant ordered posts erected 600 paces on all sides of Fort Orange. On April 1, 1652, he proclaimed the village of Beverwyck and disassociated it from the patroonship colony of tenant farmers clustered around what became known as Rensselaerswyck.

1657: Beverwyck residents who enrolled for the *Burghers Recht* paid 50 guilders for the right to hold office, which exempted them from the confiscation of property and attainder when convicted of a capital offense. Small burghers, buying the right to engage in trade and join guilds, paid 20 guilders; they had to be native-born or wed to the native-born daughter of a burgher, and keep fire and light in the community for a year and six weeks. The future Albany now growing north of Fort Orange began to take shape and substance.

1663: A smallpox epidemic at Fort Orange and Beverwyck killed about one settler each day; in the Hudson River Valley about 1,000 Indians died, joining hundreds of Iroquois killed by a plague the year before.

The English: 1664–1776

1664: Charles II, King of England, began to assert English claims to New Netherland that were based on the Cabot voyages in the late 15th century. His Majesty granted the territories of New Netherland, Long Island, New England, and land stretching to Delaware Bay to his royal brother James, Duke of York and Albany. Four warships and 450 troops were dispatched to New Netherland to settle the issue. With Stuyvesant's garrison outnumbered 6 to 1, New Amsterdam surrendered to the English without fighting. Shortly thereafter Fort Orange and Beverwyck as well were promptly renamed Albany.

1673: In the course of a third Anglo-Dutch commercial war, the Dutch retook New Netherland. Under brief Dutch rule, Albany became Willemstadt and local government was again in a state of flux. The 1674 Treaty of Westminster restored to England all "lands, islands, cities, havens, castles, and fortresses" taken by the Dutch. The English did little to disturb the bureaucratic status quo in Albany upon their return.

1675–1676: King Philip's War erupted in New England, where Indians burned a number of settlements and killed hundreds of colonists. With the Hudson frozen and 1,000 hostile Indians reported 40 miles east of Albany, the village's garrison was strengthened and the Mohawk allies sent to harry King Philip's warriors. A new fort was built overlooking Albany, with four bastions mounting 6 guns each. This installation, called Fort Frederick, stood on State Street near Lodge.

1677: In their effort to control the fur trade, the Five Nations raided the Chesapeake Bay region. New York attempted to halt these raids and held a major meeting in Albany between the Five Nations and delegates from Virginia and Maryland. A compact resulted which halted these Iroquois forays.

1678: Governor Edmund Andros issued a patent to the Van Rensselaers, confirming their possession of Rensselaerswyck but *not* of Albany, making the separation complete.

1683: Colonel Thomas Dongan, who had become Governor of New York in 1682, ordered Albany and Rensselaerswyck to send two delegates (out of a total of 18) to attend the first meeting of the General Assembly in New York. A "Charter of Libertys and Privileges" was passed, and 12 counties were established in the colony, among them Albany County, much larger than it is today.

1686: Governor Dongan, visiting Albany, was petitioned by local leaders to enlarge the town's boundaries and to give sounder guarantee to land titles. To define Albany better, he "got the Ranslaers to release their pretence to the Town and sixteen miles into the Country for Commons for the King. . . . After I had obtained this release of the Ranslaers I passed the Patent for Albany." Dongan signed the Charter on July 22, 1686, making Albany a city for the first time.

The city was given a full set of officials and divided into three wards. Pieter Schuyler was appointed mayor, "Clerk of ye market and Coroner of ye citty of Albany. . . ." Among the new government's first ordinances were prohibitions against watering horses from buckets hanging at the city wells and carrying sand from near the old burying-ground (so much had been taken that the coffins were exposed to view). And tavern-keepers were ordered to provide the constable with the name and business of any guest staying two days.

The Empire State

Pieter Schuyler, the first mayor of Albany

1689: News was received of the "Glorious Revolution" in England, which tumbled James II from the throne and replaced him with his Protestant son-in-law, William of Orange. Uprisings throughout the Dominion of New England—then including New York—ensued, and Governor Edmund Andros was arrested. During this period of wide popular unrest and dissatisfaction over the policies of James II, Jacob Leisler seized control of New York in the name of William and Mary and formed a Committee of Safety there under his leadership as self-proclaimed lieutenant governor. Leisler had arrived from Germany in 1660 in *The Golden Otter,* too poor to pay for his musket, bed, and chest. By 1689 he had become a prosperous New York City merchant who was seen as a firebrand by the conservative establishment but as a champion of Protestantism and the lower classes by others.

In Albany, William and Mary's ascent to England's throne was greeted with jubilation. At Fort Frederick "there Majts were proclaimed in solemn manner in English and Dutch, ye gunns fyreing from ye fort & volley of small arms, ye People with Loude acclamations crying God Save King Wm. & Queen Mary. . . ."

Leisler's authority over Albany, however, was rejected, demonstrating the city's growing particularism. Leisler demanded surrender of Albany's fort and garrison for resisting him. A force of Leisler's men came to Albany in three sloops, but was turned back, first by Pieter Schuyler and then by a band of Mohawks encamped on the site of Academy Park. Connecticut militia came to reinforce Schuyler against both Leisler and threatened French attack. With a Leisler plan to invade Canada and amid rumours of the Comte de Frontenac's projected invasion from Montreal, Albany finally accepted Leisler's governorship, although local government remained unchanged.

1690: After Leisler's invasion attempt petered out, the French and their Indians, 200 men in all, swept down to attack Schenectady, 20 miles north-west of Albany. "The whole village was instantly in a blaze," Mayor Schuyler wrote. "Women with child [were] riped open, and their Infants cast into the Flames, or dashed against Posts of Doors. Sixty persons perished in the Massacre, and twenty-seven were carried into Captivity. The rest fled naked towards Albany thro' a deep

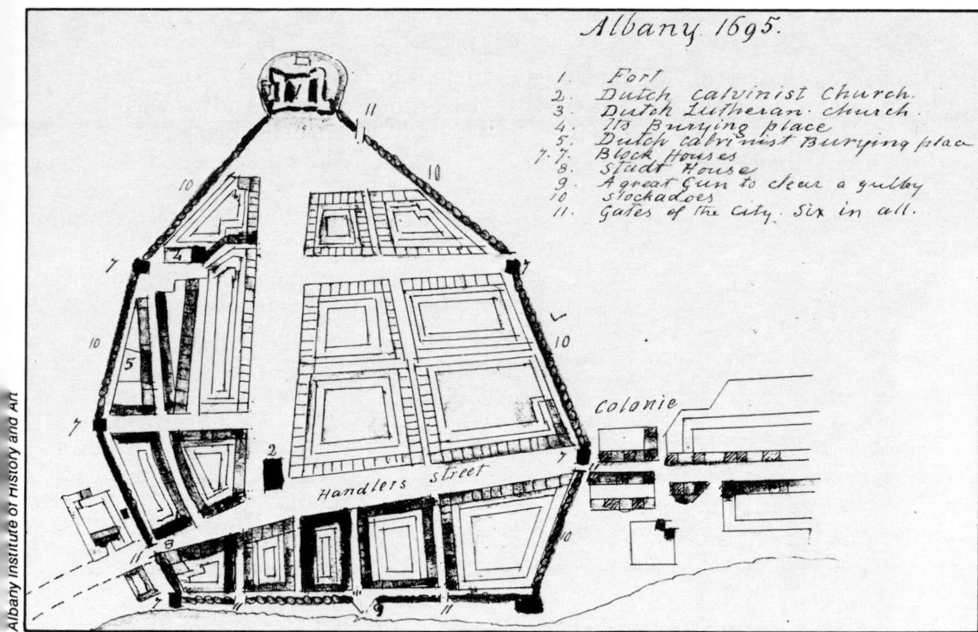

Albany Institute of History and Art

Albany in 1695

Snow which fell that very Night in a Terrible Storm; and twenty-five of these fugitives lost their Limbs in flight, thro' the Severity of the Frost." Symen Schermerhorn had ridden wounded through the night to warn Albany, which rallied for the expected French attack. The French made for Montreal, itself an epic trek, in which they ate most of the horses taken at Schenectady. The Albany militia buried Schenectady's dead and gave fruitless chase to the French.

1691: Colonel Henry Sloughter ended Leisler's Rebellion. Leisler was arrested in New York and eventually was hanged. New York concerned itself now with the war with the French, King William's War. About Albany Sloughter wrote to neighboring governors: "I need not relate unto you of how great import the preservacon of this place is, being the only bulkwork and safeguard of all Their Majesty's plantacons on the main (coast) of America. . . ."

A preventive (and vengeful) attack on French Canada was launched by Pieter Schuyler, who with Albany militia and allied Mohawks attacked and burned La Prairie de la Madeleine, killing 200. As Albany itself was increasingly fortified, thousands of pine trees were consumed.

1697: The population count of Albany County was 379 men, 270 women, and 803 children, mostly in the city of Albany. (The population of the province of New York was 18,067.) During the 1689–1697 war with the French, King William's War, 419 people had fled Albany, 84 were killed, 38 died, and 16 were taken as prisoners of war.

1700: To counter French influence with the Iroquois, the English paid court to the Five Nations, soliciting their help against Montreal. But the garrison at Albany was not turned out in a way that would impress the tribes. By the next year, however, Pieter Schuyler had succeeded in winning over the Iroquois, even though Albany's fort remained "in a miserable condition." The outbreak of Queen Anne's War in 1702 revealed that Schuyler had also made Albany's militia the only adequate unit in New York.

1708: Over four decades after the English came to power, Albany gradually began to conform to the society which controlled it. Intermarriage between the English soldiers of the garrison and the Dutch women of Albany increased and English slowly became the language of commerce and government. In 1708 the Reverend Thomas Barclay inaugurated services of the Church of England in Albany.

1710: Pieter Schuyler, after leading an abortive expedition against Canada, sailed for England, bringing four Mohawk sachems with him so they might be suitably impressed by English strength. The Indians created an immensely popular sensation, were accorded many attentions, and even received an audience with Queen Anne.

1714: The Peace of Utrecht had ended Queen Anne's War in 1713. A year later the population of Albany was 1,136, including 495 white males, 47 black males, and 528 white and 66 black women; the population of Albany County totaled 3,029, including 458 slaves.

1723: Governor Burnet reported to the Lords of Trade that he had induced Indians to bring their furs to Albany, some from "above a thousand miles to Albany from Mislimakenak which lyes between Lac Superieur and Lac Huron." Upon his recommendation, Albany built some small houses outside the stockade to shelter Indians who came to trade. Fur traders, mainly of Dutch ancestry, who had dominated both civil and economic life in Albany since the Dongan Charter, were now rivaled by an emergent class of successful general merchants who supplied the needs of the people of the upper Hudson River Valley.

1744: Once again, there was war with France. The Iroquois, Six Nations since the Tuscarora had joined their League, were at the apex of their power, their role pivotal in the perpetual Anglo-French competition for an American empire. Governor George Clinton

St. Peter's Protestant Episcopal Church

The Reverend Thomas Barclay

cautioned them against the French, and a French attack was greatly feared by Albanians, especially after the burning of Schuylerville in 1745. A terrorized Albany filled with refugees, and the three market houses became barracks. Although Governor Clinton had ordered the Iroquois out against the French, their chiefs remained reluctant until Indian Agent William Johnson brought the Mohawks to Albany and lavishly entertained them.

Again, war drained population away from an Albany too close to the enemy, and a postwar census in 1749 counted 9,154 whites in the county, down from 1737's 10,681. Albany would remain uneasily aware of its frontier exposure until the French were at last smashed in North America.

National Savings Bank

Benjamin Franklin at the Stadt Huys, 1754

1754: The famed Albany Plan of Union came about partly from Albany's significance in Colonial-Indian relations. In 1753 the Lords of Trade requested Governors of Massachusetts, New Hampshire, New Jersey, Pennsylvania, Maryland, and Virginia to send delegates to Albany for discussion of possible confederation for mutual defense against the French. In June of 1754, 24 delegates from seven colonies, including William Johnson and James Delancey of New York and Benjamin Franklin of Pennsylvania, met at Albany's *Stadt Huys,* the City Hall that stood where Hudson Avenue now meets Broadway. The Plan of Union that evolved, although never ratified by Parliament, was the first wide acknowledgment of common colonial interests and the need for concerted action to realize them.

1757: The Seven Years War, a world war known in America as the French and Indian War, had begun. The French massacre of the English garrison at Fort William Henry on Lake George again packed Albany with refugees and arriving British and colonial troops.

1758: At age 34, Lord Howe, commanding the 56th regiment, was killed in a skirmish during the advance on French positions at Ticonderoga. Howe's body was brought back to Albany, to be interred in St. Peter's Church—the only British Lord buried in North America. When another unit of Abercrombie's army, the Black Watch, was horribly mauled by the French, the army fell back on Albany.

1759: General Jeffrey Amherst camped at Albany and moved his troops north to take Ticonderoga and Crown Point, abandoned by the French. Elsewhere, after the British captured Montreal and Quebec, the French were finished as a colonial power in North America. The Iroquois from this point onward were diminished in their strategic importance. Victory brought the high point of British power, a time of elation shared with colonists who still saw themselves as English. In Albany, King George II's birthday was celebrated with a bonfire to which the municipal government provided wood.

1761: Schuyler Mansion, an Albany landmark henceforward, was constructed by British troops directed by Philip Schuyler's friend Colonel John Bradstreet. (Schuyler himself was in England at the time.) The city's leading citizen, Schuyler now led the way for integration of the Dutch into mainstream Anglo-American society. Yet in various ways Dutch folkways and vernacular would persist until today.

1765: Sir William Johnson observed that the Stamp Act—passed that year to raise Crown revenues by requiring the affixing of stamps to all commercial and legal documents—had revitalized a strong desire in the colonies for a representative form of government, such as that proposed by the Albany Congress of 1754. Unless checked, this spirit would soon be out of control. In 1766 Albany merchants, who had applied for the right to distribute these stamps, were forced to renounce their intentions by a group of young men from the Dutch merchant families then dominating city politics.

1766: Albany's Common Council voted to construct three stone docks on the Hudson River, tangibly acknowledging the benefit of the waterway to the community.

1770–1772: Albany was undergoing a transformation which shaped its future, becoming a purveyor of goods and a center for services. By 1771 the county would have a population of 42,706 persons, 3,877 of them black. In 1772, Tryon and Charlotte counties were formed from Albany County. The city's first newspaper, the *Albany Gazette,* was published, and printers James and Alexander Robertson later apologized for the irregularity of its appearance. Paper delivery came by stage coach from New York, and a heavy snowfall had frozen their paper into a large mass.

1774: Mother Ann Lee, regarded by her followers as a manifestation of God, arrived from Manchester, England, and settled four miles west of Albany. The Shaker community she founded at Watervliet would last until the 1930s. The Shakers were celibate but their sect grew through conversion and by absorbing orphans from the Watervliet area.

The old order was passing, symbolized by the deaths of Sir William Johnson and General John Bradstreet. Albany's freeholders assembled in support of the

First Continental Congress, then meeting in Philadelphia.

Revolutionary Albany: 1775–1783

1775: The news of the Battle of Lexington brought matters to a head in Albany. A meeting was held at the city's market house, "that sense of the citizens should be taken on the line of conduct they propose to hold in this Critical Juncture. . . ." The people proved enthusiastic in the cause and formed a Committee of Safety, Protection, and Correspondence. The Provincial Congress unanimously recommended Philip Schuyler as "the most proper person" in New York to be appointed a Major General. Schuyler was given command of the Army of the Northern Department and entered negotiations with sachems of the Six Nations as men straggled into Albany to join his forces. Albany was again crowded with strangers, and for the first time the Dutch Reformed Church held services in English.

1776: Popular sentiment became increasingly violent. As Mayor Abraham Cuyler and others celebrated King George III's birthday at Richard Cartwright's Tavern, another party with more radical sentiments set upon them. The swinging sign outside the King's Arms Tavern, at the corner of Green and Beaver streets, was ripped from its hinges and burned on State Street by a mob.

Albany-born Philip Livingston signed the Declaration of Independence. The Albany Committee of Correspondence

Peter Gansevoort

"Resolved that the Declaration of Independence be published and declared in this City . . . and that Colonel Van Schaick be requested to review the Continental troops in this City to appear under arms. . . ."

1777: General Burgoyne landed in Quebec with 8,000 British and German mercenary troops. Four hundred Indians joined Burgoyne, and Tory leader John Johnson was ready to advance into the Mohawk Valley. Philip Schuyler's few troops in a blocking position north of Albany desperately needed supplies of all sorts. Schuyler ordered his troops to fell trees across roads and navigable waterways on Burgoyne's line of march, cutting British speed to a mile per day. The murder of Jane McCrea by Burgoyne's Indians provided an incident with great propaganda value to the patriots. Whether McCrea's murder was cause or not, New England troops began to arrive, reinforcing Schuyler. Nonetheless, as Lord Howe (brother and successor to the title of the Lord Howe killed at Ticonderoga nine years earlier) sent his troops up the Hudson River toward Albany, Schuyler had only 2,000 troops. Soon after, General Horatio Gates replaced Schuyler in command.

At Fort Stanwix, near present-day Rome, New York Colonel Peter Gansevoort of Albany was besieged by British forces under Barry St. Leger. Nicholas Herkimer and his Tryon County Militia, hurrying to reinforce Gansevoort, collided with Indians and Tories at Oriskany in the bloodiest afternoon of fighting of the Revolution. Benedict Arnold finally came to the relief of Fort Stanwix.

In Burgoyne's path was Philip Schuyler's wife, Catherine, at the Schuylers' Stillwater Farm. Instructed by her husband to burn their wheatfields, she did so, and sent off their horses to deny them to the British.

The clash between Burgoyne's main force and the Americans came at Freeman's farm on September 19, 1777, an intense day with high casualties for the units engaged. On October 7 the Battle of Saratoga was decided at Bemis Heights, in part due to Albany's General Abraham Ten Broeck, who appeared at a critical moment with 3,000 fresh troops. Having lost his artillery, Burgoyne retreated, on his way churlishly burning Schuyler's house and outbuildings at Stillwater. On October 17 Burgoyne surrendered, escorted into captivity by Col. Henry Quackenbush and his 5th Regiment of Albany County militia. Refreshed briefly at the Quackenbush House on Broadway, Burgoyne for a time enjoyed a genteel captivity at the Schuyler Mansion.

1778: The New York State Legislature passed an act restoring Albany's municipal government, its continuity broken by the institution of the Committee of Safety, Protection, and Correspondence and by expulsion of Mayor Abraham Cuyler, last mayor by royal commission. Abraham Ten Broeck became mayor in 1779 and Philip Schuyler went to the Continental Congress.

Albany County Historical Association

General Abraham Ten Broeck

1780: Alexander Hamilton and Elizabeth, daughter of Philip Schuyler, were married at the Schuyler Mansion. The bride's father would be among Hamilton's staunchest allies in New York Federalist politics. A year later a party of Tories raided the mansion in a vain attempt to kill or capture Philip Schuyler. Another facet in Hamilton's life in Albany came in 1782, when Aaron Burr opened his law office on Norton Street two doors east of South Pearl. Hamilton would be Burr's *bête noir;* Burr, Hamilton's killer.

1783: George Washington, visiting Albany, was presented with a gold box containing the "Freedom of the City." About a month after Washington's visit, the Peace of Paris was signed, ending the American Revolution.

The New Day: 1784–1807

After the end of the American Revolution, Albany found itself an old city in a new nation. Despite gradual assimilation into the Anglo mainstream of American life, Dutch folkways—custom, language, and architecture—were still prominent. The end of French, Indian, and, for the moment, British military threats, also meant the end of Albany as a frontier community. Consequently, the city now began to outgrow the limits imposed on it, literally and figuratively, by stockades and topography. While the Hudson River remained critically important, new developments in transportation and a rapid growth in population would ultimately shift the city's axis from its traditional North and South to East and West. As the fur trade diminished in its economic importance to Albany, receding to far north and far west, Albany industrialized. New technologies and new societal stresses would transform the old city.

1784: Albany established its first post office on Broadway, north of Maiden Lane. The community was returning to normal after the war. Hard money remained scarce: at least one Albany mercantile firm, Henry, McClallen & Henry, advertised that it would take payment in wheat, corn, pease, flax, seeds, boards, planks, or peltries. Albany's Common Council proposed the demolition of Fort Frederick, its stones to be used for public improvements and in building various churches.

1786: Albany celebrated its centennial with a procession of municipal officers; 13 toasts were offered at the crest of State Street hill, and "the countenances of the inhabitants bespoke great satisfaction on the occasion." With its 550 houses, Albany was the new nation's sixth largest city.

1787: "Cherry Hill" was built by Philip Van Rensselaer on the south side of the city—today the museum of the Van Rensselaer-Rankin families.

1788: Albany's growing importance was reflected in the founding of three newspapers, and throughout the ensuing century papers would commence, merge, or vanish with feverish frequency. The political climate of the city was often volatile. When New York State ratified the Constitution, a procession celebrating the occasion was set upon by Anti-Federalists who threw stones torn from a nearby house; the city's Light-Horse troop dispersed the mob.

1790: Stage lines connected Albany with Springfield and Lansingburgh; within the next two decades Albany was the locus of most of New York State's major turnpikes. The federal census of 1790 counted 3,500 Albanians at a time when changing street names were expressing nationalist spirit. Streets named for the British heroes of the past were renamed for animals, birds, or the heroes of the American present. Some streets were paved and a new public market was erected on Broadway. Albanians formed the Albany Library.

The opening of South Ferry Street in the late 1780s was shortly thereafter followed by the laying out of a geometric grid of streets along its axis—very different from the narrow streets of the old part of Albany. Low-lying and often swampy ground, this area was formerly pasture land belonging to the Dutch Reformed Church, subsequently auctioned as building lots. The new streets were initially named for church ministers or local fish or trees. Later, as Yankee elements grew dominant in local affairs, many of the names would change to reflect more American associations, as when Frelinghuysen became Franklin Street in 1828. This Pastures area became a densely built-up neighborhood containing commercial, industrial, and residential properties, and included stores, schools, synagogues, and churches.

1793: Slaves were suspected of starting a fire in a stable which consumed most of a block bounded by Maiden Lane, State Street, Broadway, and James Street. Four slaves—a man and three women—were convicted and executed for arson, and the Common Council set a 9 o'clock curfew for Albany's slaves. Later law established a citizen night watch drawn from all males over 16. By 1799 the combined cost of this night watch, whale oil for Albany's street lamps, maintenance of the poor, and of public schools, would exceed $4,100.

1795: Because of its fortunate geographic position, Albany was, and would long remain, a conduit to the west. Stage fare for the two-day trip to New York City was $7.25, but much traffic was westward, into New York State's interior and to the "Old West." In three days, 1,200 sleighs passed through Albany loaded with families and their goods leaving stony New England for the promise of the fertile west.

1797: Albany became New York State's capital and assumed a political significance matched by its economic one. Governors and state officials gathering in the city transformed a rather staid social life and, by maintaining homes in Albany, lent the city a new sense of importance and responsibility. Growing to a work force of many thousands, the state's payroll would one day become pivotal to Albany's economic welfare. Architect Philip Hooker designed a lasting Albany landmark: the Dutch Reformed Church on North Pearl Street. Its twin spires that puncture the skyline are featured in almost all artists' views of the riverfront. The Ten Broeck Mansion was also erected in this period.

1799: Although a post road's mean and rutted track had long connected Albany with New York City, it was the turnpikes which would intimately link Albany to the west and make the city a significant emporium in westward expansion. Albany's roads soon reached north, west, and southwest; a road down the Hudson's west bank touched Catskill; by ferry across the river, the traveler could reach a road south to New York City.

The business of feeding, lodging, and supplying westward-bound emigrants coming through Albany by turnpike was lucrative; of more lasting importance, Albany's manufacturers could receive raw materials and ship products by road. River and roads gave Albany's industry a marked advantage. By 1800 Albany's population was over 50 percent larger than a decade earlier. Architect William Sander designed the State Hall, which housed New York's government in 1799.

1803: A customs house was established, indicative of Albany's commercial significance. New concentrations of population required new social services of many types. The Albany Waterworks Company

A LAW,

To regulate the Use, and restrain the Waste, of the Water of the Albany Water-Works. *Passed 21st October*, 1803.

BE **it Ordained** by the Truſtees of the Albany Water-Works, That no Perſon entitled to the Uſe of the ſaid Water, ſhall ſupply or furniſh any other Perſon, not ſo entitled to be ſupplied, with Water from any Penſtock in his or her Houſe or other Building or Lot; and that for every Neglect or Refuſal to conform to this Proviſion, the Perſon ſo neglecting or refuſing, ſhall forfeit the Sum of One Dollar.

And be it further Ordained, That every Perſon uſing the ſaid Water ſhall, at all Times during the Day Time, permit the Superintendent of the ſaid Water-Works, to enter into the Houſe, Building or Lot, in or on which any ſuch Penſtock or Aperture ſhall be erected or made, and to examine his or her lateral Pipes, Penſtock or other Devices connected with the ſaid Water-Works, without Hindrance or Moleſtation: And if it ſhall appear to ſuch Superintendent that any Part of ſuch lateral Pipes, Penſtocks or other Devices, are not well and ſufficiently ſecured to prevent the Waſte of Water, and ſuch Superintendent ſhall require the ſame to be repaired, that then and in every ſuch Caſe the Perſon entitled to the uſe of ſuch Penſtock or Aperture ſhall within ſuch reaſonable Time thereafter, as the Superintendent in his Diſcretion ſhall appoint, cauſe the ſame to be well and effectually repaired under the Direction of ſuch Superintendent; and if ſuch Repairs ſhall not have been made within the Time preſcribed for that Purpoſe, the Superintendent ſhall further require ſuch Perſon ſo neglecting or refuſing to repair, to appear before the Preſident of the ſaid Truſtees, and ſhall forthwith make Report thereof to him, and the Preſident ſhall in a ſummary Manner, enquire whether ſuch Repairs were neceſſary, and whether ſuch Notice to repair ſhall have been given and was not complied with, and in his Diſcretion, either allow a further Time to make ſuch Reparation, or cauſe ſuch lateral Pipe to be cut off.

And be it further Ordained, That no Perſon, other than the Preſident, one of the ſaid Truſtees, or the Superintendent, ſhall be permitted to open any of the Fire-Stops connected with the ſaid Water-Works, unleſs in Caſe of Fire; and that if any Perſon ſhall open any Fire-Stop, the Superintendent ſhall forthwith make report thereof to the Clerk; to the End, that the Perſons opening the ſame may be proſecuted for the ſame, which it ſhall be the Duty of the Clerk to do, as ſoon as poſſible after receiving ſuch Report.

And be it further Ordained, That if after the paſſing of this Law, any Perſon, other than the Superintendent, ſhall perforate any of the Conduits belonging to the ſaid Water-Works, or the lateral Pipes connected therewith, with intent to uſe or enable any other Perſon to uſe the Water conducted through the ſame, without the Conſent of the ſaid Truſtees firſt had and obtained, every ſuch Perſon ſhall forfeit for every ſuch Perforation the Sum of Five Dollars; and that the Superintendent ſhall not connect any lateral Pipe with the Conduits aforeſaid, unleſs he ſhall have carefully inſpected the Logs, the iron Hoops and connecting Pipes compoſing the ſame, ſo as to be ſatisfied that the ſame are ſound, well jointed, ſtrong and well calculated to prevent a Waſte of Water.

A true Copy,

PETER EDM. ELMENDORF, *Clerk.*

An Albany Waterworks Company broadside of 1803

employed large tree trunks, bored out and joined by iron collars, to bring water to the community. In 1803 the Albany Medical Society offered free "kine-pox" vaccination to the city's poor, and a County Medical Society was founded three years later.

1804: Changes were coming to Albany. Transplanted Yankee Elkanah Watson, a force for modernization not always appreciated by Albany's Dutch traditionalists, revived Philip Schuyler's concept of the Erie Canal. Watson was also prime mover in organizing the State Bank of Albany, Albany's oldest surviving bank.

The New Industrial Age: 1807–1860

1807: Significant to both Albany and to the world at large, the *Clermont* tied up at a wharf at the foot of Madison Avenue at 11:27 on the morning of September 5, 1807. Robert Fulton's sidewheeler steamboat had made the 150 miles from New York City in under 29 hours and, by harnessing steampower to transportation, ushered in the age of steam. Passage on the maiden trip: $7. A number of steamboats soon traveled the Hudson and the resultant competition over the years would cause the price of a trip to New York to fluctuate between $10 and 6¾ ¢. These boats, requiring tons of cordwood, denuded the Hudson River Valley of thousands of trees.

President Jefferson's Embargo of 1807 proved injurious to merchants, manufacturers, and workers, and its lifting two years later sparked day-long ringing of the city's bells, impromptu parades, and speechifying.

1812: Once again the nation was at war with Great Britain, and once again Albany was target of a British offensive, blunted at Plattsburg. At Queenstown Heights, Albany's Colonel Solomon Van Rensselaer was wounded four times when leading American troops against British positions, only to be forced back when New York State militia refused to cross the Canadian border to reinforce him. The war would have a dramatic aftermath for Albany.

1813: A Lancastrian School—an English system in which student proctors aided a single teacher in teaching many pupils—had also been established; by 1816, 400 students were being taught there at an average annual cost of $2.50 each. To boost local industry, the Common Council pledged $1,000 to anyone who discovered a seam of coal four feet thick within five miles of the navigable Hudson. As the forests receded, coal became a vital fuel source. In 1813, Joseph Fry issued the first city directory, a 60-page listing of 1,638 names—not quite 15 percent of Albany's population.

1815: British merchants, after the War of 1812, dumped quantities of cheap goods on the American market in an attempt to regain their dominant trading position. Many local manufacturers were ruined. Albany's newspapers—then including the city's first daily, the Albany *Daily Advertiser*—recorded financial disasters. The Common Council moved to set aside 50 acres of land on the south side of Albany for an almshouse. Debtors in the city jail petitioned the city's well-to-do "for such broken meats and vegetables as the opulent have in their power to spare." In the meantime, Albany Academy laid the cornerstone of its Philip Hooker building, still in Academy Park.

1817: Of enormous import to Albany was the bill passed by the New York State Legislature for construction of the Erie Canal, which would make Albany the terminus for the produce of the West and products of the East by connecting the Hudson River to the Great Lakes. Laborers were recruited in Ireland to build the Erie Canal, and Albany thereby gained a substantial Irish population.

At a time when there were nearly 10,000 slaves in New York State, the legislature also passed a law abolishing slavery after July 4, 1827.

1820: The Albany Savings Bank was founded, with silversmith Joseph Rice making the first deposit. Stagecoaches carried the mail to New York City; one broke through the ice and sank while crossing the frozen Hudson. Albany had five newspapers; its Apprentices' Library, founded to aid young mechanics, by 1822 had 1,585 volumes and 350 readers. Isaiah Townsend was president of Albany's first Chamber of Commerce.

1825: *The Seneca Chief* was the first boat to negotiate the full length of the Erie Canal, reaching Albany from Buffalo. Cannon were placed at intervals from Albany to New York and fired in notice of the *Seneca Chief's* arrival; it took less than an hour for this signal to reach New York and then be returned to Albany. Albany celebrated with parades, special church

Recollections of Albany

Elkanah Watson, who revived the idea of building the Erie Canal

The De Witt Clinton, *first steam passenger train in America*

services, a huge collation, and a grand ball. Seven thousand boats used the Erie Canal in its first year, almost 13,000 its second. Albany's population in 1825, nearly 16,000, would now grow dramatically, thanks to the Erie Canal. Eleven steamboats were regularly running to New York City.

1827: This year marked the emancipation of all slaves in the State of New York. . .Jesse Strang, murderer of John Whipple, was the last person publicly executed in Albany. The occasion drew an immense crowd, with 1,100 vehicles coming into Albany from the North alone. Ballads were hawked in the crowd and a largely festive atmosphere prevailed.

1828: The city was building. The Common Council received bids for leveling Robinson's Hill (Eagle Street between Hudson and Madison avenues), the soil to be used as fill in low-lying land below South Ferry Street. The contractor awarded the job was paid with three-quarters of the building lots thus created. Petitioners also requested the Common Council to improve the area of North Pearl Street between Orange and Patroon streets, where stood a row of "miserable hovels." This redevelopment, a sort of primordial urban renewal, resulted in the creation of Clinton Square, shortly afterwards the residence of young Herman Melville and his family.

1829: Both the Albany Orphan Asylum and St. Vincent's Female Orphan Society were organized. A temperance society was founded; in 1830 temperance people estimated that Albany's 415 taverns and groceries sold 200,000 gallons of alcohol annually. The city, they said, had 500 habitual drunkards, 4,000 "tipplers," and 200 deaths yearly from "intemperance." In 1829 Albanians drank 12,000 of the 42,000 barrels of beer brewed in the city, exporting the rest.

1830: The ills of urbanization were beginning to affect Albany. To maintain public services for a population of 24,238 persons, city expenditures of more than $174,000 exceeded revenues by over $18,000. Albany, author Nathaniel P. Willis quipped, looked "so well in the distance, that you half forgive it for its hogs, offals, broken pavements, and the score of other nuisances more Dutch than decent."

Most important for Albany, Stephen Van Rensselaer broke ground for the construction of the nation's first steam-powered railroad, the Mohawk & Hudson, that connected Albany to Schenectady, the first link in an eventual nationwide web of tracks.

1831: When the first train passed over the completed tracks, the people of Albany flocked to see this technological marvel, a wonder of the age. By 1833 the trains would run from the head of State Street, the cars drawn by horses to the junction of Madison and Western Avenue, where the engines were fueled. It cost $42,600 per mile to build the Mohawk & Hudson Railroad, and subscription books were immediately opened to finance a rail connection to New York City.

1832: Cholera appeared in Albany, brought in by French-Canadian emigrants. The first victim died in early July. Fearing the night air, the Common Council met by day and churches canceled evening services. Travelers avoided Albany, and boats and stages arrived half empty. Since farmers stopped bringing produce in to market, foodstocks were alarmingly low, and the bushel price of potatoes rose 300 percent. Most stores were closed; the mayor proclaimed a time of mourning. As citizens burned tar "to abate the plague," a gloomy pall of oily smoke hung over Albany. By the time the epidemic ended in mid-September, 1,147 cases of cholera had been diagnosed, more than a third of them fatal.

Recollections of Albany

The Eagle Tavern, located on Court Street

1833: With the idea of erecting a statue of George Washington there, the triangle of land at the junction of Washington and Central avenues was fenced in and named Washington Park. Its name was later changed to Townsend Park in commemoration of Mayor John Townsend.

1837: The onset of a national financial panic saw Albany's banks cease payments in specie, an action taken by New York City's banks a day earlier. Albany businessmen petitioned the Common Council to issue bills in denominations less than one dollar so that change could be made. Although State Bank of Albany was first to resume specie payment in 1838, unemployment was rife, 639 people in the city's almshouse. In three months one soup kitchen fed 1,530 persons at a cost of one third of a cent each.

1839: There was other unrest. Farmers defied the county sheriff when he attempted to collect rents due the patroonship. Turned back by several hundred assembled antirenters, the sheriff obtained the aid of Albany's militia and, after a long series of civil disturbances, was able to enforce the law. The antirenters, however, had sounded the patroonship's death-knell;

several years later a state constitutional convention abolished feudal tenure.

1840: Albany's population was 33,627 (with less than 3 percent black) and would increase by nearly 24 percent in the next five years. One May day's traffic count on a Broadway corner listed 9,762 pedestrians, 407 wagons, 146 stages, and 234 other vehicles. When the first locomotive arrived in Greenbush on the new track from Boston the next year, an all-weather route to the east was at last opened. Its Albany-bound passengers transferred from train to ferry at Greenbush.

1843–47: The Perry Stove Works opened. The stove industry became huge in 19th century Albany. City institutions were developing. Albany Hospital incorporated in 1843, five years after the medical college. The New York State Normal School, ancestor of the State University, was established in 1844. Albany Rural Cemetery supplanted several burial grounds within the city limits in 1845. In 1847 the Rev. John McCloskey became Albany's first Roman Catholic Bishop.

Albany's Irish, German, and Jewish populations were on the verge of dramatic growth. Acknowledging urban needs, in 1846 the Common Council began to search for an adequate water supply for Albany. In the same year a telegraphic link with New York City was made. Technology was beginning to shrink distance, and this communication invention owed much to Albany resident Joseph Henry's pioneering work in electromagnetic induction. In 1845 Henry was invited to become the first Secretary of the Smithsonian Institution in Washington, D.C.

1848: Albany's firemen, who were volunteers, had organized in 11 engine, two hook-and-ladder, and separate axe and hose companies. Since their rivalries were often explosive, brawls between companies, as buildings blazed, were commonplace. In 1848 large fires, including one that consumed 600 buildings on 37 acres near the river, led to a Common Council ban on construction of wooden buildings in the congested areas east of Lark Street. Another ordinance, much resented by firemen, put Albany's fire companies under command of a full-time chief, who was paid an annual $700 salary.

The Albany Republican Artillery was away in the Mexican War, in action at Chapultepec. Of the unit's 70 privates, more than one-third died. When the survivors returned to Albany, they found Albanians radically altering the topography of their city as it spread along the river and west toward the Pine Bush. Congregation Beth Jacob had built a synagogue at Madison Avenue and Fulton Street, and Joel Munsell had begun publication of his *Annals of Albany*.

An incident of anti-rentism, 1838

New York State Library

1849: Zachary Taylor made a presidential visit to an Albany whose population would soon exceed 50,000—not counting those citizens who left for the goldfields of California. Albany's real estate was valued at more than $8.2 million.

1850s: The City Water Commission in 1850 purchased land and water leases for Patroon's Creek, damming it a year later to form 40-acre reservoir Rensselaer Lake (Six Mile Waterworks).

In 1851 the first train to travel the full length of the Hudson River Railroad made the journey, New York City to Albany, in less than three and a half hours. The Albany to Susquehanna Railroad was also incorporated in that year, and by 1855 the last building east of Montgomery Street made way for a dense matrix of railroad tracks. By 1854 there was heavy rail traffic, with 2,000 immigrants passing west one day, 1,380 cattle leaving Albany another. Albany's lumber district loaded 44 cargo vessels in a day.

As a state capital at the intersection of several major transportation systems, Albany was a frequent site for conventions as well as a target of orators and entertainers. Ralph Waldo Emerson addressed the Young Men's Association in 1850; Jenny Lind first triumphantly sang in Albany in 1851; and Lajos Kossuth raised $2,000 for the Magyar cause in 1852. Black Albanians met in City Hall to discuss the Fugitive Slave Law in 1850; seven years later Albany hosted an abolitionists' convention addressed "with great earnestness" by Susan B. Anthony.

Archbishop Hughes dedicated the Cathedral of the Immaculate Conception in 1852. The widow of late Mayor Charles E. Dudley gave $63,000 toward the Dudley Observatory, built in 1856 on a northern Albany hilltop

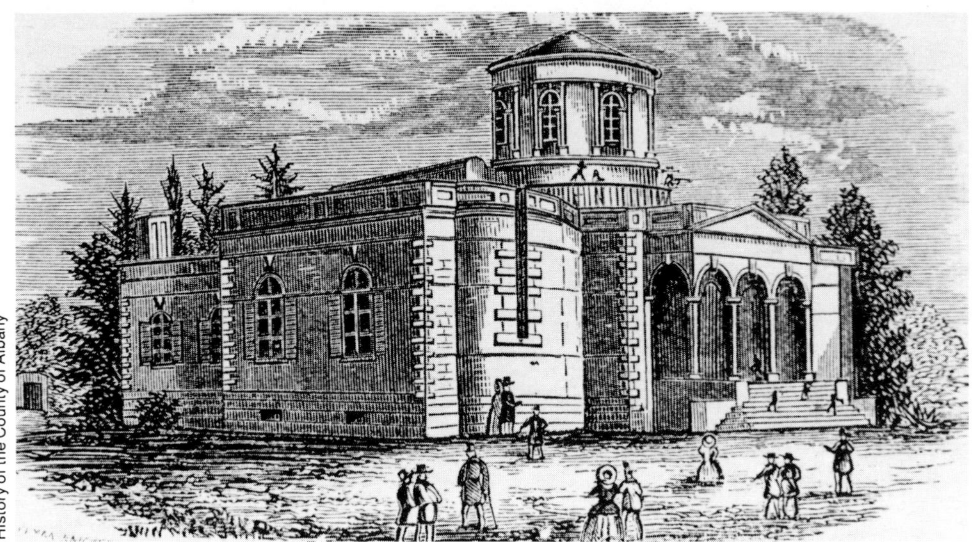

History of the County of Albany

The Dudley Observatory, located on the highest point in Albany

donated by Stephen Van Rensselaer. In 1852 Albany created a regular police corps with four precincts, succeeding the old constabulary system.

1860: Kerosene was first marketed in Albany as a lighting fuel. The visiting Prince of Wales, later King Edward VII, was lionized by Albanians. St. Joseph's Roman Catholic Church, an example of 13th-century Benedictine architecture, was dedicated—a gem in the setting of prosperous Ten Broeck Square. Also in 1860, St. Peter's present building was under construction on State Street.

Late antebellum Albany sat atop the nation's sociological iceberg; its citizens would soon participate in a four-year fratricidal war fought on safely distant battlefields.

Albany's Civil War: 1861–1865

Abolitionists had been active in Albany in an effort to arouse public opinion against the institution of slavery abiding in the South. Commerce with the South was more incidental. The possibility of Union troops' actually fighting Southern Americans was approached with much soul-searching. Thurlow Weed—publisher of the Albany *Evening Journal*, confidant of William A. Seward, advisor to Abraham Lincoln, and a nationally heard voice in Republican politics—in editorials written during the pre- and post-election months shifted his tone along with events. "No Compromise—No Back Down," he said. "It is a new and novel position, for we have been all our life showing up the dark side of the Slavery Picture. But in view of a fearful calamity, there is no want of consistency, or of fidelity, in going to the verge of conciliation with the hope of averting it." In Albany's Tweddle Hall, a mass meeting took place to promote "conciliation, concession, and compromise" on the slavery issue about to tear the states asunder.

1861: The year opened with the state's antislavery convention. Frederick Douglass, Gerrit Smith, and Lucretia Mott were among those to appear. Other cities had denied the abolitionists their rights to peaceful assembly and free speech, especially in the tense post-election period. Some Albany elements approached Mayor George H. Thacher to decline hospitality, but Thacher replied with an emphatic negative: "Let at least the Capital of the Empire State be kept free from the disgraceful proceedings which, in other localities, have brought dishonor upon our institutions. At all events, come what may, mob law shall never prevail in our good city with my consent and connivance. . . ." Local hoodlums created a riot when the convention began in the hall of the Young Men's Association, but were soon subdued by police.

A few days later Abraham Lincoln visited the city. Albany's Burgesses' Corps would act as military escort at the inauguration. When Fort Sumter fell to the Confederacy, the 25th Regiment entrained for Washington almost immediately, and the Burgesses' Corps answered Lincoln's first call for volunteers. Other Albany regiments would follow: 3rd, 10th, 43rd, and 91st, as well as the Albany Zouaves.

Mechanicsville's 24-year-old Ephraim Elmer Ellsworth, who had organized a Zouave unit of firemen, was shot pulling down a Confederate flag at an Alexandria, Virginia, hotel. Three days later a procession of 2,000 troops escorted his body to the Capitol, where it rested in state. The martyred Ellsworth's bloody uniform became a military relic. Other Albany casualties would follow, but fresh troops of eager volunteers succeeded them. When the 10th Regiment departed for the war in 1862, fervid crowds swarmed the streets, crowding windows and rooftops to watch; in this soldiers' *bon voyage,* martial music blared and women wept.

In April 1861 the first guns were fired from the batteries of treason upon Fort Sumter. The sound of those guns startled the nation, and revealed the existence of a deep, widespread and malignant rebellion. After a long period of peace, unity, and uninterrupted prosperity—during which the arts had been advanced, the resources of the country developed, manufactures and commerce increased, and the national domain extended, with a rapidity almost unparalleled in history—there burst upon us the storm of war . . .

Rufus W. Clark. *The Heroes of Albany: A Memorial of the Patriot-Martyrs Who Sacrificed Their Lives During the Late War in Defense of the Union, 1861–1863.* Albany, 1867.

Albany Institute of History and Art

The Army Relief Bazaar, held from February 22 to March 10, 1864

Ominously, by late summer Albany's recruiting offices were open on Sundays in an attempt to maintain a steady flow of replacements to add to the bloodshed in the South. To finance the war, an Internal Revenue office appeared in Albany. Meanwhile, unstable fiscal conditions caused the sudden and startling failure of four city banks.

1863: Recruiting tents were set up on State Street, and the National Commercial Bank (now Key Bank) guaranteed $3.5 million in enlistment bonuses. The 25th Regiment, returned from Washington, was called out to quash 1,000 striking dockers and railroad workers. The presence of troops quelled the disturbance. "This, we hope," wrote the Albany *Argus*, "has ended the strike—the most formidable one in our city."

1864: Between the end of 1863 and mid-July of 1864, Albany County paid well over a million dollars in enlistment bonuses as the Civil War dragged on and Union casualties mounted. An Army Relief Bazaar in Academy Park sent nearly $82,000 to the U. S. Sanitary Commission. The Common Council authorized Albany's first steam-operated fire engine. In 1864 the city had a baseball team, the Nationals, and also heard a performance of "Lucrezia Borgia," its first grand opera.

1865: At the war's end, Albany's population of 62,613 barely exceeded its total of five years earlier. On its winding way back to Illinois, Abraham Lincoln's body briefly rested in state in the Capitol. Blacks were now admitted to the Young Men's Association. Albany's regiments filtered back from a conflict which had cost their county nearly $4.5 million.

The end of the Civil War shifted civil priorities. The state legislature authorized construction of a new Capitol. The Great Western Turnpike became Western Avenue, perhaps a change in nuance as well as in name.

Albany Enters the Gilded Age: 1866–1875

As it was for the United States generally, the aftermath of the American Civil War was a time of considerable change for Albany. The city once again experienced substantial, accelerated growth in population and commerce, which strained existing urban systems and necessitated enlarged or wholly new municipal services. Industry, too, changed, and this period saw the Erie Canal dwindling in its economic significance. Albany became more specialized in many ways, more emphatically capital city and financial center, more identifiable with the Albany of the late 20th century.

1866: For decades hundreds of dockers and teamsters had worked to unload freight trains on the shores of the Hudson River, ferry the goods across the water, and warehouse or reload them on trains on the opposite bank. A $1.1 million railroad bridge was completed, although it had been strongly opposed by those whose interests it threatened. The Hudson was no longer Albany's commercial barrier to the East; freight could now ship on through trains.

Albany's horse-drawn streetcars began operating. This railway became vital to the growth of neighborhoods farther from the city's ancient core. Eventually residential areas would become differentiated from commercial or industrial ones.

Albany's Board of Public Instruction came into being in 1866. Responding to the need for a standardized education for Albany's children, new public schools were built with marked regularity around the city.

1867–69: A paid Fire Department was on the job by 1867, the Common Council also voting $15,000 to install fire alarms at strategic points in the city—75 were in place by the next year. In 1868 the center market on South Pearl Street was demolished for the erection of a new City Building to house expanded municipal services. Broadway was being paved with blocks of Canada pine, soon superseded by granite pavement. A Parks Commission was appointed in 1869, when the property tax rate was $3.54 per $100 of assessed value, with mandate to acquire the Washington Parade Ground and an adjacent cemetery, genesis of Washington Park. Like the municipal government which had outgrown its existing City Hall, New York State required a new Capitol, and its foundation commenced in 1869.

St. Agnes' Cemetery was established in 1867, the year St. Patrick's Roman Catholic Church was constructed; St. Ann's followed in 1868. Albany's Episcopal Diocese, its first Bishop 36-year-old William Croswell Doane, was set off from the New York Diocese in 1868. A $130,000 Congregational Church was dedicated in 1869, the same year that Christian Brothers

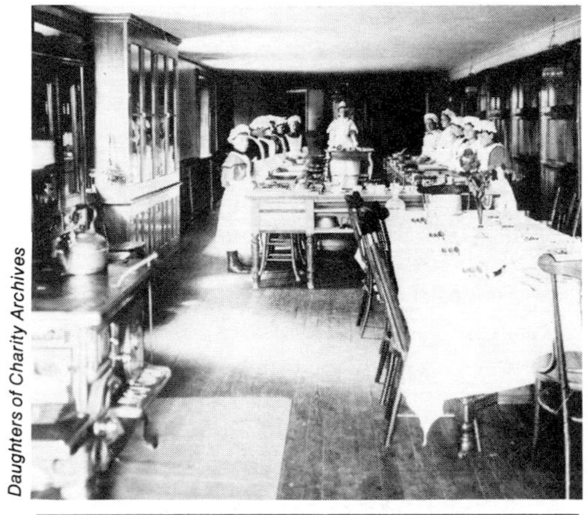

Daughters of Charity Archives

Kitchen of St. Vincent's Asylum for Girls

Academy was chartered. St. Vincent's Asylum for Girls opened on Elm Street.

1870–1875: The 1870 federal census counted 69,442 Albanians; 4.38 million people in New York State. Five years later another 17,000 persons had settled in the city and more than 16 percent of its total population was Irish-born. City government was undergoing modifications as the Dongan Charter was amended: the western boundary was fixed 4.25 miles from the Hudson River, instead of Governor Dongan's 16 mile corridor into the Pine Bush; the mayor received the power of the veto, polling places were designated, and election inspectors appointed.

Construction began on Washington Park, with bodies exhumed from the old burial ground interred in Albany Rural Cemetery—the final count was 40,000, according to one source. The Park opened in 1872; its lake was excavated in 1873, and bridged, and the original Lake House was built two years after that. In Albany's South End, School 15 opened, modeled on Boston's Shurtliff Grammar School by Albany architects Ogden and Wright. The building, dedicated in 1871 after a year under construction, was the city's first modern, scientifically planned school building, a landmark development in local public education.

The city's first high school, at Eagle, Columbia, and Steuben streets, was in operation in 1876.

Railroads were becoming increasingly important to Albany's economy. The first train crossed the Maiden Lane railroad bridge in 1871; another railroad bridge, with a 400-ton drawbridge, opened a year later. By 1875 the West Albany stockyards shipped a daily average of 103 carloads of livestock, nearly 38,000 that year, almost 25,000 of cattle, 8,500 of hogs. Rail transport was so rapid that New York City newspapers were in Albany by 8 a.m.

As the railroads waxed, the canals waned; in 1873 the Albany Dock Association adjourned indefinitely. Business along the pier and along Quay Street was at a virtual standstill, buildings there renting for half their former price, if rented at all. Through-rail transport had halted much of the warehouse business and many merchants moved to Broadway. National financial panic in 1873 hardly benefited the deteriorating basin area.

The cornerstone of the new State Capitol was laid in 1871, and in 1872 Congress authorized construction of Albany's Federal building on Broadway. Just north of the city, the Albany Gaslight Company, capitalized at a million dollars, constructed its plant.

Dennis Holzman

Three Albany boys enjoying their "bicycles"

Dennis Holzman

Architect H.H. Richardson, designer of 1883 Albany City Hall

Albany's German community celebrated Prussia's victory over France in 1871 with a *Friedens Fest*, the 10th and 25th Regiments parading for the occasion. Albany's Martin Opera House opened in 1870, and the Albany Musical Association was organized; late 19th century Albany abounded in singers and musicians.

Nation's Centennial to City's Bicentennial: 1876–1886

1876: America's centennial year was celebrated by Albanians with a midnight parade on January 1. Albany's women later sent a "magnificent state banner" to the Philadelphia Centennial Exposition. Governor Samuel Tilden hosted the first reception held at the Eagle Street Governor's Mansion. Albany's Mayor Judson, however, appealed for donations for Albany's poor—unemployed since the financial reverses of the Panic of 1873.

1877–1885: In 1880 there were nearly 91,000 Albanians, 12,575 of them Irish-born. There were 3,325 farms in Albany County and almost 9,500 horses. Dramatic population growth was reflected in the westward extension of the street railway, up Madison Avenue to Quail Street in 1877, and along Lark Street in 1885. In the course of repaving, workmen cut down the huge elm so long a landmark at the corner of North Pearl and State streets—a tree, as Albany folklore had it, planted in 1735 by Philip Livingston. There were 54 miles of paved streets in the city of 1885, 44 of those miles cobbled. That year, too, Albany contained 6,833 brick and 6,581 wooden structures and 111 "manufacturies."

The old City Hall (on the Eagle Street site of the present one) burned in 1880, but by 1881 Masons ceremoniously laid the cornerstone of a new one designed by nationally prominent architect Henry Hobson Richardson. By 1883 the building was complete, to serve as the center of city government for the century to follow. The seven million gallon Prospect Hill reservoir was completed in 1878; a public bath opened at the foot of Columbia Street in 1882. Albany's Police Department had its telephones in operation in 1877, and the next year the city had the nation's third working telephone exchange, with 100 subscribers (the first seven had been physicians). By 1879 the Commercial Telephone Company was in business; Hudson River Telephone Company in 1883. Also in that year Albany's Board of Health was endorsing municipal sewage and garbage disposal systems, visiting nurses, and vaccination of school children.

Albany Medical College obtained the Lancastrian School building in 1877, four years later granting laboratory and classroom space to Albany College of Pharmacy, the 15th college of pharmacy in the United States, second in New York; it had 21 students.

Tombstone of President Chester A. Arthur

Lou Carol Leece

The new Capitol building was officially declared such in 1878, and opened, in part, the following year. In 1879 the cornerstone of the Federal Building was laid.

Grover Cleveland, then governor, was serenaded by the 10th Regiment's Band the night he was nominated for President in 1884, while his opponent, James G. Blaine, subsequently spoke to 7,000 Albanians during a 20 minute whistle-stop. The city was spreading west; of 20 new churches built between 1872 and 1890, the majority were located in western portions of Albany. By 1885 there were more than 87,500 Albanians. "West" was west of Washington Park, and much of Madison, Western, and Central avenues was built up during this general period.

As early as 1881 the Albany Electric Illuminating Company had contracted to light city streets, generating its electricity at a Trinity Place powerhouse. The advent of electrical power launched vertical architecture in Albany; electric motors would power the elevators that made tall buildings feasible—for the first time interrupting Albany's skyline with something besides hills, steeples, and domes.

The New York Central's Broadway crossing at Colonie Street, long a danger to the frequent north-bound funeral processions, gave way to a viaduct in 1882 and a passenger bridge was opened across the Hudson. Tolls: pedestrian, 2 cents; single team, 10 cents; double team, 15 cents. By 1883 the West Shore Railroad also linked Albany to New York City, then to Syracuse and Buffalo.

1886: By now Albany had endured two centuries as a city. It celebrated its bicentennial with the innocent fervor of parades, canoe races, regattas, and a thousand school children singing a specially composed song. Books were printed and medallions struck. Albany's blacks planted a commemorative elm in Washington Park; the Germans, of course, an oak. Significantly, one day of the week-long celebration eulogized Albany's trades and manufactures.

In that bicentennial year Albany produced a panoply of Victorian consumer and industrial goods, from saddlery to dredges, drain tiles, tinwares, emery wheels, whale and elephant oils, ice boxes, monumental stonework, and sawsets.

Albany's middle class had many diversions. Rollerskating enjoyed a first popularity, as did bicycles. Albany's Wheelmen, part of a national fad, had productive goals—lobbying for better roads. There were clubs for chess, tennis, curling, canoeing, boating; baby shows and dog shows; orchestras and, inevitably, singing societies. Germans formed a Young Men's Democratic Club. Cricket was a popular game. The Holland Society, the Albany Press Club, and the Ridgefield Athletic Club were all founded in 1885. In 1886 a new YMCA was under construction on North Pearl Street; that year an Elks Club formed, as well as the Episcopal Women's Diocesan League and the Albany Historical and Art Society, the latter given impetus by the city's bicentennial celebration. The bicentennial year witnessed the funeral of ex-President Chester A. Arthur, who was buried at Albany Rural Cemetery.

Two Wars and a New Century: 1887–1916

1887–1890: The Albany Railway reduced its Pearl Street fare to a nickel in 1887; citizens were now long accustomed to the horsecars. A few years earlier, Richmond, Virginia, had experimented with electric trolleys; now electric streetcars were tried in Albany's neighboring communities. Well over four million fares in 1889 justified conversion to electricity and in 1890 the street railway sold 200 of its horses. New York's railroad workers were organizing and West Albany railroaders rioted in 1877; some Albany workers organized in the Ancient Order of United Workmen in 1878. Perhaps following the example of Jersey City and New York City railroad Knights of Labor, the New York Central's brakemen struck in 1882 as did Albany and Troy stovemolders in 1884–1885.

By 1890 the U.S. Census would count nearly 95,000 Albanians; almost 2,200 more would be added in the next two years. A north-south artery was needed further west to carry increasing traffic,

Erastus Corning 2nd

A portion of the silver presented to the U.S.S. Albany

and the Hilton Bridge Construction Company bridged the Sheridan Hollow with the Hawk Street Viaduct in 1890. Asphalt pavement was first used on Albany's streets that year, on Madison Avenue. The Albany Police Department was placed under a new Department of Public Safety. The sewer project sought by the Board of Health—Patroon's Creek—had been completed by contractors two years earlier.

The stonework began on the Washington Avenue Armory in 1889, the year William J. Milne became first president of Albany Normal School; in 1890 the Normal School was chartered as a college.

1891–1894: Mayor James H. Manning welcomed President Benjamin Harrison to Albany in 1891. In 1892 architect Marcus T. Reynolds supervised the careful dismantling, numbering, shipping, and rebuilding of the Van Rensselaer Manor House. Its site was cleared for railroad tracks and business use while the structure itself was assembled as a Williams College fraternity house. Golf was introduced in Albany in 1894 and a year later the Albany Country Club bought a Western Avenue property.

1895–1897: At this time Albany's women seemed increasingly involved in social issues. The Albany branch of the Indian Association voted to fund the education of Sophie High Dog at the Rosebud Sioux Agency. The Mohawk Chapter of the Daughters of the American Revolution organized. Other women got the loan of the Albany *Argus* for a day, proceeds of that day's edition to benefit Child's Hospital. Suffragettes Elizabeth Cady Stanton and Susan B. Anthony, frequent lobbyists in Albany, were opposed by a group of Albany women, led by Mrs. John V. L. Pruyn, and by Bishop Doane, who were against "woman suffragist agitators."

In 1896 another north-south viaduct was built, crossing the Sheridan Avenue ravine at Northern Boulevard. The police installed their signal-box system that year and the Fire Department acquired three chemical fire engines in 1897.

1898–1899: The effects of America's brief and venal little war with Spain were minimal in Albany. Albany Academy graduate Charles Dwight Sigsbee was in command of the U.S.S. *Maine* when it exploded in Havana harbor. Albanians responded with jingoistic enthusiasm to the prospect of war with Spain, feeling President McKinley held back for lack of adequate munitions. Albany Chemical Company speedily doubled its capacity, round-the-clock shifts producing a substance used in gunpowder. A year later the $25 million General Chemical Company formed, consolidating the productions of a dozen smaller Albany County firms. A Brazilian Navy cruiser under construction at a British shipyard was purchased by the U.S. and named the U.S.S. *Albany* at the petition of Albany's citizens. The *Albany*, first U.S. Navy vessel launched abroad, was finished too late for combat but remained an object of pride to Albanians, who in 1903 collected $10,000 for an elaborate silver service for the *Albany*.

The Washington Avenue Armory was crowded with volunteers taking physicals. They were to form the First Provisional Regiment and leave for Long Island, then San Francisco and Honolulu, but never see battle. The few Albany men who died in the war were in Regular Army units that fought sporadic engagements. Domestic patriotic fervor remained at high pitch. Albanians collected money and sent delicacies to its troops, presented commemorative swords, celebrated the first shots fired, the victory at Manila Bay, and the surrender of Santiago.

The State Capitol was at last finished, at a cost much greater than estimated decades earlier. The stonecutters' sheds, 20 years *in situ,* were removed and Capitol Park improved.

In 1896 Albany's street railway carried more than 9.5 million fares—on one Decoration Day a decade later, 175,000 fares totaling nearly $8,000. Albany Railway and Troy Street Railway (combined as United Traction Company in 1899), sold its franchise and assets worth $7.5 million to the Delaware and Hudson Railroad in 1905. Construction started in 1898 on the beaux arts Union Station on Broadway, which opened in 1900.

1900–1905: The new century was greeted with St. Peter's chimes ringing, cannon firing, special church services. Bishop Burke celebrated mass in a greatly crowded Cathedral of the Immaculate Conception.

Municipal Albany undertook progressive public improvements to serve its still-growing population, more than 94,000 in 1900; 4,200 more in 1905. City real property had a total assessed value of nearly $60 million. Albany Trust Company organized in

1900, as did the Chamber of Commerce and the County Bar Association.

William F. Barnes, Jr., grandson of Thurlow Weed, at age 25 became the "Boy Leader" of Albany's Republicans. By controlling the *Albany Evening Journal*, subduing intraparty factionalism, and taking advantage of Democratic schisms, Barnes rapidly gained ascendancy in Albany politics with the 1900 election of James H. Blessing as mayor.

Construction of Beaver Park was underway—later to be Lincoln Park. Dana Park was dedicated by Mayor Blessing on Arbor Day, 1901, before the Dana Natural History Society. Riverside Park, from Broadway to the Hudson River, was sodded and planted with trees two years later. Also near the river, the North Albany Filtration Plant went into operation, and in 1905 work began on a new river intake for the city water supply.

The Superintendent of Schools recommended a second high school be created in the western part of the city. The Eagle Street High School had a

Dr. Mary Walker, opponent of capital punishment

Dennis Holzman

City Hall decorated for the 1909 Hudson-Fulton celebration

capacity of 719 pupils, a daily attendance of 883, and an enrollment of 981.

Albany bicycle mechanic Christian Weeber, who in 1898 became an automotive pioneer by building a car that could carry a half-ton and in which he eventually logged 50,000 miles, established a first in 1904—a motorized honeymoon.

By 1900 motormen and conductors of United Traction Company were on strike, as were the men of the Painters and Decorators Union and the carpenters and plumbers. In 1901 United Traction Company employees struck again, the 10th Batallion patrolling U.T.C. routes and the city under martial law. Another unit, the 23rd Regiment from Brooklyn, reinforced the 10th, firing on a rock-throwing Broadway crowd, killing two men. The "White Rats" strike—Vaudeville's union—spread from New York to Albany and theaters were stilled. Stovemounters walked out of Rathbone, Sard in 1905, printers left the city's publishers, and the compositors at the *Argus* struck in sympathy. U.T.C. employees were on strike again in 1905. Master plumbers walked out in 1906.

While Governor Charles Evans Hughes actively campaigned to better the lot of workers, Albany's 157 police were coping with the gritty side of industrialized society. The freshet of 1900, 20 feet above normal, was the worst in 43 years, causing great suffering in the densely settled South End. The John G. Myers Company store on North Pearl Street collapsed, entombing 80, killing 13—all victims of negligent contractors. An army of railroad men dug in the wreckage, directed by Mayor Gaus.

Germans, who organized a Liederkranz Singing Society in 1897, figured prominently in the elaborate welcome given the Kaiser's brother, Prince Heinrich von Hohenzollern, in 1902; 1904 saw the city's first German Day with Mayor Gaus its chairman. In 1905 Albany's Italian societies paraded on Columbus Day.

In 1901 Albany mourned the deaths of Queen Victoria and President McKinley with elaborate shows of crepe; McKinley was an Albany Law School graduate. Organization of the University Club and the appearances of both Mark Twain and Irish agitator Maude Gonne also took place in 1901.

1906: The Albany Institute and the Albany Historical and Art Society merged in 1900 and in 1906 accepted the plans of architects Fuller and Pitcher for a building to be constructed on Washington Avenue near Dove Street.

Dr. Mary Walker, in her usual male attire, spoke out against capital punishment in a legislative hearing. Sarah Bernhardt appeared in two plays at Harmanus Bleecker Hall. Albany's baseball team began its season in Toronto; five years earlier it had won the State League pennant. Some young baseball players were arrested at the behest of a few Albany clergymen for playing ball in Beaver Park on Sunday. Judges dismissed the case and Sunday baseball resumed without hindrance.

1909: Albany commemorated two epic voyages: one taken at the dusk of the age of reconnaissance, the other in the dawn of the age of steam. The Hudson-Fulton celebration caught the imaginations of communities the length of the Hudson River; it was coordinated by a governor-appointed panel of persons with impeccable Hudson Valley social credentials.

Albany's Mayor Henry F. Snyder claimed he had devoted fully half his time to readying the patriotic, week-long festival. Preparations included creation of a massive, if transitory, "Court of Honor" on Broadway.

For the event, the people of the Netherlands had constructed a fine reproduction of the *Half Moon* from the plans of a contemporary sister ship and presented it to New York State. A reproduction of Fulton's *Clermont* accompanied "Hudson's" ship up the river. After the celebration, both vessels were moored near Kingston. Diminished in their mass appeal, the *Clermont* rotted; the *Half Moon* was eventually towed to Cohoes, where it too rotted and finally burned.

1910: In 1910 (and again in 1916) Albany annexed large portions of the Pine Bush area from the town of Guilderland. The population of Albany in 1910 was more than 100,000 persons, at a time when the state's residents as a whole were about 26 percent foreign born and 33 percent of foreign-born parentage. The Hudson-Fulton celebration partly expressed a long-term civic concern in Albany: the Americanization of a heterogeneous population, increasingly of Eastern or Southern European origins. (Trinity Institute, Albany's oldest settlement house, would be founded in 1912 with the goal of improving neighborhood living conditions and acculturating its clients. In planning a community center at School 14 in 1915, folk dancing and Americanization were parts of the programs; by 1920 the Board of Education annually budgeted $4,000 for Americanization classes.)

Seeking a $10,000 prize offered by the *New York World* for a flight between Albany and New York City in less than 24 hours, pioneer aviator Glenn Curtiss took off from a field on the present site of the Port of Albany. He made two refueling stops in this first long-distance flight by man in a heavier-than-air machine; the speed averaged about 53 miles per hour. Three years later, the nation's first municipal airfield was created in Albany, at his takeoff place.

Automotive technology made dramatic gains between 1900 and 1920. In 1910 there were six automobile dealers in Albany, soon to be followed by others. The increasing use of automobiles necessitated better roads, at the same time outmoding electric street cars. Albany's first concrete pavement was laid. The Suburban Transportation Bus Co. was operating in 1912, and in 1913 the Albany and Guilderland Center Bus Line charged a nickel fare. The fire horses were disappearing, and some city departments considered motorizing.

Capital Newspapers

Glenn Curtiss, early aviator

Albany Public Library

Crowd on Hudson Avenue listening to a World Series broadcast over PA system

Until about 1900, most heavy freight had been waterborne, although by then the Erie Canal no longer held prime economic importance for Albany. The Lumber District, once a major exporter of timber, had also declined, becoming moribund as the logging-off of the Adirondacks shifted the lumber industry west to the Great Lakes area. By 1910 Albany's waterfront area consisted of ramshackle, partially abandoned commercial buildings—a crumbling vestige of its active past, a tenderloin district in which nighttime travel could be hazardous. This unsightly waterfront, in view of the State Capitol, bloomed at the foot of State Street, to be traversed by virtually every arriving steamboat or railroad passenger coming to Albany. The City of Albany, the Chamber of Commerce, and the D & H Railroad, among others, coalesced in the Albany Beautiful Movement, to plan beautification of the waterfront. Under the aesthetic guidance of architect Marcus T. Reynolds, a screen of new buildings would replace the existing structures by 1916. The D & H Plaza was cleared to enable construction of the superb D & H and Albany Evening Journal buildings, both in a monumental Flemish High Gothic Style.

A contemporary Chamber of Commerce yearbook endorsed this Albany Beautiful Movement and the establishment of an Albany Barge Canal terminal. It also approved construction of low-cost housing.

1911: The Woodlawn Avenue Improvement Association petitioned the United Traction Company for trolley lines. The Albany Orphan Asylum—now the campus of Junior College of Albany—had been built in 1907, and a year later the Chamber of Commerce promoted the extension of trolley lines into the Woodlawn Avenue district, to encourage development there. But the tracks were never laid. Eventually the Association formed its own transportation corporation, a bus line.

In an epic 1911 fire, part of the New York State Capitol's premises, including the State Library, burned. The entire city fire department fought the blaze, which smoldered for a week afterward. Losses were computed in the millions of dollars, but the value of historical materials destroyed could not be calculated. Ironically, the new State Education Building, to house the State Library and Museum, was already under construction. Its plans had been selected by Governor Charles Evans Hughes after an architectural competition. In 1911 the State also acquired the Schuyler Mansion as an historic site.

In 1911 William F. Barnes became State Republican Chairman after Republican boss Thomas C. Platt waned in power. From 1912 to 1916, as National Chairman of the party, Barnes was at the apex of his political power.

1912: The mercurial William Sulzer, a Tammany Democrat, became governor of New York, but quarrels with Tammany boss Charles E. Murphy resulted in Sulzer's impeachment and conviction in 1913. Sulzer was succeeded by Albany newspaper publisher Martin H. Glynn, then lieutenant governor.

Admission to the Empire Burlesque Review cost a dime in 1912; the theater even had a ladies' matinee. Albanians, enthusiastic about baseball, had a number of teams. A large crowd of Albanians listened to the 1912 World Series between the Boston Red Sox and the New York Giants over a primitive public address system.

Albany Institute of History and Art

Flood of 1913

1913: Ice jams south of Albany caused periodic downtown flooding, and waiters at Keeler's Broadway "Hotel for Men Only" actually rowed a boat into the hotel's street-level dining room. This year's flood inundated the municipal water-filtration system, to pollute the water supply and cause a typhoid epidemic. By 1915 the cause of such flooding (near Coeymans) was removed and the Hudson's channel there was deepened.

Suffragettes were increasingly aggressive and successful; in 1913 and 1915 the state legislature passed a women's suffrage bill, to be rejected later in popular referenda. Voters finally approved it in 1917, and two years later New York State ratified the 19th Amendment to the United States Constitution.

Capital Newspapers

WWI Albany medical unit ready to depart for National Guard camp

New York State also worked to improve labor conditions, while Albany's fractious United Traction Company men struck three times between 1910 and 1916. In 1914 Albany's public schools had an enrollment well over 12,000; 97 percent attendance was the norm.

1914–1916: Charles Ogden designed the massive grey stone Academy of Holy Names on Madison Avenue in 1914. Albany's business community prospered in a time of economic growth. The Municipal Gas Company built its State Street building to Marcus T. Reynolds' design in 1915—a building now housing Niagara Mohawk. The deBeer Baseball Factory relocated from Johnstown in 1916. And in a dress rehearsal of horrors soon to come for American soldiers in the other hemisphere, Albany National Guardsmen chased Pancho Villa along the Mexican border.

The interior of City Hall was renovated by architects Gander, Gander and Gander in 1916, the year Albany annexed portions of Bethlehem and Colonie.

World War I and Its Aftermath: 1917–1920

1917–1918: Albany had a large, long-established, and prosperous German-American community. By 1913 at least two German-language newspapers were printed in the city, including the *Albany Sonntags Journal*. The widespread hysterical and vitriolic anti-German sentiment manifested in many American communities during the European conflict was tempered in Albany. When the United States itself entered the First World War, 10,000 Albany men registered for the draft; under the provisions of the Stivers Act, Albany's National Guard units were called up in July 1917.

World War I accelerated the development of some business and civic procedures. Small firms grew large and new industries evolved. "Four-minute men" made their speeches, one Liberty Loan Drive followed another, and there were plans to conserve food; "Tag Days" raised money for Armenian relief, for the Salvation Army, and for the Red Cross. Albany Hospital launched a medical unit, Base Hospital 33, which served with distinction in England. Mayor Watt appointed a War Advisory Commission. A "Melting Pot Day" was organized to collect tinfoil and scrap metal. Before the Armistice, 300 Albany men died. Henry Johnson of Albany won the French Croix de Guerre while serving with the 15th New York (Colored) Infantry Regiment. Late in 1918 and into 1919, the nationwide epidemic of "Spanish influenza" struck Albany just as the veterans of the war were filtering home.

1918–1919: The election of Alfred E. Smith as governor bolstered the spirits of New York State Democrats, who in Albany made a strong, determined effort in the 1919 municipal elections, using the issues of the high costs of Republican administration, alleged vote frauds, and the lack of basic city services such as garbage and ash collection. The new South End political team of the O'Connell brothers organized a solid reform campaign, but the Democrats narrowly lost the mayoral election, 23,553 to 22,145. Daniel P. O'Connell, however, was elected to the Board of Assessors, one of the few Democratic victors; it was the only elected office he would hold in an extraordinary political career spanning nearly six decades.

The Roaring '20s: 1920–1929

1920: Albany was at the threshold of a new era. The federal census counted 113,344 Albanians in 1920. The city budget was $3.1 million, of that more than $2.8 million to be raised through taxes. The mayor's salary was $4,000 per annum; the Board of Education's teachers, *in toto,* received more than $620,000; $2,500 was expended on truants, $70,000 for the school system's fuel. Temporary relief for Albany's indigent poor was budgeted at $15,000 in 1920, and various related activities—free dispensary, infant home, etc.—received another $4,700.

Among the things returning servicemen encountered was the prospect, at least in theory, of an Albany without alcohol. By 1914 a quarter of the states had gone "dry," and during World War I, the argument that sober servicemen and factory workers promoted victory, and that many brewers were of German ancestry, did much to advance the cause of Prohibition. In 1919 the 18th Amendment to the Constitution was ratified, in a great surge of Progressivism. The Volstead Act of 1920, providing Federal enforcement of the Amendment, went into effect on the same day as Prohibition. Overnight, some 200,000 "private" clubs opened, selling illicit liquor nationwide. In Albany saloons or "speakeasies" ranged from the desperately sordid to the elegant and were soon an open secret. Bootleggers maintained a steady supply of liquor smuggled in from Canada. Many Albany drugstores clandestinely sold liquor; Albanians made home brew or "bathtub gin."

The law-breaking climate of the times, with attendant high risks and big profits, encouraged gangsterism. The best-known incident during Albany's Prohibition era was the murder of bootlegger Legs Diamond.

Bootlegger Jack "Legs" Diamond (right), wife, and Daniel Prior

Capital Newspapers

Boss Barnes reputedly was among those Republican stalwarts in the "smoke-filled room" who, in 1920, made the cynical trade-offs that brought Warren G. Harding to the Presidency. But by this time William Barnes was slipping in his control of the Albany Republican organization because of his reactionary attitudes. Meanwhile, in the Democratic primary election of 1920, the O'Connell brothers' faction defeated that of Patrick McCabe, the oldtime Democratic boss who had worked out accommodations with Barnes. The O'Connells, now controlling the Democratic organization, prepared to challenge Barnes and the Republicans, who enjoyed a three to one advantage in voter strength.

1921: There were 98 strikes nationwide; for the men of United Traction Company, 1921 brought their fifth walkout since 1900. With the trolleys not running and 1,200 to 1,400 men striking, Albany businessmen were bound to lose money. The State Public Service Commission ordered resumption of trolley service. The company brought in strikebreakers; William Barnes supported United Traction's position. Battles broke out along the trolley lines, in the West End, along North Pearl Street and Central Avenue, and at the Quail Street trolley barns. Violence was crushed by state troopers. Public sympathy went generally with the strikers; ridership on the trolleys fell off sharply. The slack in public transportation was taken up by jitneys and autos of all sorts pressed into service as *ad hoc* cabs, and 130 taxi licenses were issued during the first 90 days of the strike. As sentiment grew for the strikers, a rift between Barnes and Republican Mayor Watt developed. By the time the strike ended months later, Barnes was an unpopular figure; his mayoral choice, William Van Rensselaer Erving, barely eked out a Republican primary victory. In its dramatic acknowledgment of the rights of labor, the Trolley Strike of 1921 was Albany's largest, and last, manifestation of Progressivism.

In the mayoral election of 1921, the Democrats nominated William S. Hackett, a lawyer and banker whose New York Mortgage and Home Building Company had aided low- and medium-income people in building affordable homes. During the campaign scandals involving fraudulent billings for coal not delivered to the city, unsafe construction of School 14, shoddy paving and sewer construction jobs became issues. When Hackett beat Erving by 7,200 votes, the Democrats returned to City Hall after an absence of more than 20 years.

1922–1924: Hackett's administration was conducted in a businesslike, cash-on-delivery manner. Consultants revamped the city's property assessment system; public schools were renovated and four new ones constructed. Ash and garbage collection was instituted and steps were taken to revamp the municipal water supply. The 1922 budget topped $3.45 million, of which more than $3 million would be raised through taxes. City revenues were close to $5 million, costs of government $5.62 million.

Albany's 1920s witnessed a continuing pattern of busline franchises encouraged by outlying neighborhoods and furthering population dispersement. The Trolley Strike had engendered a marked increase in both business and pleasure use of automobiles; gas prices rose to 35 cents a gallon. Mayor Hackett appointed a City Planning Commission to study the extension of city streets, purchase new land for boulevards, and resolve traffic problems. Traffic lights were installed in 1927. A Zoning Commission was created in 1922.

The Harmanus Bleecker Library was built in 1923 at Washington Avenue on Dove Street; in 1924 the Municipal Building was put up on Eagle Street. The College of St. Rose erected a four-story brick building in 1924; four years earlier it had begun a degree program. On New Scotland Avenue, Bishop Gibbons had chosen a 56-acre site for St. Peter's Hospital, which was joined later by Mercy College, Mercy High School, Immaculate Conception Seminary, the Motherhouse of the Sisters of Mercy, and the Villa. Governor Alfred E. Smith's statewide public works program was realized locally by construction of the State Health Laboratories on New Scotland Avenue and expansion of the State Teachers College.

1925: Governor Smith created the Albany Port District in 1925, and Congress voted more than $11 million to dredge a 27-foot-deep, 30-mile-long channel up the Hudson River capable of floating 85 percent of the world's oceangoing ships. In 1926, before the port was officially opened, it had receipts totaling about $63,000. The cities of Albany and Rensselaer expended $10 million in constructing wharves, sheds, and the world's largest single-unit grain elevator. Albany annexed Westerlo Island in the port. Both D & H and New York Central Railroads cooperated in development of the port, laying a 25-mile web of tracks; a third of the American population could be reached within a 250-mile radius of the Port of Albany.

During the 1920s Albany's last horsecar disappeared. The demise of the trolley was also approaching as buses began to replace the trolleys in the nationwide trend toward motorized transportation. Between buses and automobiles, commuting became a truly viable possibility resulting in a more convenient suburban life. In the future this trend would have immense impact on life in Albany; coupled with better roads and a national prosperity locally shared, it would be cause for a dramatic demographic change.

1926–1929: By the late 1920s Albany's Democrats had achieved a two-to-one dominance over the city's Republicans in voter registration, a reversal of the situation in 1921. Aviator Charles Lindbergh was cheered by thousands of Albanians in 1927 when he made an appearance in Lincoln Park. A year later, when Albany created the first city-owned airport in the nation, it was named "Lindbergh Field," then "Quentin Roosevelt Field."—located at the site of the present Albany County Airport.

The Albany College of Pharmacy moved into its building near Albany Hospital in 1927. The city built the John A. Howe Library in 1928; in 1929 it closed the Almshouse, transferring many of its residents to the newly opened Ann Lee Home. Albany Law School was built in 1929.

Empty Pockets: 1929–1940

1929–1934: The Stock Market Crash in late 1929 commenced the epic decline of an American economy already precarious on a foundation of overextended credit, endemic speculation, and a consumer buying power too weak to support high production and high employment. By the end of 1929, Albany had spent more than $35,000 on relief for the unemployed, an amount that would mushroom in the difficult times to follow.

In 1930, entering the Depression, Albany's population was over 127,000—98 percent white, 85.5 percent native-born.

The Depression struck with an appalling rapidity. By April 1930 an estimated 2,000 to 4,000 Albanians were out of work, up from a past average of 800 to 1,000. By November, West Albany alone had 2,000 unemployed, and 25 percent of the city's total work force was looking for work, compared to 20 percent statewide. A year after the Crash, 538 families sought aid at City Hall, where meal tickets were issued, each good for two daily meals per person. In a month, 500 men lined up for meal tickets, and the city was aiding 2,200 families. The Salvation Army set up a "Municipal Barracks" in a former Bleecker Street nightclub and served 500 meals daily.

Total wages paid Albany's work force in 1930 fell more than 27 percent; total value of goods manufactured by nearly 33 percent. By 1931 aid requests for fuel, food, and rent were up almost 38 percent at City Hall; 35 to 45 new families sought help each day. Mayor John Boyd Thacher II stretched the municipal-relief dollar as far as possible, then made funds available for labor-intensive public works projects. By 1932 the "Arbor Hill School"—Philip Livingston—was built. The Hannacroix and Basic Creeks were dammed to increase Albany's water supply, creating Alcove and Basic Reservoirs; 12.8 billion gallons were piped through a 20-mile gravity feed at a cost of $11 million. Albany built 144 miles of paved streets in 1934—28 in concrete, 40 in dressed granite, and 4 in cobbles.

Albany's Academy opened its new building on Academy Road in 1930; designed by Marcus T. Reynolds, part of its interior arrangement and woodwork duplicated the original Philip Hooker structure. (Hooker's Academy building, near City Hall, was restored five years later with the help of Reynolds and the WPA.)

The Depression at least was a golden

age for the movies. Theater attendance was high as people sought escape from a sober reality. In fact, movies were used by Albany's mayor as relief fund-raisers. In 1931 Albany's Palace Theater opened—probably the last opulent-style movie theater constructed in the city. Radio was at its zenith. WOKO, a CBS station, went on the air from the Ten Eyck Hotel in 1931, and WABY moved to Albany shortly thereafter, affiliating with the National Broadcasting System's Blue Network. (Both stations eventually relocated in "Radio Center," an Elk Street townhouse revamped in Art Moderne style in 1939.)

In 1932 the first cars poured across the Dunn Memorial Bridge, named for Rensselaer's World War I Medal of Honor winner, Sergeant Parker F. Dunn. The Dunn Memorial replaced the old Greenbush Bridge over the Hudson River at a cost of more than $2.5 million. Actively boosted by the Albany Chamber of Commerce, it could handle a daily traffic flow of 30,000 vehicles. Indicative too of the new supremacy of motorized transportation was the opening of a Greyhound terminal on Broadway in 1932; 46 buses left Albany daily, bound mainly west or south.

The Port of Albany officially opened in 1932. At the intersection of six major railroads, with miles of track of its own, the port had a capacity of 20,000 freight cars in its yards, an annual pass-through total of a million. Rail travel was ever more rapid; the Twentieth Century Limited made its record 2-hour and 35-minute New York City-Albany run in 1935. The port was also fed by the revamped New York State Barge Canal System, which in 1931 had carried 3.7 million tons of freight, an increase of 220 percent over 1918.

1935: President Franklin D. Roosevelt created the Works Progress Administration, which eventually employed eight million Americans. That year in Albany, 1,881 men and 183 women were employed by the WPA.

1936–1939: Albany's Department of Public Safety in 1936 consisted of six police precincts and a Fire Department of 200 men and 16 fire trucks. The City operated 25 public parks, a municipal golf course, skating rinks, Bleecker Stadium (converted from a former reservoir by WPA workers), the Lincoln Park Pool, and several public baths. The Public Library had 130,000 books in circulation. Albany had 20 theaters, one of them—the Palace—seating 2,800 people. There were 99 churches, 10 hotels, and 5 hospitals.

1937 aerial view of Albany

New York State Archives

The Depression ground on. In 1937 the Albany Council of Social Agencies provided Christmas dinners for 5,525 families, toys for 368. In 1939, Trinity Institute served 52,324 clients. The Depression's effects were mirrored in the statistics of the Port of Albany. Despite the decline in the number of ships, the port remained a steady source of employment in Albany throughout the Depression.

1940–1941: In the 1940 federal census, Albany's population was 130,577 persons; the city's rate of growth of 2.5 percent since the previous decade had been slowed by the Depression. Nearly 20 percent of Albany's employed men worked in transportation and communications; 16 percent were in manufacturing. Interestingly, 17.8 percent of Albany's women workers were classed as "professional," and only 6 percent of the men. New York State employed significant numbers of Albanians.

Albany had remained a large producer of iron and steel; in 1941 it had the largest machine tool repair facility in the U.S. The city with its diverse industries produced paper goods, chemicals, brushes, toys and games, caps and gowns, baseballs, pianos, billiard balls, lye, textiles, blankets, papermakers' felts, and automobile heating equipment. The total assessed value of Albany's real property was $242,525,079. John Boyd Thacher II resigned as mayor in 1941, after 14 years—then Albany's longest mayoral tenure since colonial times.

World War II: 1941–1945

1941: December 7, 1941, began as a conventional day. Jimmy Dorsey's band was headlined on the Palace Theater's marquee; and at the Leland, Charlie Chaplin's film *The Great Dictator* was playing. The Christmas tree in Capitol Park was to be lit on December 8. The New York Central Railroad advertised excursions to New York City for two dollars. Steak was 25 cents per pound, butter 35 cents, eggs 32 cents per dozen.

Many Albanians, living in peace and returning prosperity, were shocked at the news of the Japanese raid on Pearl Harbor, although many Albany men had already been conscripted and the National Guard called up. Soon blackouts and air-raid drills were

Albany Public Library

Harmanus Bleecker Hall, one of Albany's 20 movie theaters in the 1930s

supervised by Civil Defense wardens in brassards and "pancake" helmets; theater screens were filled with Pathé newsreels of the war and war movies. Flags bearing small blue (and later gold) stars sometimes hung in the windows of Albany's houses where men had left for the war. Shortages developed—of canvas, straight pins, cardboard, buttons, molding sand, paper, brushes, and mattresses. Only Albany's production of baseballs seemed unaffected as the war effort snapped up building materials and defense plants added 30 percent to the drain on Albany utilities. City government created a bombproof shelter in the basement of the police headquarters, and 500 volunteers prepared to staff it.

1942–1944: An "Avenge Pearl Harbor Day" celebrated on the Capitol steps resulted in 118 recruits being sworn into the Marine Corps and Navy. An "I Am An American Day" was held later. Stationed at Steamboat Square, a military police battalion benefitted Albany businesses by purchasing coal and groceries and paying for utilities.

Erastus Corning 2nd was elected mayor of Albany in 1942, winning by a margin of nearly five to one. Corning would eventually have one of the longest mayoral tenures in American history. In 1944 Mayor Corning entered the Army as an infantry private; under the La Guardia Act he was able to appoint an acting mayor in his absence.

Eighteen Albany-area banks participated in 1942's two-month experimental trial of ration banking; based on its outcome, ration banking went nationwide in the beginning of 1943, to prevent the counterfeiting and misuse of ration stamps. National Commercial Bank entered War Bond subscriptions of more than $238.4 million during the war; these were instrumental in financing the U.S.S. *Albany*, the last ship to bear that name (and decommissioned in 1980). Sailings from the Port of Albany diminished during the war, but revenues increased as wartime ships grew larger. By 1945 larger ships mandated further deepening of the Hudson River's channel.

Postwar Era: 1945–1959

1945–1950: By the war's end 556 Albanians had died in the service. One Albany bank alone had an investment list 94 percent committed to government bonds. The city was so geared to the war effort that disengagement would be difficult. "People expect wishfully that reconversion could be completed in less than six months after the terrific struggle which ended in August," one banker remarked. The City of Albany now found it possible, at last, to purchase much-needed equipment to replace items worn out and unavailable during the war years.

The phenomenal postwar baby boom began, the birth of a generation which by its sheer numbers would strain every institution it would encounter. Returning GIs built homes, and property owners were at last able to obtain materials for alterations and repairs. The extreme postwar housing shortage presented problems nationwide; a federal housing act in 1949 led to the creation of the Albany Housing Authority. In the early 1950s the Housing Authority began to build a succession of housing developments,

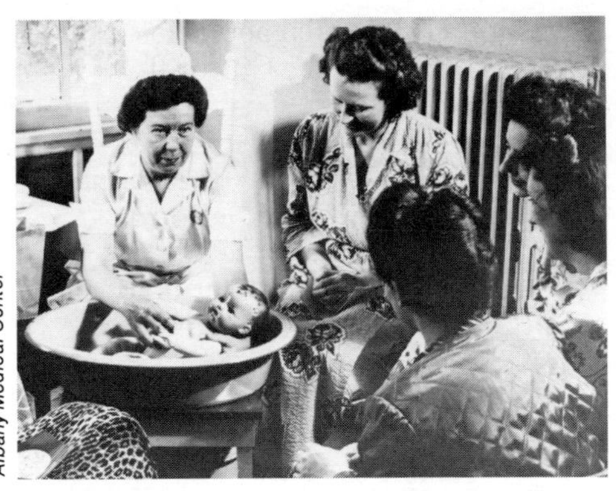

Albany Medical Center

Nurses teaching infant care classes at Albany Medical Center in the 1940s

especially in the older, congested parts of Albany.

The last trolleys ran the West Albany, Belt, Pine Hills, Delaware Avenue, and Second Avenue routes in 1946; the United Traction Company's 38 remaining trolleys and five remaining service cars were sold to a Broadway scrap dealer. Many Albany businessmen, feeling the commercial pull to go westward in the city, eventually acted on that impulse, although immediate postwar development took place along Pearl Street and other traditional commercial arteries. Albany Airport's runways were lengthened to handle larger aircraft and additions were planned for or in progress on the public schools in 1949.

1950–1954: By 1950 the population of Albany was almost 135,000. In that year 357 single-family houses were built in the city. A $100,000 supermarket and a $250,000 cafeteria were erected on Central Avenue; W.T. Grant's opened on North Pearl Street, with a "handsome television set" as door prize. The gross city debt was at its lowest since 1929 and prosperity was at hand, even though the New York Central Railroad began moving part of its West Albany shops away from the city. The opening of the New York State Thruway and other improved highways gave automotive traffic competitive advantage over railroads. In 1954 the West Albany shops closed down completely and the railroads seemed doomed.

1956–1959: Albany was changing; the character of its downtown in flux. While the Center Square Association, oldest of Albany's present neighborhood associations, was founded in 1956, many Albanians were moving to outlying residential portions of the city—notably Altamont, Voorheesville, Bethlehem, Colonie, and Guilderland. Schools followed suit. In 1958 the Albany area's first shopping centers were operating: Stuyvesant Plaza in Westmere, and Westgate on Central Avenue, "a suburban center within an urban area, bringing the advantage of a suburban center's spacious parking to city residents." Movie theaters in downtown Albany were closing. By 1958 only 168 factories were operating in the city, with some 4,900 workers.

Albany's first official urban renewal project was in northern Albany in the 1950s, the first such project to be completed in the state. School 13 and "slums" were razed on the site. Further to the north, the St. Lawrence Seaway opened in 1959, posing heavy competition for the Port of Albany, which in that year handled 867,151 tons of cargo, including huge quantities of grain and molasses, from 177 oceangoing ships, 282 barges, and 21,739 railroad cars.

Decline and Revival: 1960–1980

1960: Downtown Albany's familiar, major commercial arteries were hardening, the flow of vital economic activity beginning to slow, and Pearl Street falling slowly more silent. More stores emptied as the exodus to the suburbs and the shopping malls accelerated, as businesses decades old closed their doors or relocated. The demographic shift to the suburb was evident in the new federal census, which counted 129,726 people in Albany, down 5,200 persons since 1950. The resuscitation of decaying downtown Albany was clearly essential. Albany now created its Urban Renewal Agency, a local outgrowth of President Kennedy's newly formed Department of Housing and Urban Development.

1962: The State of New York made public its plan to acquire a large tract of land in the center of Albany for the South Mall Project. The Project was viewed with alarm and skepticism locally. Wrote Mayor Corning: "The state is planning to carve out from the heart of the city a large sterile area for a monumental group of buildings which will look spectacular on postcards all over the world, but will, in fact, hurt the people of Albany." Seven thousand people—more than 3,100 families—would be displaced by the Mall, 1,500 buildings demolished, 3.1 million cubic yards of earth excavated.

A densely settled portion of Albany now vanished as if it had never existed. In "Rockefeller's Quarry" thousands of laborers poured the 900,000 cubic yards of concrete, erected the 232,000 tons of steel and a half-million cubic feet of marble, with miles of wiring. Only in the late 1970s did this massive island of white marble begin to assume a human dimension. If the Mall's cost can ever be accurately assessed, the figures will exceed $2 billion.

Construction of the Mall reflected Albany's increasing stature as administrative nexus of an expanding State government. State jobs were an ever more important source of employment in the local economy; by

The abandoned West Albany shops, 1956

Arthur J. O'Keefe

1963 only 24 percent of Albany's work force was involved in manufacturing, well below the national average.

1967: Work began on the Northside, Riverside, and Crosstown Arterial highways—frank acknowledgments of Albany's importance as workplace to thousands of commuters. With the new Northway, they would make possible a much wider dispersion of area population away from the capital city. Within Albany, the Urban Renewal Agency had received federal approval for rehabilitation of houses on Livingston Avenue and the demolition of others for a renewal site. In 1967 Albany annexed the Karlsfeld section at the city outskirts, bringing the city line to its natural border along the Normanskill Creek.

Demonstrations for civil rights and against the Viet Nam War marked the late 1960s in Albany, making national political issues more intimate and crucial to local citizens. Despite some incidents of racial violence, the city was not badly riven as others were.

The youth culture also erupted, becoming highly visible (the first "head shop" opened in 1966). It enjoyed a short-lived flowering that faded with the less prosperous economy of the decade to follow.

1970–1980: The 1970s were marked by falling enrollments in public and parochial schools; a number of city elementary and high schools closed, casualties of a declining birth rate.

Albany High moved to its ultra-modern Washington Avenue campus; when Philip Schuyler High School closed down, its student population joined Albany High. Milne and St. Joseph's Academy closed; other parochial schools were combined.

As school enrollments sagged, jobs declined. The city's new Department of Human Resources was created to administer the federally-subsidized public employment programs that appeared again in Albany. Under one grant or another, more than 17,000 persons worked in public employment programs in the decade after 1971.

The Urban Renewal Agency developed the Pastures Preservation District, a rejuvenation of one of Albany's earliest postcolonial neighborhoods still largely architecturally intact. The State University of New York acquired the D & H, Albany Journal, and Old Federal buildings to use as its central administrative headquarters, the best form of historic preservation. Other recent and revived efforts included the colonial Quackenbush house, the Steuben Place and Ten Eyck projects, and the Water Department complex.

In 1975 the federally funded Community Development Program included the rehabilitation of housing, downtown improvements, and "economic development." Coupled with tax incentives passed by Congress in 1976, rehabilitation of Albany's older structures became feasible, attractive, and, finally, trendy; by 1981, nearly $20.5 million in Community Development money had been granted Albany. Individual houses, then city blocks, and finally whole neighborhoods began to revitalize. The post-World War II babies had grown up to penetrate the housing market; they found the ambience and convenience of the old central city attractive, especially as high fuel costs began to make suburban living, and commuting, less so. Neighborhood associations, numbering more than 20 by 1981, represented almost every geographic area; growing larger and more vocal, they are demanding, and receiving, more complex and professional services from the City of Albany.

In 1973 the new, controversial Mall had been dedicated as the "Empire State Plaza" by Governor Rockefeller. In 1976, in a flurry of local and state national bicentennial activities, the Empire State Plaza's Cultural Resources Center—housing State Archives, Library, and Museum—was opened. (In 1978, a rededication named the Mall the Governor Nelson A. Rockefeller Empire State Plaza.) As one side effect, the completion of the Mall Project meant the loss of jobs among many locals in the city's building trades, who for a decade had been busily employed.

A "Free the Panthers" demonstration on the steps of the State Capitol

State University of New York, Albany

Development of the ANSWERS Project—Albany, New York, Solid Waste Energy Recovery System—pointed one direction for Albany's future. As an old city in a climate not noted for mild winters, this unique regional facility was designed to process 750 tons of municipal solid waste daily, at once producing fuel for steam generation and recovering all recyclable materials. ANSWERS, its concepts sound, both fiscally and morally, was essentially complete by 1980.

The 1980s began with a favorable prognosis for Albany's future. New life was beginning to breathe along Pearl Street, the new State offices disgorged crowds of workers into the central city, old banks and new lined State Street. As Albany moved toward its tricentennial as a city in 1986, it showed ample signs of renewed health and vigor while yielding none of its distinctive and ancient character.

Albany D.H.R.—Historical Services

Albany D.H.R.—Historical Services

Albany Institute of History and Art. Photo by Rich Frutchey

Top
During the mid-1970s the city conducted an archaeological dig adjacent to the Quackenbush House, Albany's oldest house. The excavation produced a wealth of artifacts from four centuries.
Above
This 1840 charcoal and sandpaper drawing from Ezra Prentice depicts Mt. Hope Mansion as it appeared shortly after its construction. The home was flanked by the Rathbun estate at Kenwood and the Walsh estate, "Nut Grove," on McCarty Avenue. All three mansions have been demolished.

Albany Institute of History and Art

Above
Pemberton Corner was constructed in 1710 in traditional Dutch style on the corner of North Pearl and Columbia streets. At the end of the 19th century it was replaced with the Brewster Building (old Albany Business College). Painting by James Eights.
Right
Washington Park Lake was formed by damming up a branch of the Beaver Kill. The 1920s Dutch-Spanish lake house shown here replaced an earlier wooden structure.

Photo by Rich Frutchey

Albany Institute of History and Art

Albany Institute of History and Art

Above
This James Eights watercolor painted circa 1875 depicts the east side of Market Street (Broadway) as it appeared in 1805. Note the Public Market in the middle of the street.

Left
Dr. John Stevenson's house, built in 1780 in the Georgian style, provides a great contrast to the 1716 home built in the traditional urban Dutch fashion by Harman Wendell. The gabled end of the older house faced the street. Both houses stood on the south side of State Street just above Pearl. They were demolished in 1841. Painting by James Eights.

Clockwise from top left
The city of "Albony" was carved into this colonial powder horn, probably by provincial soldiers during the great summer campaigns of the French and Indian war.

Whitehall, shown here in an 1872 painting on brick by Ten Eyck, was destroyed by fire 11 years later. Major General John Bradstreet and the British Army used the mansion, which was seized as Tory property and became the home of the celebrated Gansevoort-Ten Eyck families.

Old Centre Market was located on South Pearl Street between Howard and Beaver streets.

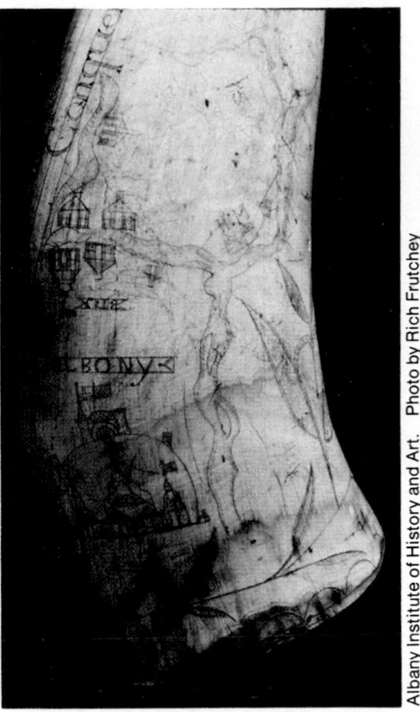

Albany Institute of History and Art. Photo by Rich Frutchey

Albany Institute of History and Art. Photo by Rich Frutchey

Albany Institute of History and Art. Photo by Rich Frutchey

Albany Institute of History and Art. Photo by Rich Frutchey

Albany Institute of History and Art. Photo by Rich Frutchey

Above
Thomas Cole painted this view of the Van Rensselaer Manor House in 1841. Constructed in 1767, the great mansion in North Albany was the location from which the Van Rensselaer family ruled one of the greatest estates in the colonies. It included most of Albany and Rensselaer counties. In 1893 the building was moved to the Williams College for use by a fraternity.
Right
A Staffordshire plate is decorated with a view of Albany from Van Rensselaers (Westerlo) Island. The design was copied from a painting by William Guy Wall, circa 1830.

Albany D.H.R. Photo by Lindsey Watson

Left
Victorian iron work decorates the roof of this Woodlawn Avenue structure.
Below
Broadway, across from University Plaza, was once a hub of Hudson River commerce.
Bottom
Albany as a city on a hill is boldly depicted in this 19th-century oil painting made after an engraving by William Bartlett.

Albany D.H.R. Photo by Lindsey Watson

McLean Gallery, Inc.

Albany Institute of History and Art

Above
James Eights painted this view of State Street as it looked from the front of St. Peter's Church, opposite Chapel Street. Its Dutch Reformed equivalent, visible at the foot of the hill, also stood in the middle of State Street.
Right
This bas relief by Charles Calverly appears on the base of the Robert Burns statue in Washington Park.

Albany D.H.R. Photo by Lindsey Watson

Albany Institute of History and Art. Photo by Rich Frutchey

Albany D.H.R. Photo by Lindsey Watson

Albany Institute of History and Art. Photo by Rich Frutchey

Albany D.H.R. Photo by Lindsey Watson

Clockwise from top
Albany's first capitol, designed by Philip Hooker, towers over the city in this 1846 painting by William Hart.

This Staffordshire bowl depicting the entrance of the Erie Canal at Albany is one of a series produced after the opening of the canal in 1825 honoring cities along that waterway. This view was taken from a watercolor by James Eights.

J. Massey Rhind's bronze statue of Moses is surrounded by smaller sculptures of several of his followers, one of which is pictured here. The statue, which stands in Washington Park, was given to the city in 1893.

The pineapple was a popular Georgian architectural detail symbolizing hospitality. This fence on South Pearl Street below 2nd Avenue incorporates the exotic fruit in its design.

Right
The Jewish Cemetery on Fuller Road memorializes an active Jewish community that has flourished in Albany from the early 19th century.
Far right, top
Pictured here is one of the carved wooden angels that looks down on the congregation of St. Joseph's Church from 80 feet above. The angels were said to remind Irish immigrants of the prows of the ships on which they came. The church, on Arbor Hill, was constructed from 1856-1860.
Far right, bottom
The third St. Peter's Church, constructed in 1856 on State Street, boasts distinctive Gothic architecture, including bronze doors, gargoyles on its bell tower, beautiful stained glass windows, painted ceiling beams, and delicate mosaic aisles, a detail of which is shown here.
Below
This depiction of State Street below North Pearl was painted by Dr. James Eights. The State Bank of Albany, whose 1806 building was designed by Philip Hooker, stands on this site today, incorporating the original facade shown in the center of the picture just above James Street. When the office building was constructed, the facade was moved up the hill to serve as the center entrance for the building.

Photo by Rich Frutchey

Albany D.H.R. Photo by Lindsey Watson

Albany D.H.R. Photo by Lindsey Watson

Albany Institute of History and Art

CHAPTER 2

COLONIZATION AND CONFLICT

Albany Institute of History and Art

Lossing, *The Empire State*

Fifteen years after Henry Hudson sailed up the great estuary that would later bear his name, the city of Albany was founded—not by a self-governing religious fellowship, as Plymouth was, nor by the Dutch government, but by a private company. The Dutch West India Company, chartered in Amsterdam in 1621, had been granted a trading monopoly that extended all the way across the Atlantic, from the west coast of Africa to the east coast of America, including the Caribbean and, of course, Hudson's River; the company was empowered to build forts, maintain a private army, encourage settlement, and establish colonial governments.

A fort had been maintained by Dutch traders at Albany since 1614, but the first real settlers arrived in 1624, under the auspices of the new company. Consisting primarily of French-speaking Walloons from the southern provinces of Hainaut, Namur, Luxembourg, and Liege, this first group of pioneer families set to work clearing a tiny corner of the seemingly endless North American wilderness, planting crops of corn and wheat on land assigned to them by the company, building their first crude shelters, and helping to fortify a new garrison for their common defense to be known as Fort Orange. Their transportation to America had been without cost but not without obligations—among them, to obey the officers of the company, to profess the approved Reformed Calvinist faith, to live only where the company permitted, and to do nothing that might jeopardize friendly (and profitable) relations with the natives. All trade for export, as well as all mining and mineral rights, remained in the hands of the company.

Scarcely three years had passed after the first settlers arrived at Fort Orange when it became readily apparent that something was wrong. The small group of Walloon families were becoming rapidly disenchanted with their new adventure in the North American wilderness. Several, in fact, had already retreated downriver to New Amsterdam, while others were casting a lingering eye homeward to the Europe they had left behind. Meanwhile, within the corporate structure of the Dutch West India

New York State Archives

Facing page
Fort Frederick, which was built in 1676 by the Crown to replace the badly deteriorated Fort Orange at the river's edge, stood just below the crest of State Street Hill for over a century. It was demolished after the Revolution and its stones were used in the construction of various churches and other buildings.
Above
In 1609 English navigator Henry Hudson, sailing for the Dutch East India Company in his 90-ton yacht Half Moon, *traveled 160 miles up the river that now bears his name.*
Right
Hudson's attempt to find the Northwest Passage to the Orient brought him to the site of Albany in 1609.

Company, opinion was by no means universal that the proper role of the company was to continue to supply, at considerable cost, a few isolated settlers in the interior of the colony of New Netherland. Was it not enough expense, many directors wondered, to provide for the garrison at Fort Orange—necessary to protect the fur trade—without taking on the additional burden of sending food, tools, and livestock to sustain a colony of would-be farmers?

Fortunately for the future of Albany, there was another opinion within the corporate mind of the Dutch West India Company—that there was a larger purpose, a more permanent mission, in the establishment of New Netherland. This opinion was shared by Kiliaen Van Rensselaer, a Dutch director of the company who had made a fortune partly by trading in gemstones. Van Rensselaer and other directors realized that there was no incentive for the average Dutch settler to go to the New World and stay for any length of time. Some organized plan had to be established that would attract colonists in greater numbers—colonists who would identify with the land and with settlement, rather than with the fur trade.

Patroonship

The plan that was developed was unique in the history of the American colonies. In 1629 the company approved a Charter of Exemptions and Privileges permitting any directors who so desired to invest their own capital in a plan of permanent settlement that would establish them as hereditary overlords of their own private fiefdoms. This was a purely voluntary plan that would not be an expense to the company; directors who did not wish to invest in colonization were free to participate in the company as before, reaping profits from the fur trade.

The Netherlands had long been dominated by foreign rulers, principally those of Spain, the dukes of Burgundy, and the Hapsburg monarchy. The great fortunes made in the lucrative trade with the East Indies and by profiteering were the fortunes of merchants and not of noblemen, based upon mercantile interests and not upon hereditary landed estates. The new plan offered these wealthy but landless men of Amsterdam an unprecedented opportunity to acquire the traditional trappings of aristocracy—a hereditary, semifeudal estate in the intriguing land of America.

Each grant had to be located along a river or other navigable body of water, extending up to 16 miles along one shore or eight miles on each side of the waterway; the depth of the estate extending back from the river or stream was open to negotiation with the Indians. The principal condition was that the investor sponsor the settlement of 50 people over the age of 15 years, to be transported to the New World within four years.

The patroon, or patron, was granted broad powers over his vassals. All mineral rights, for example, were reserved to the patroon—as they had been until recently in Holland to the Spanish king. The patroon controlled all fishing and hunting rights and could grant or deny licenses as he pleased. He conducted his own courts, serving as his own chief justice. Theoretically any case involving more than 50 guilders could be appealed to the directors of the company, but settlers were made to agree in advance of coming to the New World that they would not appeal the decisions of the patroon. Settlers coming to the patroon's estate were promised 10 years free of taxes, but, like the serfs of old, they were denied the right to move from one estate to another or to quit the land by moving into a town.

Lossing, The Empire State

Albany's first settlers, 18 families of Walloons, arrived aboard the ship *New Netherland* in 1624. Commanded by Captain Adriaen Joris, the ship carried 260 tons.

Trade on the estate was controlled in every detail. Industry of any kind, including grain and lumber milling, was strictly the prerogative of the patroon. Even handicrafts, such as blankets or clothing woven by the wife of a settler, had to be offered first to the patroon's agent before they could be sold to a next-door neighbor. The discouragement of industry in favor of agriculture in its purest form, in addition to enhancing the power of the patroon, was designed to protect Holland's home industry, in which the directors of the Dutch West India Company also had personal interests.

The patroon for his part invested heavily in establishing the settlers upon his land, providing labor to help clear the forest, as well as livestock, tools, and initial supplies of food. African slaves were to be provided for all who wanted them—supplied, of course, by the Dutch West India Company, from ships that they had captured. In order to assure the safety of the settlers and to keep peace in the patroonship, the company required that Indian claims be satisfied through purchase before title to the land would actually be granted. The company further required that the religious needs of settlers be met by a "comforter of the sick," to be followed as soon as possible by a minister of the Dutch Reformed Church.

Once the plan had been approved by the States-General of the Netherlands, Kiliaen Van Rensselaer wasted no time. He instructed Sebastian Jansen Krol (Crol), comforter of the sick and head of the garrison at Fort Orange, to purchase the land that would later be known as Rensselaerswyck. The Van Rensselaer grant—which was to prove the only successful patroonship in the Hudson Valley—extended from the Cohoes Falls southward along the Hudson River to Beeren Island in the vicinity of present-day Coeymans, ultimately extending back 24 miles on each side of the Hudson River, encompassing most of today's Albany County and southern Rensselaer County. The holdings were expanded by subsequent generations of Van Rensselaers through additional purchases, particularly in present-day Columbia County, until they totaled more than a million acres. Van Rensselaer knew what he was doing when he chose this particular location for his estate. It was situated at the head of the tidewater of the Hudson River, and it had the military protection of Fort Orange.

As soon as title to some land was obtained, an elaborate advertising campaign was launched in Holland and other parts of northern Europe. Rensselaerswyck was described in glamorous broadsides as a "Heaven in the Wilderness"; maps were drawn to show settlements presumably already in existence. The first party of Van Rensselaer settlers arrived in March 1630.

In 1640 Van Rensselaer and his partners reevaluated their plan of settlement and made major reforms, granting a new charter to their tenants. Under the extreme paternalism of the old system, particularly the restraint in trade, recruitment in Holland had been successful only among the impoverished, failing to attract prosperous, established farmers. The revised charter for the first time allowed the resale of Dutch goods, the trade of homecrafts between the settlers without the aid of a Van Rensselaer agent, and the exploitation by settlers of fisheries and salt deposits. Some degree of self-government, carefully supervised, was also introduced. And for the first time tenants, as well as other independent traders, were permitted to engage in the fur trade.

Van Rensselaer would have preferred that the majority of his tenants settle on the east bank of the Hudson, where present-day Rensselaer is

located and where the original Fort Crailo was built. Settlement there, it was hoped, would divert some of the fur trade from Montreal by establishing relations with the Mahican Indians—deadly enemies of the Mohawks, who brought their furs from the west. Nonetheless, most of the settlers wanted to be on the west bank, if only for the protection of Fort Orange.

In 1646 Kiliaen Van Rensselaer died, without ever having visited his American holdings. He had not only assured the continuation of the colony, but he had established a unique American dynasty that would endure well into the 19th century. Even today in the deeds of properties in Albany and Rensselaer counties, it is not uncommon to find a requirement that the owner provide annually to the successors of the Van Rensselaers 34 bushels of wheat, two fat fowl, and the use of a wagon and team one day per year as tribute to the patroon.

Fort and Manor

In 1648, shortly after assuming the governorship of New Netherland, a crusty, peg-legged Pieter Stuyvesant visited his northernmost outpost at Fort Orange. The affairs of the surrounding patroonship of Rensselaerswyck were then in the hands of Brant Aertse Van Slichtenhorst, who had been appointed director of the domain in 1646. As stubborn in defense of the prerogatives of the patroon as Stuyvesant was in the assertion of those of the Dutch West India Company, Van Slichtenhorst was to prove a formidable adversary in the forthcoming conflict between the company and the patroonship.

The principal focus of the conflict was the question of jurisdiction over the small settlement, then known as the Fuyck, that had sprung up in the immediate vicinity of Fort Orange—and indeed over the site of the fort itself. Settlers under the jurisdiction of the patroon sought to build their houses as close as possible to the fort—not only for the meager protection it offered, but also in the hope of cashing in on the fur trade. Stuyvesant insisted that no further building should take place within range of a cannon shot from the fort (approximately 1,000 yards)—ostensibly in the name of military security, but also presumably in an effort to defend the company's profits. As a matter of fact, soldiers and settlers alike, equally disloyal to their respective overlords, participated in the smuggling of furs to Connecticut, where the rival English held sway.

The conflict dragged on year after year, with Stuyvesant's agents posting notices and Van Slichtenhorst tearing them down, new buildings being

John J. McEneny

Albany Institute of History and Art

Above
Fort Crailo, on the east bank of the Hudson, was erected in 1680 by Hendrich Van Rensselaer. During the French and Indian Wars Albany residents inhabited the stockaded grounds for protection. This view of the building, which appeared on an 1848 sheet music cover, was made when it was used as a private academy for boys.
Right
Pieter Stuyvesant, known as "Old Wooden Leg," served as Dutch governor of New Netherland from 1648 to 1664. He upheld the rights of the Dutch West India Company against the equally obstinate patroon's agent, Brant Van Slichtenhorst, by establishing, in 1652, Beverwyck as an independent municipality with a "city line" one cannon shot's distance from Fort Orange.

The Dongan Charter

The significance of the city charter granted by Governor Thomas Dongan to the people of Albany on July 22, 1686, cannot be overstated. The document, conferred in the name of his "Most Sacred Majesty," James II, confirmed the importance of Albany as the second largest city in the province of New York and ended the claims of the Van Rensselaer family to ownership of the land and authority over the people resident within the city boundaries.

Stating that Albany was "an ancient town" even then, the charter reaffirmed old rights and privileges that had been granted to the burghers of Beverwyck, Fort Orange, and Willemstadt by a series of civic and military officials representing Dutch and British governments over several decades of development. It confirmed public ownership of property and land used by the people in common, including the Stadt Huys (statehouse), the burial grounds, the adjacent palisades, the watch house, and the pastures south of the old fort, and bestowed on the city control over the ferry rights to Greenbush. The economic security of Albanians was guaranteed by the granting of all fishing, hunting, and mining rights to the city government (with the specific exemption of any gold or silver mines, which were presumably reserved to the Crown). Permission also was granted to purchase from the Indians meadowland at "Schaittecoque" and "Tionondorogue," which could later be sold to farmers as a means of raising revenue.

Albany Institute of History and Art

Left
The first seal of the city of Albany was affixed to the 1686 Dongan Charter. The crown, symbolizing British royalty, surmounts the lettering ALB. Seals that were adopted in 1752 and 1797 incorporated the beaver to symbolize the city's early history as a fur trading center.

Facing page
The Staats House was originally constructed in 1667 as a double house on the corner of State and South Pearl streets. It was a typical Dutch urban town house and was the traditional birthplace of General Philip Schuyler. Half demolished for the widening of South Pearl Street, the building was finally removed for the construction of a bank building in 1881.

The municipal offices established by Thomas Dongan were those of mayor, recorder, chamberlain, six aldermen, six assistant aldermen, town clerk, sheriff, coroner, clerk of the market, high constable, three subconstables, and a sergeant-at-mace. Albany's city government traces its roots to this ancient document, thus making Albany the oldest city in the original 13 colonies still operating on its original charter.

There have been changes, of course, over the last 300 years. The size of the Common Council has been increased on several occasions, while the office of assistant alderman has been dispensed with. The mayor is no longer nominated "upon the feast day of St. Michael the Archangel," and the recorder and clerk no longer require the appointment of the lieutenant governor of New York before taking office. The chamberlain (treasurer) is now chosen by the people at the polls rather than by the mayor, and the sheriff's office maintains a separate existence within the county's bureaucracy. The duties of the clerk of the market each Wednesday and Saturday have also been removed from the responsibilities of the mayor—a change that no doubt brings much relief to the modern incumbent of that ancient office.

Most radically changed is the administration of justice—once dispensed by several city officials acting together on cases ranging from the short-weighting of groceries to capital offenses—now carried out by individual, elected judges serving on a variety of specialized courts. City Court, Police

Howell and Tenney

The seeds of disaffection between colony and mother country were being sown. From a European perspective, the defense of the struggling colony seemed a great burden and expense, of lesser importance than matters closer to home; to the colonists, the paltry amount of aid that finally made its way up the Hudson Valley seemed woefully inadequate, reflecting a distant monarch's unconcern with the reality of North American survival.

The population of Albany and its environs fluctuated wildly during the colonial wars of the 17th and 18th centuries. During King William's War alone, the population shrank by 25 percent, leaving many areas populated largely by male settlers and slaves. Women and children were routinely sent down to New York City for safety, while slaves harnessed to the task of clearing the wilderness lacked the mobility to leave the dangerous frontier territory even if they wanted to.

King William's War (1688–1697) was soon followed by Queen Anne's War (1701–1714). The next quarter-century of relative peace was marked by the ongoing competition between French and English for the fur trade and, even more important, for the loyalty of the Indians that each side hoped to use as its pawns in the next round of battle that was sure to come. During this period the French succeeded in making considerable inroads with the Indians, gaining the firm allegiance of the Senecas, the westernmost tribe of the Iroquois Confederacy, and some support from other tribes.

War broke out again in 1739, this time under King George II. The European issues were of little interest to the citizens of Albany, the majority of whom wished only for peace. In 1745, however, the reality of the situation was brought home with a shock. In the month of November, at a time folklore refers to as "Indian summer," French, Canadians, and Indians fell upon old Saratoga (now Schuylerville) and obliterated the settlement there, killing or capturing more than 100 people.

Still the Indian commissioners at Albany were reluctant to take definite action. The assembly voted more money to strengthen defenses on the frontier, but no action took place. By 1746 the lack of credibility with the Indians on the part of the British government had become a major problem.

What finally tilted the tables was the coming to power in the Mohawk Valley of William Johnson. Born in Ireland, Johnson had come over as a young man to protect and administer the large landed estate of his uncle, Admiral Sir Peter Warren. Acquiring land in his own name, he imported Scottish and Irish settlers from whom he won great loyalty and admiration. At the same time, he gained a remarkable rapport with the Six Nations of the Iroquois, in some ways becoming almost one of them. By 1746 he controlled the whole western frontier, and Johnson and his Indian followers assembled at Albany for a great march up to Canada that summer.

Once again, as in the two previous wars, the great hope of conquering Canada was dashed upon the rocks of international politics. The European war was not going well for the British, and the luxury of sending a fleet up the St. Lawrence—ships that could be better used in Europe—was an expense the admiralty was not about to bear. The fleet was canceled, and to the great mortification of Governor Clinton and Colonel Johnson, the news had to be spread to the Indians that King George had once again failed to send the promised help and all soldiers and warriors were to disband.

Knox Family

From his baronial seat at Johnson Hall in the Mohawk Valley, west of Albany, Sir William Johnson maintained the balance of power between the British and French empires by earning the loyalty of the Iroquois Confederacy. His mansion, shown in this E.L. Henry painting, was the site of frequent gatherings of Indians from the time of its construction in 1763.

The Treaty of Aix-la-Chapelle which ended the war in 1748 did not impart much feeling of confidence or security to the settlers of the Hudson Valley. Most people knew that it would be only a matter of time before France and Britain would be at war again.

The British government did little to ease the colonists' fear of renewed attack, as the French established garrisons at Crown Point on Lake Champlain and at Niagara, regularly penetrating the British sphere of influence in the West and wooing the Indians with French trade and religion. It seemed to the colonists that the British Crown was more interested in the future of Gibraltar, Madras, and the Caribbean than in the wilderness defense of a less glamorous North America. Ineffectual and disunited, the colonists could do nothing alone, while their appeals to London seemed to fall on deaf ears.

By 1753 a few colonial leaders, recognizing that Great Britain could no longer be relied upon for their defense, were arguing for greater military and political organization and mutual support among the American colonies. A plan for common defense, one that would be initiated and controlled by the colonists themselves, became more and more the subject of discussion in the coffeehouses and meetinghouses of America. This movement, spearheaded by Benjamin Franklin, found its first public forum at the Albany Congress of 1754, called to negotiate a new general treaty with the Iroquois Confederacy. The result was the highly prophetic Albany Plan of Union.

The French and Indian War

Even as the delegates discussed the need for a strong common defense against the French and their Indian allies, far to the west of them, after a 10-hour siege in the forests of the Pennsylvania wilderness, a force of 150 young Virginia militiamen commanded by a 22-year-old lieutenant colonel named George Washington, were forced to abandon the hastily erected Fort Necessity and return home in defeat. The date of Washington's defeat was a prophetic one—July 4, 1754.

Dictionary of American Portraits

The final chapter in the epic battle between Bourbon France and the British Empire of the German-speaking Hanoverian kings had begun. At its end, in the Treaty of Paris of 1783, the French threat that had so long shadowed Albany's history and retarded its growth was removed for all time.

British military strategy during these years depended on Albany as the headquarters and quartermaster of the northern department. The city designated as the assembly point for armies marching on to Canada also served as a supply depot, winter quarters for regular troops, and a behind-the-lines hospital for the inevitable wounded and dying of armies all too vulnerable to epidemics of typhoid, typhus, smallpox, and dysentery.

In 1755, as soon as the spring planting season was over and young farmers could be spared from the land, an army composed of militiamen from New York, New Jersey, and New England was formed at Albany to march against the French Fort St. Frederic (Crown Point), a small castlelike structure whose ruins have lately been excavated on the banks of Lake Champlain. The expedition, augmented by a small contingent of British regulars as well as the usual warriors from the Iroquois Confederacy, was placed under the command of William Johnson.

The army met the enemy at Lake George in a bloody confrontation that saw the death of the aged chief, King Hendrick, one of the Mohawk sachems who had traveled to England with Pieter Schuyler nearly half a century before, as well as the enemy commander, Baron Ludwig August Dieskau, a German mercenary in command of French and Indian troops.

Albany Institute of History and Art

In a year filled with British defeats, the victory at Lake George was welcome news, and Johnson was made a "Baronet of the British Empire in New York"—a title still held by his descendants in Canada today. Following his victory, Johnson built Fort William Henry, named diplomatically after two dukes of the royal family; for the next two years the log fortress would stand as Albany's northernmost bulwark against the inevitable onslaught of New France. The French, for their part, further narrowed the no-man's-land to the length of Lake George by building the log citadel of Fort Carillon at Ticonderoga. Albany's role in supplying Fort William Henry as well as a fort at Oswego overshadowed all other considerations in the northern colonies.

From their great country mansion at Whitehall, whose foundation now supports an apartment house on Whitehall Road in Albany, the British commanders planned and launched several attacks against the French. War was conducted almost exclusively during the summer months, when the primitive military roads were not muddy, washed out and, most important, when the boys and young men could be spared from the farms. War or no war, the worst enemy was crop failure, which in those days meant famine.

Albany Institute of History and Art

Facing page

Top

Indian commissioner William Johnson was extremely well liked by the Iroquois. In 1755 he led an expedition of British soldiers and Iroquois warriors to victory over the French at Lake George and earned the title of Baronet of the British Empire in New York.

Bottom

Decorated with handcarved drawings of various Northeast forts, this soldier's pewter-top powder horn dates from the French and Indian Wars.

Right

Chief Hendrick was one of the four Mohawk sachems brought to London to the court of Queen Anne in 1710 with Colonel Pieter Schuyler to plead for more military aid to the colonies. This mezzotint, one of several made after the celebrated visit, was widely circulated among Europeans, who were fascinated by the Indians of North America. Years later, in 1755, Hendrick would serve as a portly and aging senior officer to William Johnson at the Battle of Lake George. There he would meet death by a French bullet while still wearing a medal given him by the Queen.

The Albany Plan of Union

In 1754, startled into action by reports of the imminence of what was to be the French and Indian War, the Lords of Trade in London called for a convention of colonial leaders in Albany to negotiate a new general treaty with the Iroquois. Known today as the Albany Congress of 1754, this conference was by far the most significant gathering in Albany in colonial times.

A total of 24 delegates, including military leaders, public officials, lawyers, and clergymen, represented seven colonies—New York, Massachusetts Bay, Pennsylvania, Rhode Island, Connecticut, New Hampshire, and Maryland; the southern colonies of Virginia and North Carolina, unable to send delegations over such a long distance, also asked to be considered as participants. The conference met from June 9 to July 25 in Albany's Stadt Huys on the northeast corner of Hudson and Court streets (today's University Plaza).

The Iroquois, by now clearly skeptical of the colonies' ability to fend for themselves, were slow in arriving. Their leader, the aged Mohawk chieftain known as King Hendrick, delivered an eloquent oration in which he spoke as much to the British monarchy as he did to the colonial leaders:

" 'Tis your own fault, brethren," the chief declared, "that we are not strengthened by conquest, for we would have gone and taken Crown Point, but you hindered us. You have no fortifications about you, no, not even to this city. 'Tis but one step from Canada thither, and the French may easily come and turn you out of doors.

"Look at the French, they are men, they are fortifying everywhere—but, we are ashamed to say it, you are all like women."

Despite this harsh rebuke, King Hendrick entered into the new treaty, and the delegates, stung by his words, turned their attention to the need for a common colonial defense.

The debate, which went on for days, soon moved beyond creating a union of colonial defense to creating a colonial union. Benjamin Franklin, then a 48-year-old Pennsylvania provincial assemblyman, had brought with him to Albany a plan of unity appropriately reminiscent of Hiawatha's Confederacy. At a time when separation from Britain was undreamed of, Franklin was about to plant the seeds of a national government for America.

Franklin's plan called for a general government of 11 colonies, with a Grand Council of 48 members presided over by a President-General—the first hint of an American Presidency. The colonies would jointly maintain an army and levy taxes to pay for a united colonial defense.

On July 9 the delegates agreed "that there be a union of His Majesty's several governments on this continent, to act against their common enemy." The following day Franklin's "Plan of a Proposed Union of the Several Colonies" was approved and forwarded to the colonial assemblies—all of which ultimately refused ratification.

The idea of a united America was born out of the colonists' recognition that they could survive against the common enemy, France, only by standing together. Twenty-two years later, Benjamin Franklin, still devoted to the concept of unity presented at Albany, would sign another declaration in Philadelphia—only this time the common enemy would be not France, but England.

Franklin's divided snake illustrated the importance of the Albany Plan of Union.

Dictionary of American Portraits

During the French and Indian War, General James Abercrombie led his British troops to horrible defeat against the French garrison at Ticonderoga.

The disruption of the city by the quartering of troops in the homes of its burghers, the arrogance and revelries of unruly soldiers far from home, and the congestion of its narrow streets with a seemingly endless procession of cannon, military stores, and barrels of food and provisions were reluctantly tolerated, as Albanians contemplated the possible alternative. Too well they remembered the massacres of Schenectady, Deerfield, and old Saratoga. The war had grown particularly brutal since both sides had offered a bounty for the scalps of their respective enemies—a practice engaged in by whites and Indians alike.

In August 1757 a new wave of horror swept through the city. Not only had the famed Fort William Henry fallen, but—in a catastrophe related in James Fenimore Cooper's *Last of the Mohicans*—almost its entire garrison, along with several hundred unarmed men, women, and children, had been massacred by scalp-hungry Indians, completely out of control, who comprised the greater part of the army of the outraged but helpless Marquis de Montcalm. As the shattered survivors of the massacre trickled into Albany from their original haven at Fort Edward, the citizenry was in a state of near panic.

But the disaster was not without its benefit to the British cause. From within the British Parliament, a strong leader arose in the person of William Pitt, a magnificent orator and devoted friend of the American cause. Pitt's commitment to defend the colonies, coupled with the righteous longing of the colonists to revenge the bloody massacre at Lake George, led the following year to the formation in Albany of the largest army yet assembled on North American soil. In the early summer of 1758, some 15,000 troops, plus a motley assortment of camp followers, gathered under the command of General James Abercrombie, filling the fields near Whitehall and above Fort Frederic, as well as much of Greenbush on the east bank of the Hudson, with an accumulation of humanity that exceeded by five times the resident population of the city.

Abercrombie's mission was to advance northward along the traditional "Warpath of Nations," first defeating the French garrison at Ticonderoga, then effecting a similar victory at Crown Point, and finally moving on north to take Montreal and, if possible, Quebec. The mission failed. Wave after wave of the massive force, marching to the wail of Scottish Black Watch bagpipes, were horribly cut up by the grapeshot and musket fire of the much smaller but well-entrenched Ticonderoga garrison, by now protected by massive stone walls.

But the days of the French in North America were numbered. The vast empire of New France was held together by an extensive chain of forts strategically placed along the waterways that encircled the British colonies from Quebec to New Orleans. This thin line of French civilization was protected by alliances with most of the surrounding Indian tribes, reinforced by the zealous efforts of missionaries and trappers. Farmers and settlers, however, were rare indeed outside the narrow trading/military corridor. The French, unlike the English, had never created a large reservoir of dissidents, such as the suppressed Scots and Irish, anxious to emigrate to America; because of their long-standing commitment to the spread of Roman Catholicism throughout the New World, in fact, they had driven one potential immigrant group, the Huguenots, into the camp of the enemy. As a result, French settlers in North America were outnumbered by their British counterparts 10 to one, and there was simply no appreciable native militia to mobilize in defense of French territory.

In the next expedition based in Albany, in 1759, some 9,000 troops under the command of Lord Jeffrey Amherst produced a series of victories that placed both Ticonderoga and Crown Point under the Union Jack. The fall of Montreal and Quebec the following year ended a long and painful chapter in Albany's history.

Dictionary of American Portraits

The victories of 1759 were overshadowed by the loss of a great friend of Albany and the American colonies, Viscount George Augustus Howe, who had been killed in 1758 at Ticonderoga. Howe had a genuine sympathy with the colonists's feelings of estrangement from the mother country. Displaying none of the arrogance shown by so many other commanders, he got to know the provincial leaders and local militiamen with whom he fought the common enemy. He appreciated the ways of the forest by which the Americans lived and fought, realizing that the close-order lines and formal discipline of European soldiery had little place in America. He encouraged his men to simplify their elaborate uniforms, to cover their gaudy colors with mud, and to hide behind the trees and rocks of the Adirondacks. Had he survived, the course of American history might well have been different. As it was, however, his remains, brought back to Albany by Philip Schuyler, were laid to rest beneath St. Peter's Anglican Church, and the question of future Anglo-American relations would be left to lesser men of little vision.

New York Historical Society

Albany in the Revolution

Following the signing of the Treaty of Paris of 1763, the people of Albany experienced a peace they had not known for generations. The new sense of security from external attack, however, made them less tolerant than ever of British officials, military or civil, at the same time that Britain was determined to begin recouping some of the huge expenses of defending and maintaining her American colonies.

The Navigation Acts, on the books for decades but enforced with new vigor after 1763, infuriated Albanians, to whom smuggling was a time-honored tradition. The Stamp Act, passed by the British Parliament in 1765, intruded even more directly into the lives of the people, and opposition throughout the colonies was virtually unanimous. In Albany a group of young men, many of them members of the city's most prominent families, began calling themselves the Sons of Liberty. Protected by older relatives on the Common Council, they regularly harassed would-be tax collectors, effectively blocking implementation of the act. Over the next few years, Committees of Correspondence disseminated to the most remote settlements news of the mounting confrontations between the American colonists and British officialdom.

Lossing, The Empire State

The reality of armed revolt was brought home to Albany on May 1, 1775, when the news of Lexington and Concord reached the city. That afternoon members of the local Committee of Correspondence addressed a large crowd at the old marketplace, located in the middle of today's Broadway in front of the present post office. A new Committee of Safety, Protection, and Correspondence was formed, with full powers to act in support of the patriot cause. Chaired by Abraham Yates, this extralegal committee almost immediately began filling the void left by a vacillating and generally pro-British Common Council under Mayor Abraham Cuyler. Meeting daily in the old Stadt Huys, the committee regulated everything from fire watches and the raising of militia to price gouging and the suppression of conspiracies.

Albany's role in the War of Independence was essentially the same as it

Dictionary of American Portraits

Facing page
Top
In 1759, as commander-in-chief of the British forces in America, Jeffrey Amherst and his troops drove the French from Lake Champlain. He completed the conquest of Canada the following year when he captured Montreal. Painting by Joseph Blackburn.
Middle
Major General Philip Schuyler, who served as quartermaster general of the Northern Department of the Continental Army, was the father-in-law of Alexander Hamilton. This portrait of Schuyler was painted by John Trumbull in 1792.
Bottom
Lord George Augustus Howe, who accompanied James Abercrombie on his expedition against Ticonderoga, was killed in battle at the age of 34. He was buried beneath St. Peter's Church.
Above
In 1775 Richard Montgomery became a brigadier general in the Continental Army. When Albany's Philip Schuyler became ill during the siege of St. Johns, he turned over command of the Montreal expedition to Montgomery. After capturing the city, he joined forces with Benedict Arnold. On December 31, 1775, Montgomery was killed during the attack on Quebec.

had been in the earlier wars against the French. Its geographic position remained pivotal, and once again the city served as a vital center of military supply, intelligence gathering, and Indian diplomacy.

In June of 1775, the great stone fortress at Ticonderoga was taken by Ethan Allen and the Green Mountain Boys of Vermont. In the same month, the Continental Congress commissioned Albany's Philip Schuyler a major general and, in a replay of previous wars, directed him to attack Canada before the British could move south and capture the Hudson Valley, thus splitting the colonies in two.

The generations-old trading connections of Albany merchants engaged in the illegal smuggling trade with Canada would prove invaluable to the invasion force. Even so, the going was slow. The American troops, despite the blandishments of the increasingly unpopular General Schuyler, were poorly trained and undisciplined. The problems of supplying an army extended so far into the wilderness were staggering. Dysentery, smallpox, and other diseases were rampant. In the siege of St. Johns, which lasted into November, Schuyler became so ill that he turned over his command to General Richard Montgomery, the Irish-born son-in-law of Robert Livingston, who 16 years previously, as a British adjutant under General Amherst, had traveled the same path northward against the French army of Montcalm.

While Schuyler saw to the badly disrupted supply lines from his base at Ticonderoga, Montgomery pushed on to capture Montreal in mid-November. At Quebec he joined forces with General Benedict Arnold, whose weary troops had defied all odds by penetrating the still uncharted wilderness of northern Maine. With barely 800 men left, they advanced against Quebec in a desperate New Year's Eve attack. The gamble failed, Montgomery was fatally wounded, and the army retreated back down its invasion route to the Champlain Valley. Nearly 5,000 American soldiers had lost their lives in the ill-fated expedition, the overwhelming majority having perished from disease or exposure.

The one bright spot in the winter of 1776 was the successful movement of 59 pieces of ordnance from Ticonderoga over an arduous route down Lake George and the old military road to Albany, across the frozen Hudson, and through the Berkshires to Cambridge, where they played a key role in the siege of Boston. A bronze plaque in Albany's Loudon Shopping Center is one of several that mark that tortuous journey, made with the help of ox-drawn sleds, which gave new hope to the patriot cause and led to the British evacuation of Boston that March.

Meanwhile the loyalist mayor and Common Council remained in office, seemingly oblivious to the daily recruitment of troops and frantic garnering of supplies to support the Continental Army to the north. Albany County, like most of the country, was at least one-third loyalist, with perhaps as many again uncertain which side to support. Many families were disunited; Mayor Cuyler, in fact, was a first cousin of General Schuyler. Sheriff Henry Ten Eyck refused use of the jail for loyalist prisoners being questioned by the Committee of Safety, which used two rooms of the deteriorating Fort Frederick instead.

This strange dual administration lasted until June 5, 1776, when the mayor and several of his followers, ignoring all patriotic sensibilities, publicly celebrated the king's birthday at Cartwright's Tavern, at the corner of today's Green and Beaver streets. The offending loyalists were

CHAPTER 3

PATTERNS OF SETTLEMENT

The street patterns of downtown Albany still retain much of the 17th-century character created by their Dutch builders. The lower blocks of Hudson Avenue and little Beaver Street still curve to parallel a log stockade that has long since faded into history.

To the native as well as the visitor, the great breadth of State Street seems an anachronism. Most people are unaware that, in the middle of the street, the foundation ruins of the city's first Reformed and Anglican churches sleep undisturbed beneath the macadam world of modern Albany.

Albany Institute of History and Art

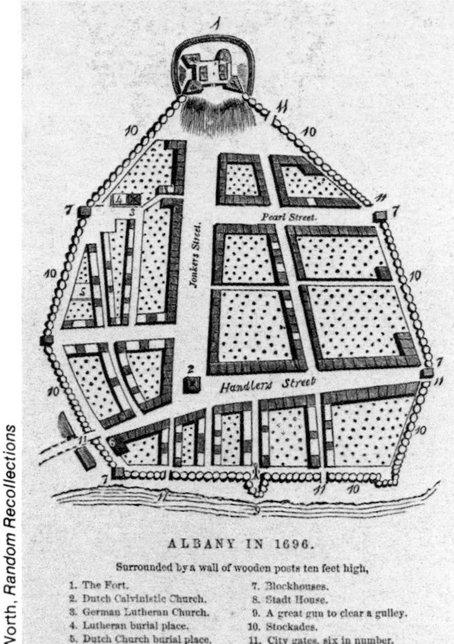

Worth, *Random Recollections*

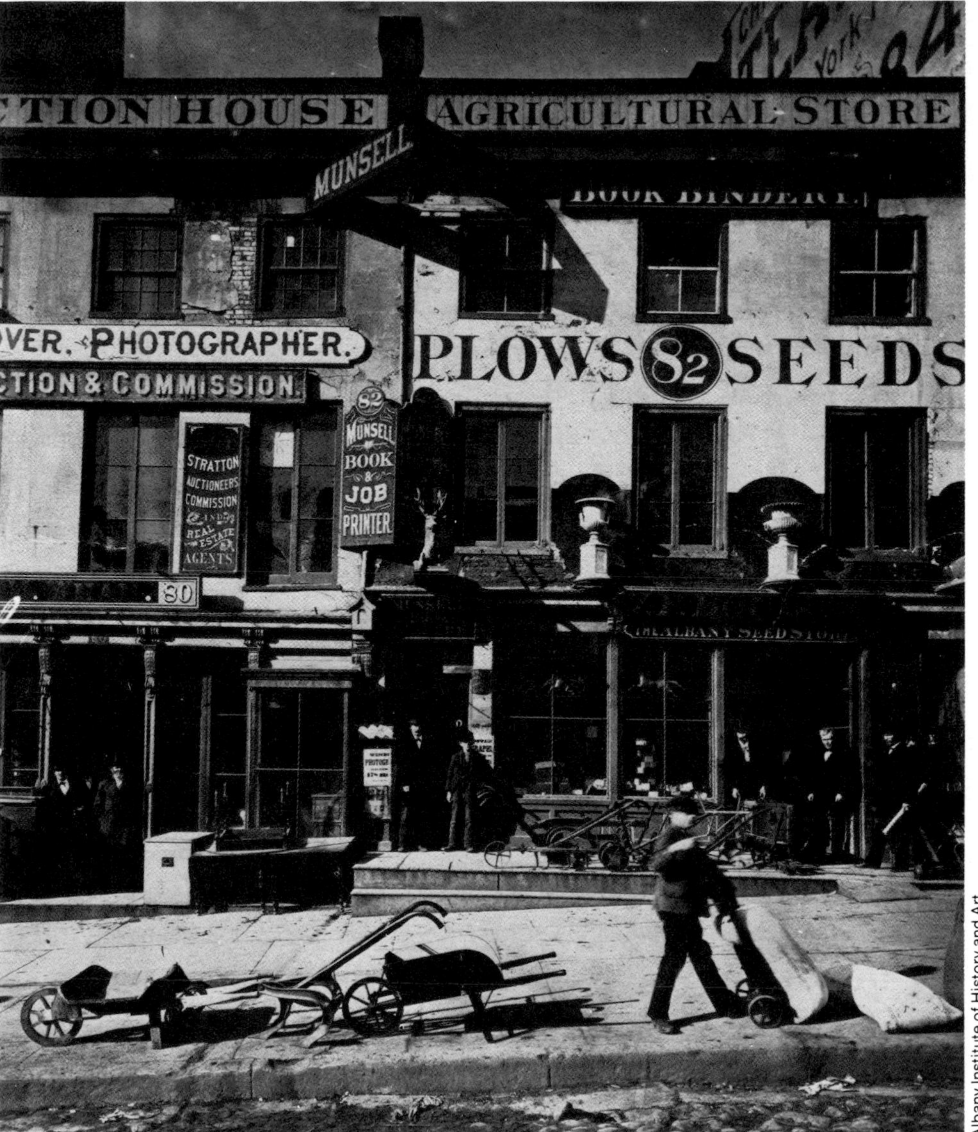

Albany Institute of History and Art

Facing page
This 1848 watercolor by John Wilson depicts State Street as seen from Broadway (then called Market Street). The spire of St. Peter's Church and the State Capitol, both designed by architect Philip Hooker, can be seen in the distance.
Above
In 1696 Albany was surrounded by a 10-foot-high wall of wooden posts. This plat of the town shows the fort, Dutch Calvinist Church, German Lutheran Church and cemetery, Dutch Church cemetery, and blockhouses.
Right
State Street storekeepers in the late 1800s apparently had no compunction about using their own stoops and city sidewalks to display their wares. Joel Munsell Books and Printing, V.P. Douw's Albany Seed Store, T.J. Wendover, Photographer, and Stratton Auctioneers and Real Estate occupied 80 and 82 State Street, circa 1870.

North Broadway, from State Street to Union Station, also retains a width uncommon to the age of its origin—a legacy of its function as the "Market Street" where colonial and early 19th-century Albanians bought and sold produce, poultry, and small livestock from an open-air market in the middle of the street. North Pearl Street is also comparatively wide, in this case belying its traditional role as a prime residential, professional, and commercial street that with State Street formed the principal crossroads of downtown Albany and the capital district.

Excluding these three major streets, the urban map contains exceptionally narrow streets with a design more comfortable in the 17th century than our own. The narrowness of Maiden Lane and James, Norton, Beaver, Steuben, and Division streets remains as a visible legacy of a people who kept their homes, shops, and gardens huddled together within a small area for mutual protection from the wilderness. Progress and commerce have not always been compatible to this weblike pattern. In recent years several of the streets have been closed off to traffic or obliterated entirely to accommodate large building projects such as the new Ten Eyck Project on State Street. Other streets, such as South Pearl Street—the original "Cow Lane," the path to the common pastureland in the city's South End—retained a narrowness so extreme for modern traffic that they could only be widened by demolishing the buildings along one side of the street.

Howell and Tenney

One frequently heard lament is that nothing remains of the riverfront streets that must surely have existed between University Plaza and the waters of the Hudson. The fact is that for all of its history Broadway has been the city's "River Road." The blocks to the east of it, the great rows of warehouses and wide piers, the quays, docks, railroad tracks, and modern arterial highways are virtually all built on land created by filling in the Hudson River in an attempt to service the city's ever-expanding business and commercial needs. No ancient cobblestoned streets or crumbling foundations lie beneath Interstate 787—only the same river bottom and mud flats that have always existed in the natural environment.

Colonial Times

One of the earliest descriptions of Albany comes from Jasper Danckaerts, a Dutch missionary who visited the area in 1680—after the British had assumed control of the colony but before Albany received its charter from Governor Dongan. Danckaerts' journal entry for April 30, 1680, includes the following observations:

Before we quit Albany, we must say a word about the place. It was formerly named the Fuyck by the Hollanders, who first settled there, on account of two rows of houses standing there, opposite to each other, which being wide enough apart in the beginning, finally ran quite together like a "fuyck" [a funnel-shaped fishing net], and, therefore, they gave it this name, especially the Dutch and Indians living there. It is nearly square, and lies against the hill, with several good streets, on which there may be about eighty or ninety houses. Fort Orange, constructed by the Dutch, lies below on the bank of the river, and is set off with palisades, filled in with earth on the inside. It is now abandoned by the English, who have built a similar one behind the town, high up on the declivity of the hill, from whence it can command the place. From the other side of this fort the inhabitants have brought a spring or fountain of water, under the fort, and under ground into the town, where they now have in several places always fountains of clear, fresh, cool water. The

Albany's Old English Church was located east of Fort Frederick.

town is surrounded by palisades, and has several gates corresponding with the streets. It has a Dutch Reformed and a Lutheran church. The Lutheran minister lives up here in the winter, and down in New York in the summer. There is no English church or place of meeting, to my knowledge. As this is the principal trading-post with the Indians . . .there are houses or lodges erected on both sides of the town, where the Indians, who come from the far interior to trade, live during the time they are there.

Perhaps the best-known description of the city in colonial times is that of Peter Kalm , the Swedish naturalist, who visited Albany in June of 1749. After 85 years of British rule, Dutch influence was still clearly apparent.

The town extends along the river, which flows here from N.N.E. to S.S.W. The high mountains in the west, above the town, bound the view on that side. There are two churches in Albany, one English and the other Dutch. The Dutch church stands a short distance from the river on the east side of the market. It is built of stone and in the middle it has a small steeple with a bell. It has but one minister who preaches twice every Sunday. The English church is situated on the hill at the west end of the market, directly under the fort. It is likewise built of stone but has no steeple. There is no service at the church at this time because they have no minister, but all the people understand Dutch, the garrison excepted. . . .The town hall lies to the south of the Dutch church, close by the riverside. It is a fine building of stone, three stories high it has a small tower or steeple, with a bell, and a gilt ball and vane at the top of it.

The houses in this town are very neat, and partly built of stones covered with shingles of white pine. Some are slated with tile from Holland, because the clay of this neighborhood is not considered fit for tiles. Most of the houses are built in the old Frankish way, with the gable-end towards the street, except for a few, which were recently built in the modern style. . . .The eaves on the roofs reach almost to the middle of the street. This preserves the walls from being damaged by the rain, but it is extremely disagreeable in rainy weather for the people in the streets, there being hardly any means of avoiding the water from the eaves. The front doors are generally in the middle of the houses, and on both sides are porches with seats, on which during fair weather the people spend almost the whole day, especially on those porches which are in the shade. . . .The streets are broad, and some of them paved. In some parts they are lined with trees. The long streets are almost parallel to the river, and the others intersect them at right angles. The street which goes between the two churches is five times broader than the others and serves as a marketplace. The streets upon the whole are very dirty because the people leave their cattle in them during the summer nights. There are two marketplaces in town, to which the country people come twice a week. There are no city gates here but for the most part just open holes through which people pass in and out of the town.

Twenty years later, in 1769, Richard Smith of New Jersey, a native-born American and later a member of the Continental Congress, recorded his impressions of pre-Revolutionary Albany.

At Half after 10 oCloc we arrived at Albany estimated to be 164 Miles by Water from N.York and by Land 157. In the afternoon we viewed the Town which contains according to several Gentlemen residing there, about 500 Dwelling Houses besides Stores and Out Houses. The Streets are irregular and badly laid out, some paved others not, Two or Three are broad and the rest narrow and not straight. Most of the Buildings are pyramidically shaped like the old Dutch Houses of N.York. . . .

We did not note any extraordinary Edifices in the Town. . . .The Fort is in ruinous neglected Condition and nothing now to be seen of Fort Orange built by the Dutch but part of the Fosse or Ditch which surrounded it. The Barracks are built of Wood and of ordinary Workmanship; the same may be said of the King's Store Houses. The Court House is large and the Jail under it. . . .There are 4 Houses of Worship for different denominations and a Public Library which we did not visit. Most of the Houses are built of Brick or faced with Brick. The Inhabitants generally speak both Dutch and English and some do not understand the latter. The Shore and Wharves 3 in Number abounded in Lumber.

Facing page
Right
In this 1913 view of Arbor Hill, the spire of St. Joseph's Church towers over the neighborhood.

Imposing Order

After the American Revolution, Albany was the sixth largest city in the United States and growing rapidly. The extension of the ancient, haphazard street pattern of Beverwyck was a practical impossibility.

In an attempt to impose some sort of order on the development of the city, the Common Council adopted the comprehensive grid pattern of straight streets and rectangular blocks upon which subsequent generations of Albanians have placed their homes, businesses, and institutions. This division of the vast uptown plains of the city into a simple grid provided clear reference points from which the farms and forests to the west might be developed and absorbed into the settled community. In recent years, this post-Revolutionary street plan has become familiar to area residents in the form of a 1794 map of the city by Simeon De Witt, which was used as a paper placemat at Farnham's restaurant downtown.

Starting from the site of the city's west gate in the now-demolished palisade, the grid pattern divided the entire city—more than a mile wide and 16 miles long—into spacious city blocks and larger "great lots," to be developed at a later date. Roads leading away from the old city were named after animals; only one of these, Elk Street, remains today. Crossing these streets were the "bird streets"—Eagle, Hawk, Swan, Dove, Lark, Snipe (now Lexington), Quail, and Partridge.

The grid system, however, made no provision for the natural terrain of rolling hills that lay to the west of the original settlement. Great ravines and wide bogs formed by the numerous streams that meandered through what is now Pine Hills and midtown Albany were all crisscrossed by "paper streets." Such undesirable land was inevitably developed last or not at all, leaving great gaps in the development of neighborhoods. Interruptions in the grid pattern, many of them now occupied by highways, parks, and campuses, have long caused confusion to postmen, cab drivers, and visitors. Albany is no doubt unique in having, for example, three Spring Streets, four Providence Streets, and five Hudson Avenues—each of which is actually a single street with vast gaps in house numbers.

The original city lines, as described in the Dongan Charter of 1686, coincided with Clinton Avenue and its imaginary extension on the north side, and on the south side, with an imaginary line running through Gansevoort Street, Woodlawn Avenue, and Cortland Street. When Arbor Hill, the former village of Colonie (1806–1815), was annexed as the city's fifth ward, it too gained a grid system, which, while allowing for some

City Engineer's Office

Rutgers University Fine Arts Collection

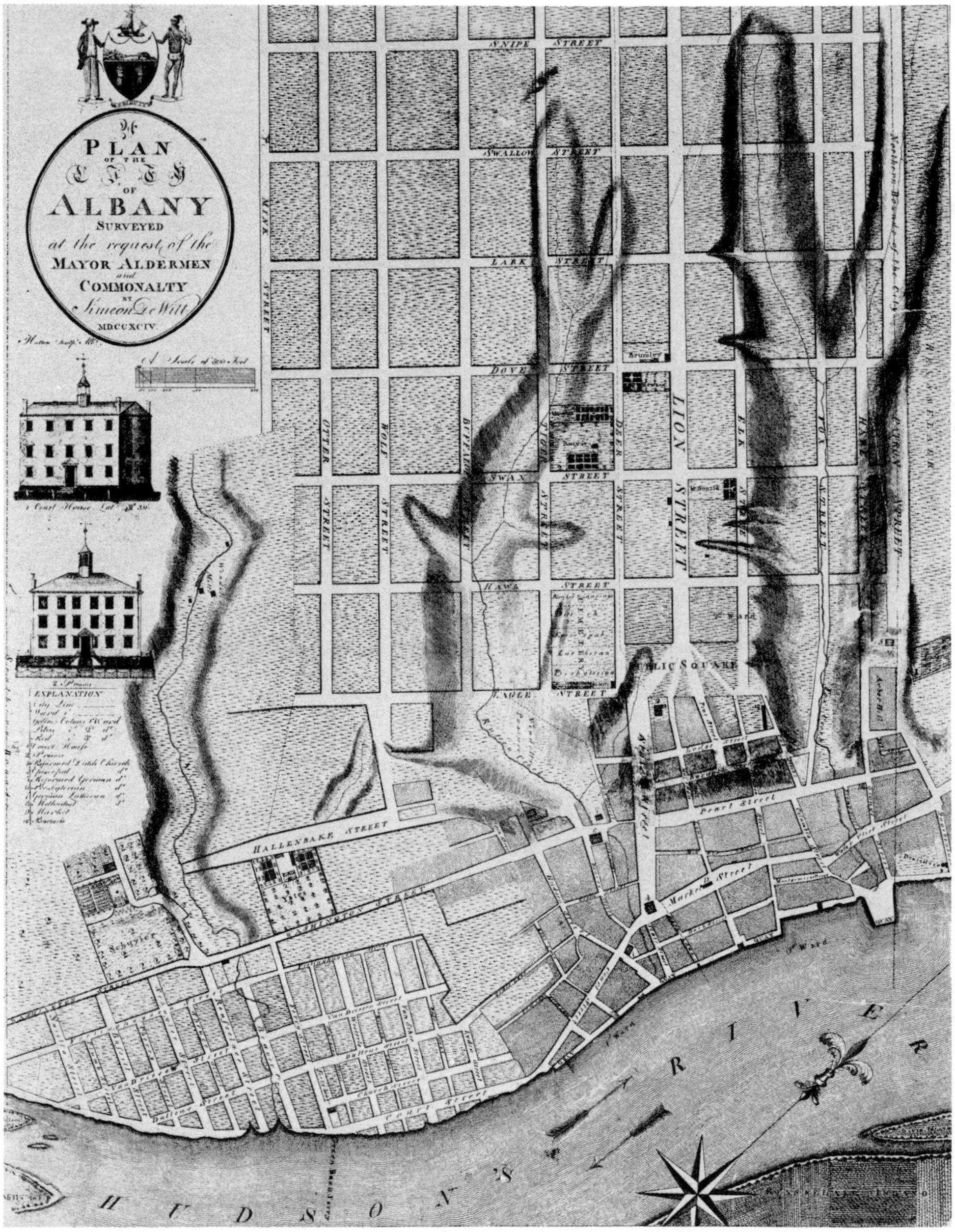

Albany Institute of History and Art

Above
Simeon De Witt was responsible for mapping Albany's grid pattern in the late 18th century. Ezra Ames painted this portrait of the cartographer.
Right
Simeon De Witt's 1794 map shows the grid-like organization of Albany's streets. Note the "bird" and "animal" street names.

Albany Institute of History and Art

longer blocks and narrow service alleys, remained equally as monotonous and inflexible as the street pattern of Capitol Hill and beyond. When West Hill, from Oak Street to beyond Quail Street, was annexed in 1870, the system was extended, even eliminating the back alleys. By the final quarter of the 19th century, Victorian Albany had expanded well into Pine Hills, where at Allen Street the old system would be completely abandoned.

Arthur J. O'Keefe

One of the main reasons that the grid system had to be altered was that public and charitable institutions, as they moved out of older neighborhoods downtown, required more land to carry out their functions. These institutions frequently absorbed paper streets and land not yet developed or poorly developed into their campuses. In effect, by closing streets they created "superblocks."

Ringing the older neighborhoods of the city are several such superblocks that have been created over the past century or so. Albany High School, La Salle School, the Armed Forces Reserve Building, the Brady Building, and St. Catherine's Home share one such block, which once included St. Mary's Cemetery. These blocks unwittingly play a significant role in the lives of the city's people. In many cases they serve as preservers of open spaces or "greenbelts," marking the end of one neighborhood and the beginning of another, and helping to break up the pattern of the city into a network of intimate neighborhoods rather than one large, impersonal urban sprawl.

The largest of the superblocks, University Heights, had its roots in the original street pattern as Alms House Square, which extended from Lark Street to Perry Street (now Lake Avenue) and from West Ferry Street (Myrtle Avenue) south to the city line.

Facing page
Top
This early view of Washington Park was taken prior to the demolition of homes on Lake View Terrace. The park was established in 1869 through the consolidation of the abandoned State Street Burial Grounds, the parade grounds, and the purchase of many private residences such as those shown here. Some people were persuaded to sell their homes by park commissioners who promised them land on the south side of Madison Avenue.
Bottom
This Washington Park gazebo, no longer in existence, reflects the exotic Near and Far Eastern style that was popular in Victorian America.
Right
Washington Park Lake was a popular leisure spot for families and young couples during the 1880s. The first lake house can be seen in the background.

Dennis Holzman

Originally the square was devoted exclusively to public institutions: the county poor farm, which remained there until the 1920s; the county pest house, a rather unattractively named quarantine hospital for people with communicable diseases; and the county jail, located approximately where the Hackett Middle School is today. During the Civil War the jail was used as a prison camp for Confederate soldiers, and for many years after the jail paid for itself by taking in federal prisoners from as far away as the Carolinas. Most of these functions have now been moved to the old Shaker farms in Colonie, and in their place three hospitals, two nursing homes, a home for children, three private schools, several colleges and graduate schools, a regional psychiatric center, and the National Guard armory all share a common location in the very heart of the city they serve.

Creating the Parks

Just to the north of the old Alms House Square is Washington Park. Designated as a park in 1869 and preserved from residential or commercial development, this 98-acre expanse of land in the heart of downtown Albany has proved one of the great legacies of 19th-century Albanians to their 20th-century descendants.

Following the Civil War the North began to prosper again, and the tide of immigration resumed into Northern cities such as Albany. Industry, which had expanded greatly because of the war effort, now attracted more and more workers who crowded into neighborhoods already short of land and open space. Washington Park, then on the outskirts of the settled city, was intended as a place where people of all classes could spend their Sunday afternoons.

The city appointed a board of park commissioners, consisting of representatives of the better educated and wealthier families of Albany society. The commissioners then embarked on an ambitious project to expand the relatively small parade grounds, a legacy of colonial times, that extended from Madison Avenue to State Street below Knox Street (Northern Boulevard), which at that time extended in a straight line through Washington Park. A pedestrian walkway today marks where the original Knox Street formed the western boundary of the park.

In the northern part of present-day Washington Park were the State Street Burial Grounds. These burial grounds had been laid out at the time of the American Revolution and by the mid-19th century were almost completely occupied. Psychologically they retarded development in the area—as was also the case with the Van Rensselaer burying ground next to St. Joseph's Church on Ten Broeck Street—because few prospective home buyers were willing to settle in a neighborhood where they could sit on their front stoop and watch the daily burial of their fellow citizens. In the 19th century, with infant mortality so much higher than it is today, funerals were a much more constant factor than they are in present-day life. A city law, in fact, banned the pealing of church bells at funerals because of their inordinate frequency.

The State Street Burial Grounds also presented a problem of vandalism. Street gangs, predominantly German and Irish, were active in Albany in the 1860s, and rival gangs would battle one another in isolated, undeveloped areas of the city, including the cemetery. At the same time, the concept of the rural cemetery was beginning to take hold. Albany Rural Cemetery was established in nearby Menands in 1841, and the adjoining St. Agnes Cemetery in 1866. These cemeteries, and that of Jewish Beth Emeth, would eventually service several generations of Albanians; in fact, more people are buried in these cemeteries than live today in all of Albany County.

The State Street Burial Grounds, already filled to capacity, had little future in the city's grand scheme. The bodies were exhumed at Common Council expense and their remains moved to the newer, more suburban cemeteries to the north, outside the city limits.

The burial grounds coupled with the parade grounds now provided a substantial expanse of land in the very heart of the city. Meanwhile the railroad tracks, originally located to the south of Madison Avenue, were relocated in the 1840s to Tivoli Hollow, far north of this section of the city. All that remained was to expand the western part of the park southward to Madison Avenue, then all the way west to Perry Street (Lake Avenue).

Below
After the Civil War enterprising real-estate speculators constructed Martinville on the site of an old brickyard. The neighborhood, shown in this 1892 photo, was built on land not well suited for residential construction. It was obliterated around 1910 for the development of Lincoln Park.
Facing page
In 1866 geologist and paleontologist James Hall was appointed director of the Museum of Natural History in Albany. In 1893 he was made state geologist of New York.

Morris Gerber

Dictionary of American Portraits

The park commissioners completely displaced a new housing development known as Lakeview, replacing it with gardens and the famous statue of Moses that is so dear to the hearts of most Albanians. The lake was formed by damming up a natural stream, a branch of the Beaver Kill that ran down today's Elberon Place which was once the site of a cotton mill. What the commissioners were not able to do was to displace the millionaires who had built their homes on Englewood Place and Thurlow Terrace; a number of these mansions can still be seen today. The fact that several residents of these two streets were also members of the park commission may have had some direct bearing on the fact that the park was never expanded to its "natural boundaries" of Lake and Western avenues.

At one point the park commissioners were able to buy out the rights of the old Great Western Turnpike Company, and in so doing they gained title to all the land on both sides of Western Avenue from Washington Park up to Manning Boulevard. Even today, it is a responsibility of the city of Albany to plow the sidewalks on Western Avenue from Manning Boulevard to Washington Park because of this long-forgotten purchase by the park commissioners.

The city's other major park, Lincoln Park, was originally known as Beaver Park—the name of an estate situated near present-day Morton and Delaware avenues, where the tennis courts are today. The workshop or studio of James Hall, the noted geologist and paleontologist who trained a generation of scholars in the field, was built there in 1848 and still remains in the park.

At the beginning of this century, the upper end of today's Lincoln Park was known as Delaware Square. It included a stream, barely visible today at the bottom of the great ravine to the south of Park Avenue, with a pond at the bottom known as Rock Ledge. The adjoining Hinckel (later Dobler) Brewery dumped its effluent suds into the water supply, thus giving the area its more common descriptive name of Buttermilk Falls.

The eastern part of Lincoln Park, which today serves as an athletic field in a bowl, was once a community known as Martinville—an extremely poorly planned ghetto of wooden row houses built upon the ruins of an abandoned brickyard. A predominantly Irish neighborhood paralleling the now-defunct ways of Martin Street and Johnson Alley, it was mercifully destroyed about 1910 to create the present Lincoln Park. The park shrank in size in the 1960s when, as part of urban renewal, the extreme lower end of the park was converted into Lincoln Park Homes, a high-rise public housing development.

Lincoln and Washington parks were overwhelmingly popular and are still successful additions to the urban environment. A less successful experiment occurred on the north side of town, where abandoned Water Department property was turned into Tivoli Park. The area proved to be just too much land for the city to develop and maintain, and in recent years Tivoli Park has been relegated to the status of a nature preserve.

Swinburne Park, named after a popular Albany doctor and Republican mayor, also comes from the the conversion of the old water system into a more usable facility. Two large reservoirs had previously been utilized—one above and one below Manning Boulevard. In the 1930s, the lower body of water, known as Bleecker Reservoir, was cut through in four places by WPA workers and then turned into the stadium that it is today.

Albany Public Library

Albany High School and Bishop Maginn High School use it for their athletic contests. The stadium has also served a variety of uses for Twilight League baseball, and at one time it was the principal parade ground for Christian Brothers Academy.

Turnpikes and Growth

The first major assault on the grid pattern came, however, not from institutions or parks but rather from the development of turnpikes which, like arteries carrying the economic lifeblood of the region, radiated out from the city and ultimately determined how and where the original settlement would grow to form new neighborhoods.

From the close of the Revolution to the opening of the Erie and Champlain canals, the state government placed great emphasis on the development of the vast expanse of western lands seized after the war from the Iroquois, who along with their Johnson family allies had remained loyal to the Crown. Land companies and land speculators abounded, with the full blessing of the state, as Yankee emigrants from the declining farms of New England, Revolutionary veterans, and immigrants from abroad turned their sights westward.

"By 1795," according to Albany historian Codman Hislop, "the tide of migration through Albany to the West was so great that in one day a citizen counted over five hundred sleighs crowding up the State Street hill. . . .Twelve hundred sleighs went through Albany in three days during that winter, loaded with whatever their owners thought was necessary to begin life on their new land." Albany soon found itself adapting to a new role as banker, teamster, and general store for the tens of thousands of pioneers who made the journey west.

The lack of adequate roads was sorely felt by the emigrés from Yankee New England. Narrow, decaying military roads from the colonial wars, with their "corduroy" paving of logs thrown across muddy stretches,

The Western Avenue tollgate was located a few yards west of the junction of Manning Boulevard and Western Avenue. After the rights of the Great Western Turnpike Company were purchased by the park commissioners in the late 19th century, the green belts along either side of Western Avenue were maintained from this point to Washington Park.

placed travelers completely at the mercy of the weather. Lengthy travel had to be deferred until the winter months when the ground was frozen.

The solution to the problem proved to be the turnpike—a vastly improved type of road built and maintained by a private company that charged a toll for the use of its facility. A far cry from the washed out, rutted roads of colonial New York, the turnpikes were, by early 19th-century standards, broad and well graded; they were surfaced with dirt, crushed stone, or heavy wooden planks. Tollgates, or "turnpikes," placed at intervals of approximately 10 miles, were used to collect the fees, which varied greatly according to whether the traveler was on horseback, in a stagecoach, or driving cattle, sheep, or hogs to market.

The popularity of the turnpikes was immediate. By 1815, every major valley in the state had one, and virtually all of them eventually fed into a turnpike leading to Albany.

Albany soon became the turnpike center of the state. Central Avenue (Route 5) was started in 1797 as the Albany-Schenectady turnpike, linking the commerce of the Hudson and Mohawk rivers while providing safe portage around the Cohoes Falls. As a direct result of this development, the old Kings Highway—which had been strategically placed in the city's Pine Bush to keep the Albany fur trade out of the jurisdiction of the surrounding manor of Rensselaerswyck—now became all but obsolete, condemning the area to the status of an obscure backwater for the next century and a half.

Western Avenue (Route 20), the Great Western Turnpike, was started two years later and eventually carried the bulk of stage and freight traffic through the heart of the state to Buffalo. Great, lumbering stagecoaches were developed that could transport a dozen passengers from Albany to Buffalo in the breakneck speed of six days.

The Albany-Lebanon Turnpike (Routes 9 and 20), which dates from 1798, carried travelers from New England to the village of Greenbush, where for the next half-century a ferry franchised by the city brought traffic across the Hudson to Albany. Other major roads dating from this period were the Bethlehem Turnpike (now Route 144), the Delaware Turnpike (now Delaware Avenue), and the Schoharie Turnpike (now New Scotland Avenue).

The significance of this lively travel to Albany cannot be overstated. All roads led to Albany, not just in a geographic sense but in an economic sense as well. The typical Yankee settler moving with his family from Massachusetts to the fertile valley of the Genesee would not only traverse toll roads owned in part by Albany investors but would often purchase land held by Albany speculators and mortgaged to Albany bankers. Once settled, he would clear his land with Albany tools and supply his farm with provisions ordered from Albany merchants and factories.

The turnpike and stagecoach companies enjoyed a symbiotic relationship with numerous other industries that sprang up along the routes they followed. Livery stables dotted the roadways, providing frequent changes of horses, and roadside inns offered welcome shelter and refreshment to weary travelers tired of sitting three abreast on a wooden plank seat for upwards of 60 dusty miles a day. For sustenance, financial backing, and even newspapers, innkeepers and tradesmen, like the travelers and farmers they served, looked in only one direction—Albany.

Great fortunes were made by the Dutch and Yankee merchant princes of old Beverwyck. By the mid-1790s Dutch had ceased to be the majority language of the populace. The city was growing, and as it expanded it became more and more Yankee and less and less Dutch. The population tripled from 3,506 in 1790 to 10,762 in 1810, almost entirely as a result of the Yankee invasion; by 1830 the figure had more than doubled to 24,238.

Wide sidewalks and streets characterize Madison Avenue east of Dove Street in this photograph taken circa 1915.

Entire neighborhoods had to be developed to accommodate the city's growing population. Narrow streets were laid out paralleling the new Albany-Schenectady turnpike, the principal source of the new prosperity; the formal grid pattern was largely ignored. The lower part of present-day Central Avenue was known as the Bowery because it led to the "bouweries," or farms, of the Dutch. Present-day Sherman, Elk, West, and Bradford streets served as working-class neighborhoods for the people who earned their living along the turnpike and in its related industries.

In 19th-century Albany, as in all of urban America at the time, the typical citizen commonly worked a 10 to 14-hour day for six days of every week. Public transportation was rare, and if a man wished to spend any time with his family it was an absolute necessity that he live close to his place of work. This was true not only for the least skilled worker but for the senior manager as well. In the case of women, common household chores were difficult and time consuming, and the days left little time to be wasted in traveling long distances for everyday goods and services.

Albany's street patterns were designed to respond to this common need.

That portion of the lot not occupied by the building is set apart for recreation purposes, and has been properly graded and paved with the "Scrimshaw pavement," a patent concrete pavement, and presents a very clean appearance.

The girls' portion, which is on Herkimer street, contains about three thousand square feet. The boys' playground is on Franklin street and contains 4,830 feet, and is separated from the girls' ground by a strong fence nine feet high.

In each of these playgrounds are the necessary privies, urinals, etc., all of brick, with floors of flag-stone, and proper screens in front to secure privacy.

The exterior of the building, which is both imposing and pleasing, is constructed of the following materials: The water-table and lintel course of the basement is Grawacke stone; the trimmings and belt course to first and second story windows are of cast iron; the main cornice and dormer windows are of wood and are very ornamental. The French roof is covered with slate banded in two colors, while the roof is surmounted with a neat cornice and ornamental iron cresting. The wood and iron work is painted and sanded to imitate the stone.

Albany Argus, August 29, 1871.

City Engineer's Office

Each neighborhood, as it was laid out, provided appropriate housing for all of its requisite personnel. Worker and manager, servant and master, immigrant and Brahmin, all lived within a few yards of one another.

Each neighborhood met this challenge by utilizing essentially the same solution—the creation of an alternating rich street/poor street residential pattern, interspersed with corner shops, groceries, drugstores, and saloons. In some cases the centermost building of a block also contained a store at ground level. This pattern is readily apparent in the neighborhoods established in Albany prior to 1850.

A prime example is the north Pastures District, that part of the South End closest to downtown. It extended from Madison Avenue to South Ferry Street and from South Pearl Street to the river. From 1794 on, the Dutch Church, by much dredging and filling in of what had been oft-flooded common pastureland, developed the land into a neighborhood that still contains nearly 90 buildings listed in the National Register of Historic Sites. It is completely depopulated now, with the goal of rebuilding the neighborhood through restoration and in-fill housing.

The Pastures is typical of the rich street/poor street pattern. The wide street of Madison still contains the Sanders Mansion (built in 1808), the executive mansion of Governor Joseph Yates (built in 1812), and the classic Federal row houses built by the prominent Dublin-born merchant Dudley Walsh between 1817 and 1821. To the south, Herkimer Street has the remains of a prominent Jewish synagogue and the city's first modern public school, built in 1871. Westerlo Street boasts an unbroken row of Federal homes designed by architect Henry Rector, of the New York State Court of Appeals. South Ferry Street contains the pretentious homes of the Boyd family, whose large brewery once provided employment to scores of men in the South End. A Schuyler family mansion also still stands on South Ferry Street—a building considered so elegant that it sold for $28,000 in 1865 at a time when $7 a week was considered a living wage. Around the corner on Green Street, Philip Hooker, Albany's foremost architect of the time, maintained an office from which the city's most prominent buildings were designed.

But these silent surviving examples of Federal architecture, with their wrought-iron railings, multipaneled doors, leaded-glass sidelights, pillared dormers, and sandstone or marble trim portray only half the story of the neighborhood. Gone from today's Pastures are the "poor" streets. John, South Lansing, and Bleecker streets, and even little Franklin Street—whose narrow passage, like Green and South Pearl streets, once extended

By 1810 there were more than 200 sloops on the Hudson; by 1850, despite the advent of steam, there were 400 to 500 sloops in regular service between Albany and New York. The average size was about 60 tons; one of the largest, at 220 tons, was the *Utica,* built at Albany in 1833. After 1850 the number of sloops decreased, and by the time of the Civil War no new sailing vessels were being built. Even so, in 1900 there were still about 200 sloops in service along the Hudson; the last one was reportedly destroyed by a hurricane in 1938.

Development of Industry
Early industry in Albany was generally oriented toward meeting the demands of local consumers and the export market through the processing

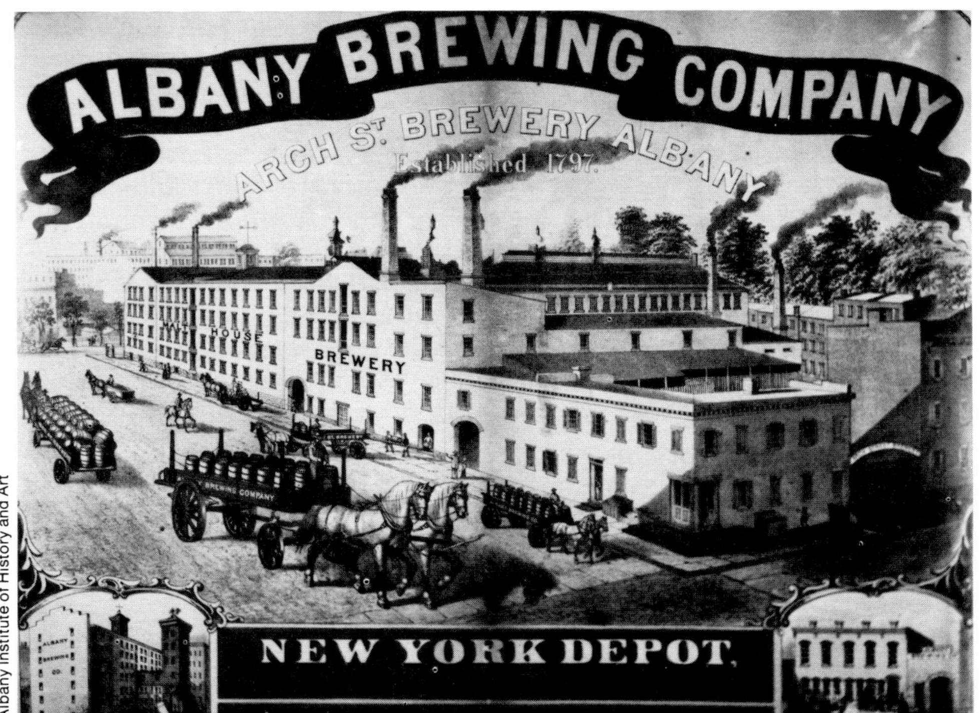

Albany Institute of History and Art

Albany Institute of History and Art

Albany Institute of History and Art

Book of Commerce

Facing page
Top left
Breweries provided jobs for hundreds of Albany residents throughout the 19th century. The Albany Brewing Company was established in 1797.
Top right
The building on State Street that housed the Albany Hardware and Iron Company gives a good indication of the size and diversity of the company's inventory.
Bottom
The West Albany cattleyards, established in 1850, were of great importance during the latter part of the 19th century. Until refrigerated boxcars made it unnecessary to transport live animals, cattle were driven down Central Avenue to the yards. The cattleyards were later replaced by the West Albany shops and the West Albany Industrial Park.
Below
Albany merchants imported tea from China. Agents were sent to the Orient to purchase the tea from merchants. Once purchased, the tea would be shipped to Albany.
Below right
Albany's lumberyards, established in 1850, were located between the Erie Canal and the Hudson River, extending northward from the entrance of the canal into North Albany. From this location, Adirondack timber was sent to points throughout the United States and Europe. At the turn of the century, the lumber district's business declined due to the scarcity of Adirondack lumber from exploitation and a major fire in the lumber district in 1908.

of primary products: the milling of flour and of lumber, the processing of meat, and—from earliest colonial times—the conversion of grain into beer and spirits. Brewing in particular, thanks initially to the Dutch and German presence, was a significant local industry up until quite recent times.

Among the more prominent breweries of the 19th century was the Dobler Brewery, originally the Hinckel Brewery, located in a complex of shops and industrial buildings that extended from Elm Street to Park Avenue along both sides of present-day Swan Street. Part of the old Hinckel Brewery still stands overlooking Lincoln Park and is considered one of the finer examples of 19th-century industrial architecture remaining in the city.

George Amsdell's great brewery still stands, too, although few Albanians would recognize it today. During Prohibition it was converted into the Knickerbocker Apartments, which occupy the block between Lancaster and Jay on Dove Street.

The Hedrick Brewery, started in 1852, was famous for its ownership by the late Daniel P. O'Connell, longtime political patriarch of the city's Democratic organization. The brewery was located at 400 Central Avenue, the present site of the high-rise apartment building known as Central Towers.

Another of Albany's political figures, Michael Nolan, the city's first Irish Catholic mayor, initially achieved fame and fortune as the president of

Albany Institute of History and Art

Quinn and Nolan, later known as the Beverwyck Brewery, in North Albany. Purchased by Schaeffer and Sons, it was the city's last remaining brewery until the early 1970s, when it was closed down and the building demolished.

For many years the Schaeffer Brewery was known for its all-night Beer Fountain, where many a late-returning worker or city newspaper reporter would stop in for a final toast to the evening, and also for the great statue of King Ganbrinus that stood with foaming stein aloft looking down on the hundreds of North Albany workers who daily produced the sudsy brew.

Like many of the breweries, a number of 19th-century distilleries were associated with the names of politicians—among them, city aldermen Evers, Tracy, and Boyd. Their distilleries, in the days prior to modern zoning, stood in the midst of residential neighborhoods in Sheridan Hollow and in the city's South End.

Just as the city's hardware stores and bankers supplied and financed the westward expansion of the American people, so too did the distillers and brewers earn their fortunes by sending uncountable barrels and hogsheads of porter, ale, whiskey, and beer to the thirsty farmers and other settlers in the western part of the state.

A smaller but nonetheless interesting local industry, which survived until the 1930s, was tobacco rolling. In the 19th century it was not uncommon for Albanians to buy their tobacco by the leaf and to have bunches of tobacco leaves hanging in the attics of stores such as Coulson's on Broadway, where entire floors were maintained as great humidors. As the need arose, the discriminating tobacco smoker would order that a leaf be taken off and given to a tobacco roller, who would then make hand-rolled cigars for his use—an art that is virtually unknown in the United States today.

Another long-standing Albany industry, and one that survives to this day, is publishing. For much of the 19th century, Albany was second only to Boston in the number of books produced, particularly in the fields of law and religion. The first steam-driven printing press in the United States was installed at Albany in 1828. City directories of the mid- and late 1800s list large numbers of morocco workers in and around the central downtown area—the number of morocco workers, of course, reflecting the use of leather binding in the books produced at that time. The printing industry survives today on a greatly reduced scale in the northern part of the city, oriented primarily toward the production of government reports and other documents related to the role of Albany as the state capital.

The 19th-century industry most closely associated with Albany and its sister city of Troy was iron casting—most notably, the fabrication of cast-iron stoves. The Albany Institute of History and Art recently exhibited a major collection of stoves gathered from all over the country, almost all of which were manufactured in Albany.

The iron industry had its foundation in the city of Troy and was controlled by men with interests in both cities, including Henry Burden and Erastus Corning, Sr. The Upper Hudson Valley was an ideal location. Limestone from the banks of the Hudson served as flux; coal was brought in by the Delaware Canal from eastern Pennsylvania; and iron ore, mined in the Adirondacks, was transported down the Champlain Canal.

Below
Joel Munsell (1808-1880), printer, publisher, antiquarian, collector, and author of books about printing, was a native of Northfield, Massachusetts, but quickly developed a personal devotion to the history of Albany. His 10-volume Annals of Albany *and a 4-volume* Collections on the History of Albany *are considered invaluable historical reference works. His 58 State Street firm became a nationally prominent printing and genealogical publishing house.*

Albany Institute of History and Art

Albany Institute of History and Art

Right
At the reins of their delivery wagon, employees of the Beverwyck Brewing Company stop in front of the office. Formerly the Quinn and Nolan Brewery, the Beverwyck Company later became the Schaeffer Brewery.
Below
The Quinn Ale Brewery was operated by James Quinn from 1845 until 1866 when Terrance J. Quinn and Michael N. Nolan succeeded him. Their partnership lasted until Quinn's death in 1878. The business was operated by Michael Nolan until 1917. This 1902 watercolor of the brewery was painted by J. MacGregor.
Below right
Joel Munsell, one of the nation's leading genealogical publishers in the 19th century, printed this Albany bicentennial broadside. Local historians still use his Annals of Albany.

Albany Institute of History and Art

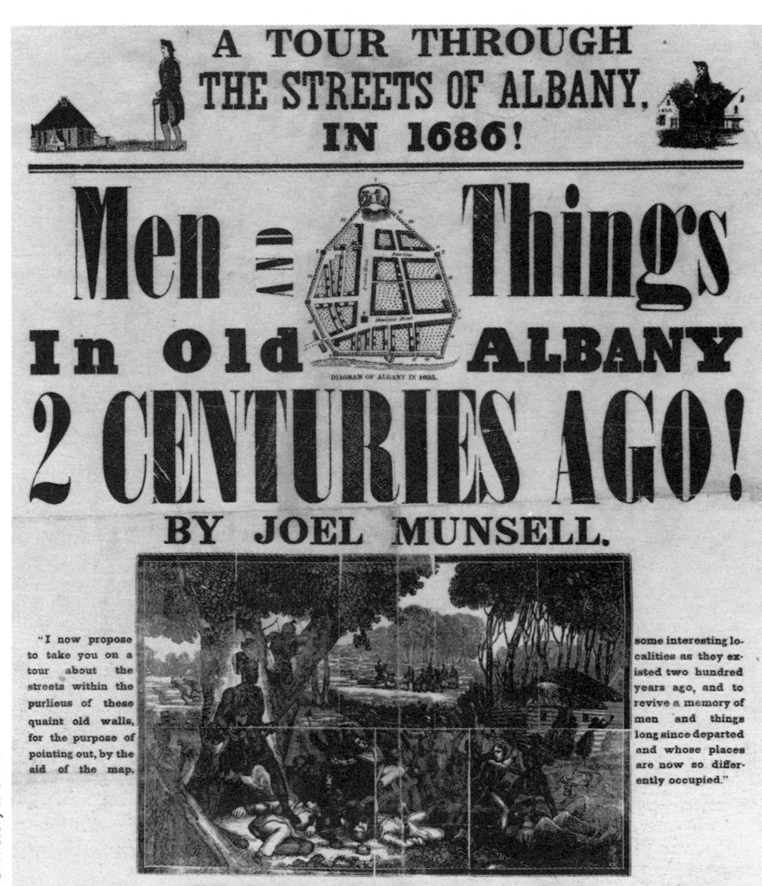
A TOUR THROUGH
THE STREETS OF ALBANY,
IN 1686!

Men AND Things
In Old ALBANY
2 CENTURIES AGO!
BY JOEL MUNSELL.

"I now propose to take you on a tour about the streets within the purlieus of these quaint old walls, for the purpose of pointing out, by the aid of the map, some interesting localities as they existed two hundred years ago, and to revive a memory of men and things long since departed and whose places are now so differently occupied."

FOR SALE BY
All BOOKSELLERS and NEWSDEALERS,
And by the Publishers, JOEL MUNSELL'S SONS, 82 State St.
PRICE 25 CENTS.

Albany Institute of History and Art

Cast-Iron Stoves

When the Albany Institute of History and Art recently exhibited a major collection of cast-iron stoves, nearly all of them manufactured in the Albany area, it made a timely display. Today's energy crisis has caused Americans to rediscover, and reconsider, the wisdom and craftsmanship of past generations in this fuel-efficient heating and cooking technique. The coal-burning cast-iron stove—initially, Albany's response to a serious wood shortage in the 1820s brought on by overconsumption of local timber by steamboats and factories—impresses present-day observers as a model of sound technology, usefulness, and careful design.

In 1833 the editor of the Albany *Daily Advertiser* stated that the "manufacture of iron castings was brought to a greater perfection in Albany than any other place in the country, or even Europe." Cast iron, a moldable and durable metallic material that could both accept and radiate high temperatures, proved the ideal replacement in the 19th century for the fireplace as a domestic heating and cooking device. Raw materials basic to the production of cast iron were plentiful in Albany. Iron ore, limestone, charcoal, and silicon (sand) were either available locally or easily acquired from nearby counties in the Hudson Valley and the Adirondacks. Because of its high percentage of pure iron, the ore was of exceptional quality. Charcoal, produced locally, was used as fuel for the air blast furnaces; coke, serving the same function later for the cupola furnaces developed in Albany, came from Pennsylvania via the Delaware and Hudson Canal to the Hudson River. The excellence of the castings themselves was chiefly due to the fine-quality molding sand available in the region.

In the early 19th century new ideas were rife in the burgeoning industrial revolution, and inevitably the cast-iron stove challenged American innovators. Rensselaer Polytechnic Institute, founded in Troy in 1824 as the nation's first school of engineering, concentrated on practical applications of the physical sciences. Undoubtedly RPI supplied technical knowledge to the cast-iron stove designers and manufacturers in Troy and Albany, who were making the region the center of the industry.

Artisans in Albany and its sister city Troy contributed their own special talents to the development of the cast-iron stove as a parlor heater or kitchen range. Especially important were the patternmakers, whose designs molded into the iron were trademarks as well as decorations. The stoves of mid-19th century America simulated the Victorian Age's taste. Ornate decorations were possible in both flask casting (in which imbedded flasks received molten iron to form stove parts) and the new cupola furnace. Thus, stoves featured stylistic niceties found in castles, cathedrals, and Italian villas. There were elaborate floral and patriotic motifs; details from Greek, Roman, Gothic, Egyptian, and rococo revival architecture; Gothic and Palladian windows and columns shaped like dolphins; grapes and grapevines, leaves, acorns, and fruit baskets adorning the cast-iron stoves. After 1850 most stoves were given romantic names, such as "Venetian Parlor,"

"Castle," and "Temple Parlor," which enhanced their allure while helping the buyer identify the stove of his choice when ordering from a catalog.

By 1875 there were 15 stove foundries in Albany. The Perry Stove Company, one of the largest in the U.S., covered five acres of ground, employed almost 1,800 workers, and grossed about a half-million dollars a year from its production of some 40,000 parlor stoves, kitchen ranges, and furnaces. Ransom and Rathbone was another major manufacturer during this period when Albany's cast-iron stoves were achieving worldwide recognition. Indeed, the area had proved a perfect breeding spot for the industry, not only because of the availability of materials and artisans, but also because of the transportation facilities by both ship and rail. The completion of the Erie Canal in 1825 gave access to the fast-growing settlements in the Great Lakes area. And the port of Albany along the Hudson River made it possible to ship stoves to New York City and thence to other American cities and to Europe. No wonder Albany was called the "Crossroads of the Northeast and the Gateway to the West." The introduction to the Perry Stove Company's catalog of 1876 was written in English, French, and German, indicating the far-flung recognition accorded the Albany craftsmen and manufacturers.

Ultimately, however, after many productive years, the combination of unionization with tough competition from the Midwestern stove industry—which was partly launched as branches of Albany and Troy companies—brought an end to the lucrative operation. The Mesabi Range in Minnesota, too, offered a high-quality, low-cost source for iron ore that was depleted now along the Hudson. By 1900 most of the Albany area foundries had shut down or moved to the Midwest. Albany's last foundry, Rathbone, Sard and Company, closed in 1925.

Today the renewed popularity of cast-iron stoves, antique or newly made, is much in evidence. Appreciation of this uniquely American invention encompasses both its practical value and superior design with decorative appeal.

(Special credit to Tammis Kane Groft of the Albany Institute of History and Art and photographer William Knorr.)

The prosperity of the iron industry in both Albany and Troy was legendary. Iron foundries in Albany were located in the city's north and south ends, where generations of immigrants and their descendants served as ironmongers, puddlers, and molders of stoves that were sent all over the United States and Europe. Production flourished until the 1890s, when a combination of unionization and the opening up of the great Mesabi Range in Minnesota started its gradual decline.

The older neighborhoods of the city reflect this once great industry—from the earliest Federal buildings, with their iron acorn railings, to the square, boxy ironwork of the Greek Revival period, to the post-Civil War cast-iron lintels over windows and doors. The city's builders seldom had to look far for these cast-iron fixtures; most of them were fabricated right in Albany by Albany craftsmen.

These industries, plus the port, the canals, and later the railroads, begot other industries, including wholesale and retail trade, services of all kinds, and construction. Continuing expansion of the city required new housing, indeed whole new neighborhoods, with their corner stores, churches, and schools. Public and private buildings alike sprang up where once Dutch cattle and hogs had grazed, providing more employment for the Albanians they were destined to house and serve.

Steamboat and Canal

The key to economic prosperity in 19th-century Albany, however, lay not in industry but in transportation. The city that began its existence as a trading post and inland port flourished as the Hudson River traffic moved from sail to steam and the Erie Canal funneled raw materials from the great western hinterland out through the thriving port of Albany.

The first commercially successful steamboat, Robert Fulton's *Clermont,* ventured forth from New York harbor on the afternoon of August 17, 1807, reaching Albany two days later. The 133-foot vessel, powered by a pair of boiler-fired 12-paddle sidewheels, achieved the upriver passage in 32 hours and the return in 30 hours—compared with the three days to a week by sloop, depending on the wind and tides.

On September 4, 1807, the *Clermont* began regular passenger service between Albany and New York. The venture, like the development of the steamboat itself, was financed by Robert R. Livingston, who had first become acquainted with Fulton in the 1790s in Paris, where Livingston was serving as minister to France and Fulton was earning his living as a portrait and landscape artist while tinkering with new applications of the developing steam engine. The *Clermont*, in fact, was named for Livingston's country estate along the Hudson River in southern Columbia County.

The Fulton-Livingston service, granted a monopoly by the state, proved to be a huge success. In 1808 there were three steamboats in regular service between Albany and New York, and by 1811 there were eight. In 1824 a Supreme Court decision broke the Fulton-Livingston monopoly, and steamboat service mushroomed—from a total of 12 vessels in 1825 to more than 100 in 1840. By this time, travel time between Albany and New York had been reduced to 10 hours or less; by the 1860s it was down to seven hours. At the same time, the size of steamboats was increasing. The *New World,* built in 1848, was 352 feet long, and with overnight berths no longer a requisite, carrying capacity was vastly increased. In 1851 more than one million passengers traveled by steamer from Albany to New York; in 1884, despite the competition of the railroads, the figure was 1.5 million.

Clockwise from top left
The steamboat Rip Van Winkle, *owned by the Albany Line, ran nonstop between Albany and New York City. According to this 1847 broadside, the boat was "fitted up with staterooms in superior style." Thomas Schuyler, an agent for the line, was one of several family members who earned his livelihood from the river traffic.*

Hudson River sloops and steamboats as well as packet boats destined for the Erie or Champlain canals abound in this mid-19th-century lithograph of the Albany Basin.

Few people are aware that John Wesley Hyatt of Albany first fabricated celluloid as a substitute for ivory in the production of billiard balls in 1866. Hyatt and his friend Peter Kinnear formed the Hyatt Billiard Ball Company, which became the Albany Billiard Ball Company, shown above in this circa 1913 photograph. The plant is still in operation today on Delaware Avenue.

Rathbone, Sard & Company factory workers catch iron from a cupola with hand ladles in 1911.

This Rathbone, Sard & Company employee is seen ramming up a mold by hand.

Robert Fulton, who designed the steamboat Clermont *for service on the Hudson River, painted this self-portrait from a miniature by Benjamin West.*

1847.

ALBANY LINE.

INDEPENDENT OPPOSITION!

Albany to New-York.

THROUGH WITHOUT LANDING.

THE NEW STEAMBOAT

Rip Van Winkle

CAPT. GEORGE B. RIGGS.

The splendid Steamboat RIP VAN WINKLE, will run between Albany and New-York the ensuing season; Leaving Albany and New-York at 7 o'clock P. M.

The Steamboat RIP VAN WINKLE is fitted up with STATE ROOMS in superior style, and will run as a Regular Passage Boat during the season. The patronage of the Travelling Public is solicited.

For Passage or Light Freight apply to Captain on board, or at the

OFFICE 29 QUAY-STREET, ALBANY.

Office on the Dock, foot of Robinson-st. N. York.

THOMAS SCHUYLER, Agent.

Albany Institute of History and Art

New York Historical Society

New York Historical Society

Capital Newspapers

New York State Archives

New York State Archives

The problems of traffic continue to be of a major nature. On a long range basis there are clear-cut indications of relief. I am hopeful that the waterfront arterial highway can be started this year. When completed it should eliminate from our streets a tremendous amount of heavy traffic, as well as make it possible for the City to provide in connection with it more than one thousand parking spaces between Madison Avenue and Columbia Streets. In the meantime we must recognize that many of our streets are narrow, that we have many hills, and that our main business section is at the eastern limit of the City. We must make every effort to maintain a balance between the natural wish of people to drive their cars into this congested area, and the need to keep our streets as clear as we can so that public transportation may move as smoothly, promptly, and efficiently as possible. . . .

Message of Mayor Erastus Corning 2nd to the Common Council of the City of Albany, January 1953.

first train of the Hudson River line, which followed the east bank of the river, arrived from New York in the record time of three hours and 45 minutes, having achieved an average speed of 40 miles an hour. The New York and Harlem, which followed an inland route, initiated service the following year. Cornelius Vanderbilt later gained control of both railroads and joined them to the New York Central system. The journey from New York to Albany that had taken four days by sloop could now be accomplished—summer or winter, fair weather or foul—in the space of four hours.

In the 1850s several north-south lines were built connecting the New York Central with the Erie Railroad, the most important of which was the Albany and Susquehanna (later the Delaware and Hudson). In 1883 the West Shore Railroad was completed between Albany and Jersey City, and passengers and freight thundered along both banks of the mighty river, even as sloops and steamboats—now doomed to extinction—continued to ply its waters.

The railroads opened Albany to once seemingly inaccessible parts of the country. The city of 50,000 took on a cosmopolitan air in the early 1850s as the rich and famous, enjoying travel in increasingly comfortable railcars, transferred at Albany for other destinations. Albanians delighted in playing host to their transient guests, including President-elect Lincoln and his wife, who arrived in Albany in February 1861 en route from Illinois to the inaugural in Washington, D.C.

The convergence of rail lines also brought fame to several Albany hotels, including Stanwix Hall at Maiden Lane and Broadway and the nearby five-story Delavan House, whose owner, E.C. Delavan, scandalized his fellow temperance workers by selling intoxicants to guests over the hotel's elegant bar.

For a decade and a half after the completion of the Hudson River Railroad- -two and a half decades after the Albany and West Stockbridge—travelers still had to cross the Hudson at Albany by ferry. This anomaly was the result of political pressure by the merchants of

Right
The last of the Delaware and Hudson Railroad steam engines made their way to the scrap yards on September 24, 1953. A riverfront arterial highway system surrounding the city now covers the area pictured here.
Far right
Locomotive 999 of the NYC & HRRR became famous for establishing a new speed record. In 1959 the locomotive was exhibited at the foot of Columbia Street.
Below
The bridging of the Hudson River in 1866 finally ended the race for commercial dominance between Albany and Troy. Prior to this, rail and foot traffic from the south and east had to cross the river by ferry.

Troy, who sought to maintain the commercial advantage afforded by the city-financed Troy-Schenectady Railroad which bridged the river at Waterford. Enlisting the support of the steamboat and canal interests, Troy politicians successfully blocked legislative approval of a bridge at Albany until 1856, when a charter was finally granted. The bridge—nearly 2,000 feet long and supported by 21 stone piers—was not completed until 1866, giving New England a direct rail link at last with the burgeoning American West.

The new bridge led to the construction in 1872 of Union Depot on Montgomery Street. By the mid-1800s more than 200 passenger trains passed through Albany every day; in the single month of May 1885, nearly 160,000 passenger tickets were sold at Albany.

The century of railroad growth climaxed with the opening, in December 1899, of the mammoth Union Station on Broadway. Occupying the site of the old Delavan House, it stood as an ornate, spacious symbol of Albany's gilded age of transportation. In 1968 the station was abandoned by the state of New York, its original function transferred to a more utilitarian prefabricated structure across the river in Rensselaer. Today this once magnificent edifice stands forlorn and half boarded up—its copper roof stripped by thieves, its fine plasterwork crumbling onto the floor some 60 feet below—awaiting a new role as the focal point of a rejuvenated historic Albany.

Arthur J. O'Keefe

Arthur J. O'Keefe

New York State Archives

CHAPTER 5

THE PEOPLE OF ALBANY

Dutch and Yankee, German and Irish, Polish and Italian, black and Chinese—over the centuries Albany's heritage has reflected a succession of immigrant nationalities. Its streets have echoed with a dozen languages, its neighborhoods adapting to the distinctive life-style and changing economic fortunes of each new group.

Dutch and English

From earliest colonial times Albany was peopled by a mix of nationalities. The first boatload of settlers to arrive in 1624 under the auspices of the Dutch West India Company, in fact, consisted of French-speaking

New York Historical Society

Memoirs of An American Lady, Munsell edition

Walloons, Protestant refugees from the southern provinces then beleagured by Catholic Spain. Throughout the colonial period the Albany fur trade, as well as nearby farmland, attracted a range of European nationalities that included Germans, Scandinavians, English, Scots, Irish, Poles, and Italians, as well as Dutch.

The dominant nationality of colonial Albany, however, was clearly Dutch. Dutch dominance at first was by sheer numbers, but even with the later influx of New England Yankees, Dutch language and culture remained strong. Even today names ending with *-kill* (creek), *-bush* (woods), *-wyck* (district), and *-vliet* (stream)—not to mention Van Zandt, Ten Broeck, Gansevoort, and many more—remind modern Albanians of their Dutch heritage.

"The inhabitants of Albany and its environs are almost all Dutchmen," wrote Peter Kalm, with some slight exaggeration, nearly a century after the British takeover of New York. "They speak Dutch, have Dutch preachers, and the divine service is performed in that language. Their manners are likewise quite Dutch"—manners of which Kalm, a Swede, evidently did not approve.

In their homes the inhabitants of Albany are much more sparing than the English and are stingier with their food. Generally what they serve is just enough for the meal and sometimes hardly that. The punch bowl is much more rarely seen than among the English. The women are perfectly well acquainted with economy; they rise early, go to sleep very late, and are almost superstitiously clean in regard to the floor, which is frequently scoured several times in the week. Inside the homes the women are neatly but not lavishly dressed. The children are taught both English and Dutch. The servants in the town are chiefly negroes.

Facing page
Johannes Schuyler and his wife Elizabeth Staats Schuyler were among the many Dutch residents of Albany in the 17th and 18th centuries. This painting of the Schuylers is attributed to John Watson.
Above
Anne Grant (1755-1838) of Laggan, Scotland, visited Albany as a child in 1768. Her descriptions of the town at the twilight of the British Colonial period tell us much about social customs of the area's Dutch families.

Negro slaves as well as free blacks were a part of life in Dutch Albany and throughout colonial New York, which in fact had a larger slave population than any other colony north of Maryland. A number of slaves worked as domestic servants and farmhands; others were skilled artisans enjoying varying degrees of freedom. In 1714 the population of Albany was approximately 10 percent black (113 out of 1,136), while that of the surrounding county was about 15 percent black.

The change of administration from the Dutch West India Company to the British Crown in 1664 had very little practical effect on the Dutch way of life at Albany. The terms of surrender, followed in 1686 by the Dongan Charter, guaranteed to the inhabitants their language, religion, material possessions, and even their Dutch laws. Beverwyck was renamed Albany, in honor of James II's Scottish title as Duke of Albany, but virtually all the Dutch settlers elected to stay and life went on pretty much as before.

A century later, however, the tide of westward migration that swept through New England following the American Revolution threatened to inundate the Dutch with new settlers of English descent. Great swarms of Yankees passed through Albany on their way west, and many settled in the environs, leasing their farms from patroon Stephen Van Rensselaer. It was a group of New Englanders who founded the city of Troy in 1787, promptly capturing much of the trade of the Upper Hudson Valley and initiating a deep-seated rivalry with Albany that would last for generations. Another contingent of New Englanders founded the city of Hudson, chosen as a safe inland port from which whaling ships embarked on regular voyages to the Antarctic.

Worst of all, from the point of view of many old Dutch families, was the invasion of Albany itself. The New Englanders were energetic, ingenious, enterprising—and frankly intolerant of all that was not. Elkanah Watson, who arrived in 1789 and later became one of Albany's leading entrepreneurs, clearly expressed the Yankee view of the Dutch city and its inhabitants. "I settled in Albany, an old traveler, in the midst of the most illiberal portion of the human race—sunk in ignorance—in mud—no lamps—water spouts projecting several feet into the streets—no pavements—no library—nor a public house—or a private boarding house deserving the name." By 1803 Yankees outnumbered the Dutch, and an ordinance was passed requiring that those famous Dutch rainspouts be cut off short—to many traditionalists, a terrible blow indeed.

The political influence of the New Englanders extended far beyond the question of rainspouts. They helped push through a liberalized state constitution that extended the vote to all adult white males (a property qualification was retained for blacks), and by the 1830s most of the state's prominent political leaders were of Yankee stock. Among the Democratic leadership known as the Albany Regency, only Martin Van Buren was descended from an early Dutch colonial family; the others—including Silas Wright, William L. Marcy, Azariah C. Flagg, and John A. Dix—were of Yankee descent. Similarly, the leadership of the Whig and later the Republican party—men such as William H. Seward, Thurlow Weed, Hamilton Fish, and Horace Greeley—represented the tide of immigration from New England.

Over time the obstreperous Yankees mellowed, the original Dutch, Germans, and Scandinavians lost their accents, and monied members of both groups tended to merge into a single economic and social aristocracy. By the 1840s a new wave of immigrants, primarily Irish, cemented the alliance, as good old "American" Protestants prepared to defend themselves against what they saw as the onslaught of Catholicism.

Immigrants of the 19th Century

Irish immigrants, in the city since colonial times, together with a number of French Catholics, built St. Mary's Church in 1797—the second Roman Catholic church in the state of New York. After the turn of the century, the Irish began to arrive in ever-increasing numbers, drawn by the work of building and maintaining the turnpikes, the canals, and later the railroads. In the 1840s, the stream of immigrants became a flood, as famine at home forced thousands upon thousands of families to flee Ireland in search of a better life. By the end of the century, the Irish were the most numerous immigrant group, and Irish neighborhoods were to be found in every ward of the city—most notably, in North Albany, Arbor Hill, Sheridan Hollow, Cathedral Hill, and the South End. Albany elected its first Irish Catholic mayor, Michael M. Nolan, in 1878—two years before Boston followed suit.

Germans had also been a part of Albany since colonial times, but their numbers increased substantially in the 19th century. At first they tended to concentrate downtown in the vicinity of Holy Cross Church (since torn down) at the corner of Hamilton and Philip streets. In the course of the 19th century, German-speaking Albanians established a number of other neighborhoods. One revolved around Central Avenue, where Our Lady of Angels German Catholic Church still stands opposite St. John's German Lutheran Church; the area from West Street to Livingston Avenue was commonly known as Cabbage Town—a name that remained in use when Poles came to the neighborhood toward the end of the century. Another German neighborhood was along Second Avenue in the South End, in the

Albany Institute of History and Art

Above
This cover illustration from Leslie's *depicts the parade of bobbing clubs, one of many events that took place at the Mid-winter Carnival at Albany in 1888.*

Facing page
Top left
From 1800 to 1830 the city's population quadrupled, primarily because of an influx of Yankees from New England. Mercantile establishments like the Relyea & Wright clothing store transformed State, Pearl, and Broadway streets into a fashionable shopping center.
Top right
In the reenactment of a 1650s Dutch wedding pageant during Albany's tercentenary celebration in 1924, Anna Hamlin and Huybertie Hamlin were bride and mother, respectively.
Bottom
Also participating in the mock Dutch wedding were other representatives of the city's Yankee-Dutch first families.

FASHIONABLE C..OTHING STORE.

RELYEA & WRIGHT,
DRAPERS & TAILORS,
IN THE ATHENEUM BUILDINGS,
No. 371 NORTH MARKET-STREET,
Opposite the Mechanics' and Farmers' Bank,
ALBANY,
Have constantly on hand, an extensive and elegant assortment of articles
in their line, which they will make up on reasonable terms, on short notice, and in the
MOST FASHIONABLE MANNER.
They also, constantly keep .n elegant assortment of
FANCY GOODS,
Consisting of the following articles, viz: Spitalfield Handkerchiefs;
fashionable Cravats, both white and coloured; sil. ..itto, of different kinds; Silk and Kid Stocks;
ditto, Suspenders; fine Linen Collars; Black and White Silk Hose, plain and ribbed;
Black and White Silk Gloves; and all other articles in their line.
Albany, October, 1828.
John B. Van Steenbergh's Print.

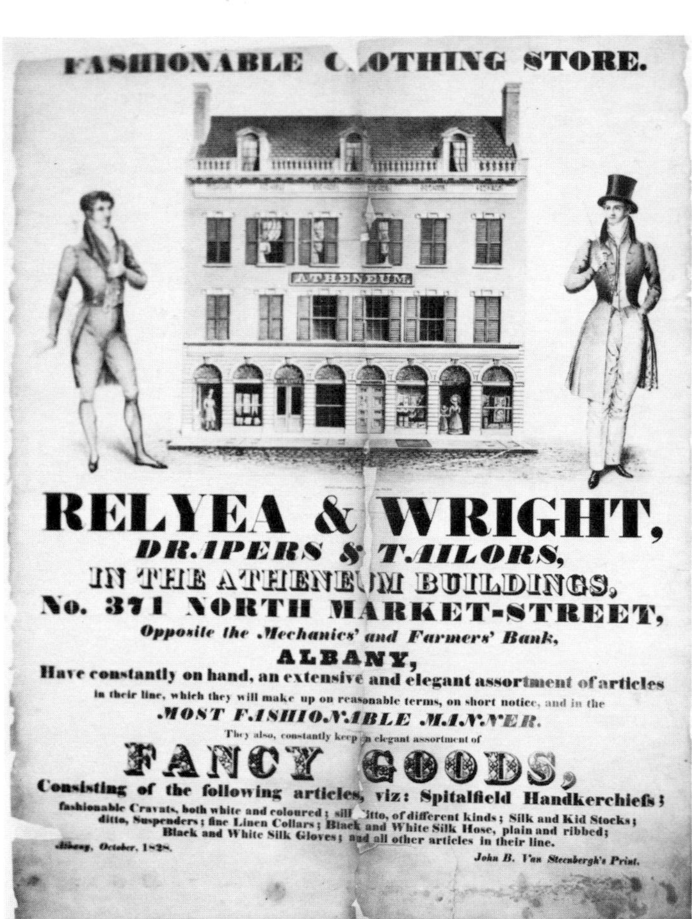

Albany Institute of History and Art

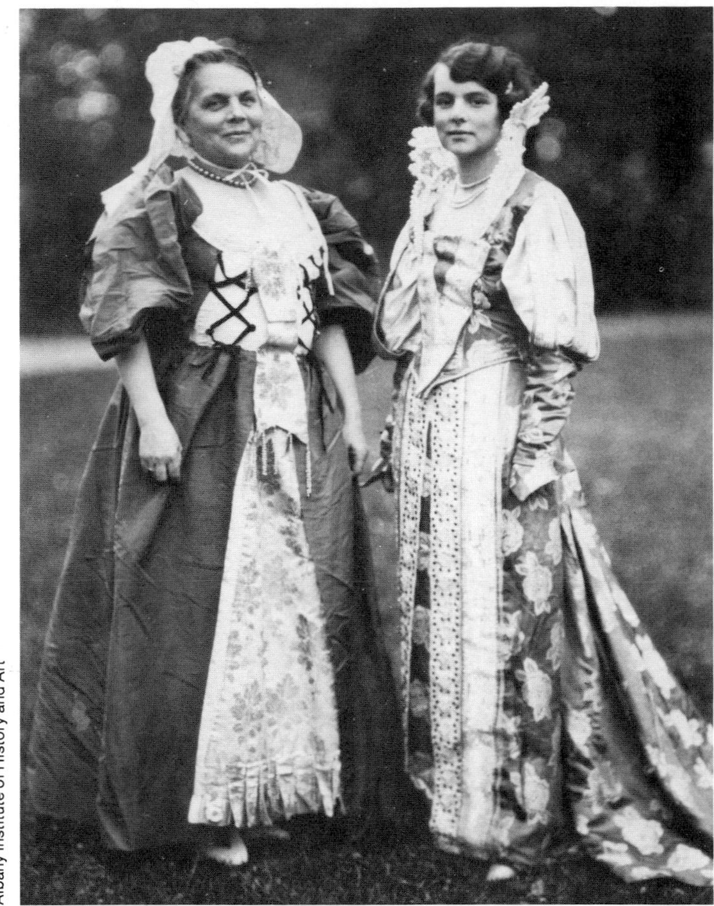

Albany Public Library

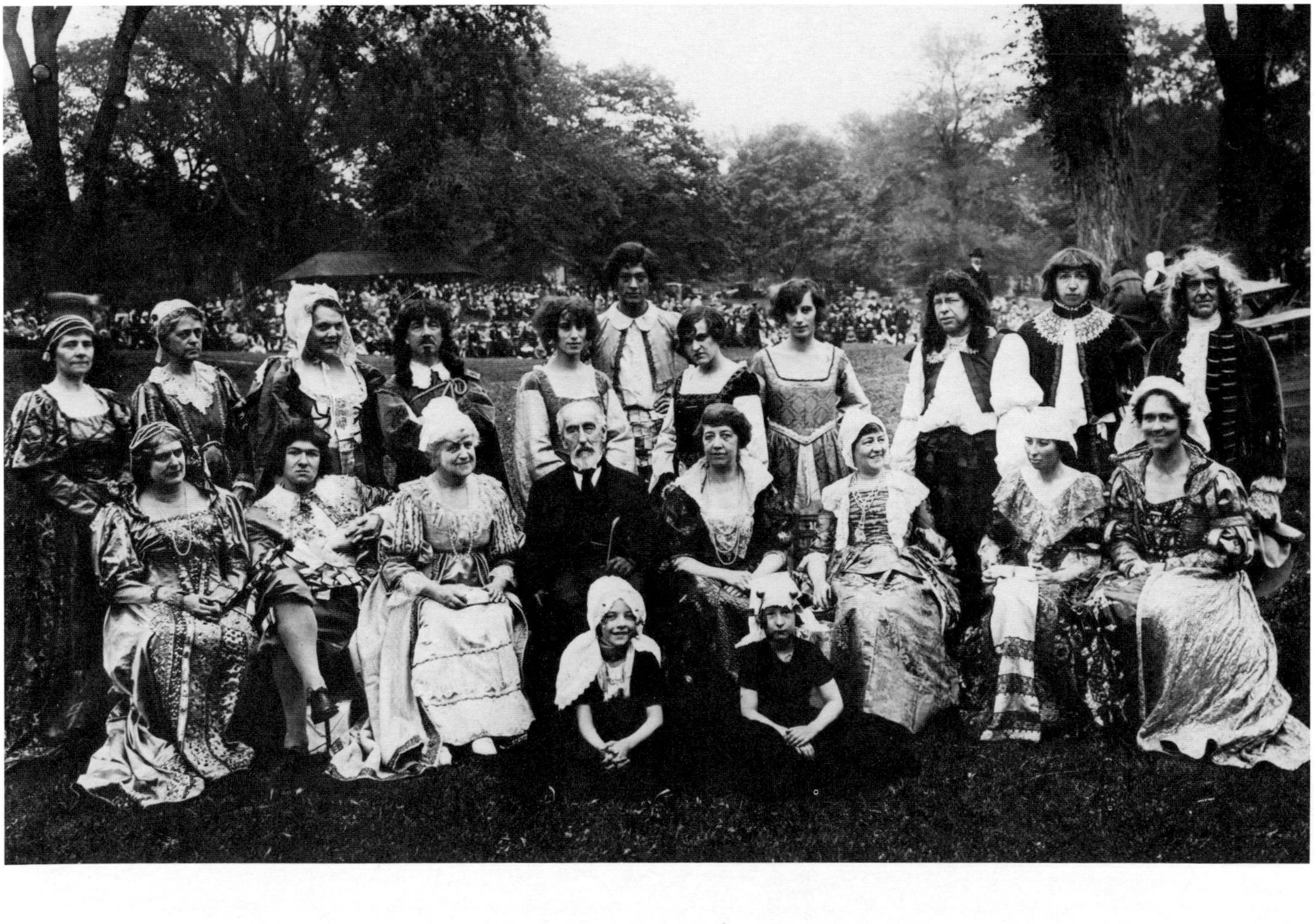

Albany Public Library

former village of Groesbeckville, annexed to the city in 1870. German neighborhoods were typified by side-by-side Protestant and Catholic institutions—churches, Sunday schools, and fraternal halls.

Morris Gerber

The German community up until World War I produced a number of German-language newspapers, the most prominent of which was the *Freie Blaetter.* Of 7,000 copies of the *Albany City Record,* detailing the proceedings of the Common Council and city government, published every week at the turn of the century, 3,000 were printed in German. As recently as the late 1940s, one Sunday school of a Protestant church in the South End still conducted classes in German. The cemeteries on Krumkill Road and at Eagle Hill on Western Avenue are full of inscriptions in the German language.

World War I was a particular tragedy for the German-Americans of Albany, as it was for all Americans of German descent. Even though their contribution to the U.S. war effort was as great as that of any other group, the wave of anti-German feeling that swept the country forced many families and community organizations to suppress their German heritage. In a sense, an entire ethnic group went "underground." German was dropped from the curriculum of Albany High School, books were banned from the library, and the colorful German street bands were heard no more.

Capital Newspapers

Temple Beth Emeth Archives

Facing page
Top
In the 1920s the area of the South End, now known as the Pastures District, was teeming with first generation Italian and Jewish families. In this view of Green Street from Herkimer, it is clear that the lack of open space provided by the layout of a century earlier forced children to regard the streets as their playground.
Bottom
Employees pose outside the German Publishing and Printing Company building.
Above
Rabbi Isaac Mayer Wise was the first rabbi of Congregation Anshe Emeth, which was established on South Pearl Street opposite Herkimer Street in 1850. Wise, who interspersed the English and German languages into his services, was frequently at odds with older Orthodox Jews who had established their congregation on nearby Fulton Street in the 1830s. His attempts to accommodate more simplified Reform methods with those of traditionalists caused great strife in Albany's Jewish community. At one Passover service it was said that law enforcement officials had to be called in to calm the heated debate. In 1854 Wise and some of his Albany followers settled in Cincinnati, Ohio, where Reform Judaism flourished.

During the war many German families found it advisable to instruct their children to cite their heritage as Dutch rather than German—ironically imitating the long-practiced Anglicization of the German word *Deutsch* into *Dutch.* Thus Our Lady of Angels school was referred to as "the Dutch college," and the Osborne Road/Delaware Avenue neighborhood as "Dutch Hollow." The Fifth Dutch Reformed Church of Albany was in fact a German-speaking congregation.

Germans and Irish lived in close proximity in Albany's South End; the two elements came together politically after the war in support of Daniel P. O'Connell, a fourth-generation South End Irishman. O'Connell's father, John, was the popular owner of a saloon at the corner of Fourth Avenue and South Pearl Street—a neighborhood in which a bartender had to speak fluent German if he wanted to stay in business. The intersection, popularly known as Beatitudes Corner, was in its way a microcosm of the city that existed before the automobile revolutionized the American lifestyle. On these four corners, O'Connell's bar gave drink to the thirsty, Machwirth's grocery fed the hungry, Belser's dry goods store clothed the naked, and the Barry Brothers Funeral Parlor buried the dead.

The Jewish community of Albany also dates back to colonial times, indeed probably to Dutch times when a number of Sephardic Jews settled in New Netherland (including one patroon, named Gomez, in the lower Hudson Valley). The Jewish population of the city became clearly identifiable in the early 1800s when German Jews established their synagogue on Fulton Street. A culturally rich Jewish community was well established by 1840 when Rabbi Isaac Mayer Wise tried unsuccessfully to plant the seeds of Reform Judaism at his temple on South Pearl Street. Meeting with almost total rejection—a Passover service erupted into a fistfight that had to be broken up by the Albany County Sheriff's Department—Rabbi Wise and a number of his followers retreated westward to Cincinnati, where the movement took hold and flourished, returning to Albany at a later date.

The tradition established by the German Jewish families who settled in the South End near the present Pastures Preservation District and along Broad and Clinton streets was continued by Eastern European Jews, who began arriving in substantial numbers in the 1890s and early 1900s—a tradition reinforced by the Orthodox Jewish requirement that families walk rather than ride to Sabbath services. Meanwhile the older German Jewish families became the founders of the Pine Hills neighborhood, where many of their homes still stand along Madison Avenue across from and just above Washington Park.

Numerous Jewish cultural and benevolent associations flourished, along with the prestigious Adelphi Club, the Colonie Country Club, and later the Shaker Ridge Country Club. Today's Jewish community is still found in Pine Hills and off Delaware Avenue but centers primarily along New Scotland Avenue and Whitehall Road.

Polish and Italian immigrants began arriving in the latter part of the 19th century. Their numbers were relatively small in Albany compared to many other eastern cities, probably because the employment opportunities offered by the General Electric Company, established at nearby Schenectady in 1875, attracted many immigrants there instead. A similar diversion occurred of French-speaking immigrants from Canada. Albany had one French-Canadian church on Hamilton Street (destroyed to create the approaches to the Empire State Plaza), but by and large the French-Canadians were detoured away from Albany by the managers of the Harmony Mills in Cohoes—a city where as recently as the 1960s one could still hear older residents speaking French in the streets and see French-language advertisements in the windows of insurance agents.

Settling at first in the downtown immigrant neighborhoods, the Poles in the 1890s built St. Casimir's Church on Sheridan Avenue just above Northern Boulevard, and thereafter most Polish families strove to live within its figurative shadow. When a split occurred within the Irish-dominated Roman Catholic church and the Polish National Church was formed, it too remained within the established Polish neighborhood, founding its new church on Clinton Avenue just two blocks from St. Casimir's.

Similarly the Italians, once numerous in lower Sheridan Hollow, established St. Anthony's Parish in 1908 with its church at the corner of Grand Street and Madison Avenue. From that day forth the neighborhood was known as Little Italy; its characteristic street festivals continued until the advent of the South Mall in the mid-1960s. Many Italian families displaced by the Mall have since moved into the adjoining parishes of St. James, St. Margaret Mary, and the most Italian neighborhood of all—West Albany, just at the edge of the city in the town of Colonie.

The McCarran-Walters Act of 1924 effectively closed off new immigration from abroad. For evidence of its impact, one need only drive up Livingston Avenue and look at St. George's Lithuanian Church—still confined to basement level as it has been since 1917, when the war and the change in immigration policy cut short what had started out as a significant influx of Lithuanians.

Another group that was once numerically significant, but whose growth was cut off by changing immigration policies, was the Chinese. Albany's Chinese community, dating from the late 19th and early 20th century, was concentrated in an area of downtown that included lower Hudson Avenue, Green Street, and Division Street, where it coexisted—as in Boston, New York, and elsewhere—in close proximity with the city's Little Italy. For years the Chinese characters could be seen on an old Federal-style building between Green and North Pearl on Hudson Avenue that housed a Chinese benevolent society.

Today the Chinese community is so widely scattered throughout the greater Albany area as to have only a fraction of the visibility it had earlier in this century. Nearly 1,000 Asians live within the city limits, including Filipinos and Taiwanese as well as more recent refugees from Southeast Asia, the majority of whom are Ethnic Chinese.

The Black Community

The story of Albany's black community is different from that of other ethnic groups. At first a substantial minority of the city's population, Albany's black population remained fairly stable throughout the 19th century, at a time when white immigration—first from New England and then from Europe—was increasing rapidly. As a result, the proportion of blacks fell to less than one percent of the city's population. Since World War II this trend has been reversed, and blacks have made up an ever-increasing proportion of the Albany community.

The percentage of blacks in the city during colonial times was much greater than most present-day Albanians realize. Slaveholding was quite common among the Dutch settlers of Albany and the surrounding area

Greater Albany Jewish Federation

City Engineer's Office

Top
South Pearl Street was a thriving commercial area that included numerous Jewish proprietors in the 1930s. H. Margulies owned this kosher restaurant and hotel. Note the discrepancy in the spelling of the owner's name on the signs.
Above
A Broadway shop window displayed these help wanted notices offering jobs to 1600 people circa 1915.
Facing page
Top
Following the opening of St. Anthony's Church on Grand Street and Madison Avenue in 1908, the area below Cathedral Hill became a mecca for Italian religious and cultural events. Celebrations in honor of Saint Anthony, the Blessed Mother, and Saint Rocco attracted thousands of residents, Catholic and non-Catholic alike.
Bottom
Albany residents displayed their enthusiastic interest in their European roots with an International Fair at the State Education Building.

Albany Institute of History and Art

St. Nicholas Ukranian Orthodox Church, Troy

CHAPTER 6

SOCIAL AND CULTURAL INSTITUTIONS

Albany Institute of History and Art

Albany's diverse ethnic background and strong political position, coupled with its economically strategic location, have made the city a logical home for innumerable cultural, educational, humanitarian, religious, and medical institutions. Albany is the capital of the Empire State, the county seat of a metropolitan county, and the regional headquarters for numerous nonprofit organizations. As such, it enjoys a cosmopolitan atmosphere beyond what might be expected in a city of its size.

Facing page
Enlargement of the Protestant Dutch Church in 1715 consisted of constructing the new addition around the shell of the old church.
Top
The oaken pulpit of the First Dutch Reformed Church was brought from Holland to Albany in 1656. It was used for 150 years.
Above
The two-steepled North Dutch Church on North Pearl Street was erected in 1798. Architect Philip Hooker designed the building that today houses Albany's First Church.

Religion

Albany today has more than 100 houses of worship representing dozens of denominations. Despite its long history of religious toleration, however, the town of Beverwyck originally had only one official or "established" church—the Dutch Reformed.

The colony's first spiritual leader was Dominie Johannes Megapolensis, who arrived on August 13, 1642, aboard the *de Houltyn*, along with Abraham Staes (Staats), a surgeon, and brewmaster Evert Pels—all of whose services would soon be much appreciated by the residents of the fledgling settlement.

Dominie Megapolensis delivered his first sermon in the patroon's warehouse, next to the fort, which was later converted into the colony's first church. In 1649 he left to become pastor of the church in New Amsterdam, and in 1652 Dominie Gideon Schaets arrived as pastor, first as an official of the patroon and then under the jurisdiction of the newly created town of Beverwyck.

Dominie Schaets inherited a congregation of about 130 members, though Sunday services—still conducted in the patroon's remodeled trading house—were generally attended by 300 to 400 residents of the town and the patroon's domain. In 1655 it was agreed that a new and larger church should be built. The patroon subscribed 1,000 guilders, the town appropriated another 1,500 guilders out of court fines, and a new site was chosen in what is now the middle of State Street at its intersection with Broadway. On June 2, 1656, one of the town magistrates, Rutger Jacobsen, laid the cornerstone with all due ceremony before the assembled officials and inhabitants of Beverwyck and Rensselaerswyck. A temporary pulpit was installed but was soon replaced by a carved oaken pulpit sent over from Holland by the Dutch West India Company, which also provided a small bell for the steeple. The pulpit, now in the First Church in Albany (Reformed), survives today as the oldest pulpit in the United States.

In 1715 a new and larger church was built, using a rather ingenious method of construction. The old church was left standing and the new one built around it, with the shell of the old church not dismantled until the very last. By this means the old church was kept in active use almost up until the dedication of the new one; in fact, only two Sundays' services were missed in the transition. This new church on the old site served until 1806, when it was torn down and the stone and other materials used to build what was known as the South Dutch Church, between Hudson and Beaver streets. The North Dutch Church—today's First Church in Albany (Reformed)—on the west side of Pearl Street, was designed by architect Philip Hooker and constructed in 1798.

Even during the Dutch period, however, not all residents of Beverwyck belonged to the established church. Lutherans met for their worship services in private homes—despite the objections of the local authorities—as they had been permitted to do in liberal 17th-century Holland. After the English takeover in 1664, the Lutherans were able to build a church of their own, on the southwest corner of present-day Howard and Pearl streets. Their first minister was the Reverend Jacobus Fabricius, succeeded in 1671 by Bernardus Arensius. Lutherans, like everyone else, however, were still required to pay taxes for the support of the established Dutch Reformed Church.

The Reverend Thomas Barclay began preaching the Anglican service, in had once again descended on the city's terrified populace. The establishment of zones or "swine lines" eventually limited hog-raising to the less settled areas of the city, and even today keeping hogs is a tradition in the Rapp Road area of the city's Pine Bush.

The year of the last great cholera epidemic, 1854, was also the year that Albany's first real hospital began accepting patients. Advocated since 1830 by Dr. Alden March, Albany Hospital—known today as the Albany Medical Center—has the commonly accepted founding date of 1849. Its first home was on the corner of Madison Avenue and Dove Street in a row house that is still standing. Then, in 1852, the former county jail on the southeast corner of Eagle and Howard streets was purchased and the prisoners moved to a new facility located in what is now the backyard of the city hall. By August of 1854, at the height of the epidemic, the old building had at last been refitted to the point where it could accept its first patients. The new hospital stood directly opposite the street where the Albany Medical College 15 years earlier had acquired the old Lancastrian School, and from that day forth the two institutions became virtually one in the minds of the Albany populace.

Albany Institute of History and Art

Education

Albany's first schoolmaster, in 1648, was a local tailor by the name of Evert Noldingh; evidently his efforts did not last very long. In 1650 a schoolhouse was built, a simple wooden structure 34 by 19 feet, and Adriaen Jansen Van Ilpendam was engaged as teacher. The curriculum consisted principally of reading, arithmetic, proper manners, and "the true Christian religion."

228 ALBANY DIRECTORY

MEDICAL.

LIFE! LIFE!! LIFE!!!

SIGHT FOR THE BLIND.

Hearing for the Deaf,

AND

NEVER FAILING REMEDIES

FOR

CATARRH AND CONSUMPTION.

H. A. OAKS, M. D.,

Is a graduate of the London Medical Colleges, and has practiced in Europe and America for more than eighteen years, with unparalled success in the treatment of

Deafness and Catarrh,

Noises in the Head, Dizziness, and all Diseases of the Eye and Ear, Throat, Lungs, Heart, Liver, Kidneys, Chest, Spine,

BRONCHITIS, CONSUMPTION, SCROFULA, CANCER, DYSPEPSIA, PILES, RHEUMATISM, &c., &c., &c.

The Doctor having a large and extensive practical experience in the treatment of Diseases generally, he is prepared to receive patients for medical treatment on the most approved and modern principles, and to treat their diseases ina very superior and satisfactory manner, and in the majority of cases to far exceed the most sanguine expectations of the patient, without resorting to any unpleasant or torturing processes.

Dr. OAKS treats successfully all Diseases of the

EYE AND EAR,

on the most improved principles, whether European or American, with entirely new remedies, and with little or no suffering to the patient.

The Doctor may be consulted the first seven days of each month, at his Rooms,

Nos. 6 & 7, White Marble Building,

No. 55 State Street, Albany, N. Y.

Office hours from 9 A. M. to 12 M., and from 1 P. M. until 6 o'clock P. M. Sundays from 9 A. M. to 10 A. M., and from 1 P. M. until 4 o'clock P. M.

CONSULTATION ONE DOLLAR.

Albany Medical Center

Albany Medical Center

Shortly after Beverwyck became Albany, Governor Nicolls granted a license to the town's first English schoolmaster, Johan Shutte, as well as to Dutch schoolmaster Jan Jeurians Becker. The next schoolmaster of whom anything is known was Johannis Glandorf, engaged by the city in 1721 "for teaching and instructing the youth in speling, reading, writeing, and cyffering." A house was provided rent free, but his salary came from the fees paid by his pupils' parents. Free public education was still more than a century away.

The 19th century saw the creation of Albany's well-known private academies. Albany Academy, originally chartered in 1813, held classes at first in a frame house at the corner of Lodge and State streets, under the headmastership of the Reverend Benjamin Allen. Its own building, on the south side of present-day Elk Street, was started in 1815—the cornerstone was laid by Mayor Philip Van Rensselaer—and occupied in 1817. Like so many public buildings of its day, the school—now the headquarters of the Albany Board of Education—was the work of architect Philip Hooker.

Classes began at the new school in September of 1817 under a new headmaster, Dr. Theodric Romeyn Beck, and by 1830 it had 200 pupils. The curriculum included Latin, Greek, history, geography, English, geometry, "cyphering," and "natural philosophy"—what we would call general science. Joseph Henry, whose work in electromagnetics made possible the Morse telegraph, was a teacher at the Albany Academy.

The Albany Female Academy opened just a year after the boys' school in a small building on Montgomery Street, with Horace Goodrich as principal. In 1834 the school moved to a new building, complete with classic columns and portico, on the west side of North Pearl Street. The curriculum of the girls' school included reading, writing, music, and needlework; tuition ranged from $12 to $32 a year.

My previous visit to Albany having been very brief, I now remained some time in the place, to see its state house, public libraries, and normal school establishment. The State House, situated on the top of the rising ground on which the city has been built, is a conspicuous and elegant structure, devoted to the meetings of the legislatures of the state of New York. In connection with it, I was shown a library of 30,000 volumes, for the use of members, and open to the public. A considerable number of the books are of the best English editions, no expense being spared to procure works of the highest class in general literature. Adjoining is an extensive law-library. Among the more interesting works shown to strangers, is a series of large volumes, embracing the printed legislative proceedings since the English organization of the colony. It is interesting to observe in the series, how at the Revolution, the British royal arms and styles of expression are quietly dropped, and followed by the republican forms, as if no break had taken place in the course of procedure.

William Chambers. *Things As They Are In America,* 1853. Reprinted in Joel Munsell's *The Annals of Albany,* Vol. VII, 1856.

Clockwise from top
Dr. Albert Vander Veer received the degree of M.D. from the Albany Medical College in 1869 and settled in Albany. That same year he was made attending surgeon of Albany Hospital and elected professor of general and special anatomy in the Albany Medical College.

Improved conditions in the Albany Medical Hospital included such things as this private room with a brass bed, circa 1925.

A Shaker bentwood rocking chair and an ornate dressing screen furnished Room 2 of the Albany Hospital in 1896.

This 1865 advertisement from the Albany Directory *is an example of the sorry state of the medical profession at the time of the Civil War. Reliable doctors fought in earnest for increasing education and legitimate licensing. Their efforts improved the quality of medical care available to Albany citizens.*

City Engineer's Office

City Engineer's Office

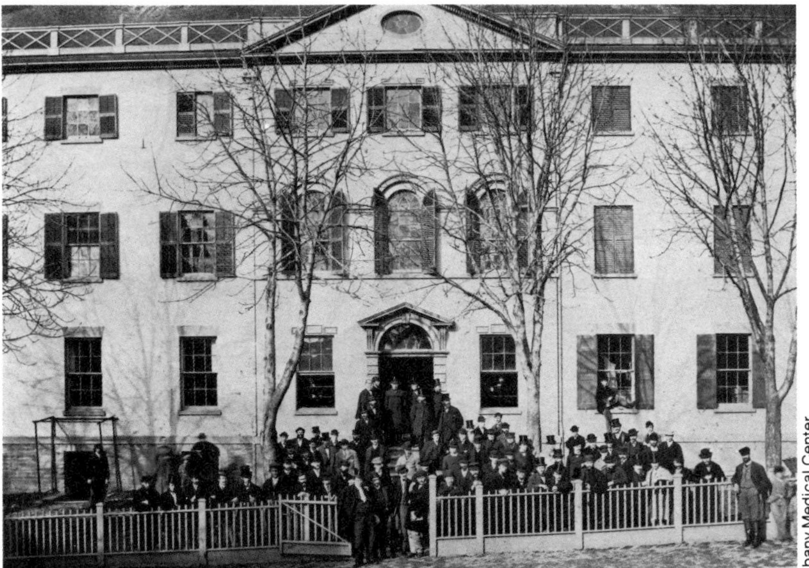

Albany Medical Center

Mrs. John Horan McEneny

State University of New York, Albany

Today, as the State University of New York at Albany (SUNYA), the former State Teachers College still includes the old campus on Western and Washington avenues but is now headquartered in a massive uptown campus, designed by Edward Durell Stone and completed in 1970, whose white cement columns and familiar quartet of dormitory towers dominate the landscape. SUNYA is one of four university centers in the state system that award doctoral degrees. Over 14,000 students pursue more than 100 degree programs in the sciences, business, and the liberal arts.

Arts and Culture

When British officers staged Albany's first play in 1760, the event was looked upon as something of a scandal, evoking from the outraged Dutch Reformed Dominie, Theodorus Frielinghuysen, a scathing sermon on the sinfulness of the thespian art. The following morning a stick, a pair of old shoes, a crust of bread, and a dollar were left at his doorstep in hopes of sending the minister packing. Frielinghuysen did indeed leave the city soon after to return to his native Holland, only to drown on the voyage home.

The disapproval of theatrics was common throughout the northern colonies. A few professional acting companies did come to the city on occasion to play in the old colonial hospital, where the parking lot for the County Courthouse is now, but it was not until 1813 that a permanent theater was constructed on Green Street, under the management of John Bernard.

The new theater—a subject of much controversy—lasted only five years, after which it was sold and converted into a Baptist church. In 1852 it would be rededicated to the thespian art as the celebrated Green Street Theater.

Clockwise from top
The Yardboro Avenue School, shown here in 1922, was attended by well behaved, young students.

John Joseph Gaffie, a member of the Class of 1909 of the Christian Brothers Academy, poses during his sophomore year at the school. Established in 1859 as a private school to provide revenue for St. Vincent's Orphan Asylum, Christian Brothers Academy has maintained a military program since 1891, as has its secular equivalent, Albany Academy, since the 1880s.

Teacher, critic teacher, and superintendent of the primary department of the model school are pictured in 1896 with the first grade class. The school was part of the New York State Normal School at Albany.

The Albany Medical College Class of 1868 poses in front of the former Lancaster School building. Designed in 1812 by Philip Hooker, the building was occupied by the Albany Medical College from 1838 to 1927. It was the first schoolhouse to adhere to Joseph Lancaster's educational system, promulgated at the turn of the century, in which one teacher instructed scores of pupils.

Meanwhile the precedent had been established, and the Albany stage was destined to remain. In 1824–25 a new theater opened on South Pearl Street, where the old Leland Opera House would later be located. Because of the city's proximity to New York, stock companies readily made the journey upriver to test what was to become known as the "coldest audience" in the country. Until recent memory, it was said among theatrical circles that if a production was received well in Albany, it would do well anywhere.

Theaters were established throughout the 19th century. They survived with mixed economic success, degenerating occasionally, as in the case of the Gayety, into a saloon concert hall as part of a "Great White Way" already well established by the time of the Civil War. By the turn of the century, burlesque was in its heyday and Albanians would sneak into theaters like the Empire on State Street to see "Sliding Billy Watson" and other notables of risqué humor and merriment.

Attempts at establishing respectable theaters, often in converted churches whose congregations had moved out of downtown, generally failed until 1888, when the legacy of Harmanus Bleecker provided for construction of a new theater on the site of the present Albany Public Library on upper Capitol Hill. It was the first theater built outside the downtown theater district that centered around Green, Division, and South Pearl streets. Harmanus Bleecker Hall would survive as a respectable place for first-run plays and benefits into the mid-20th century.

Moving pictures, introduced before the First World War in nickelodeons like the Hellman's Fairyland on South Pearl Street, the first of a chain of such institutions, revolutionized the entertainment business. Movie theaters sprang up everywhere. In the city's South End, films were available in Yiddish and Italian. In some cases, the theaters were open air, utilizing courtyards, as was the case where the Lark Tavern is now located. In other experiments, the roof of the theater rolled back to expose the sky and let out the hot summer air from the crowded aisles below.

By the 1920s burlesque was dead and movies were no longer an experiment—they were big business. Large, elaborate theaters were built to accommodate 1,000 or 2,000 patrons. The Ritz, a converted municipal building on South Pearl and Howard streets, the Grand, the Strand, and, queen of them all, the Palace, all sprang up within a new theater district near Clinton Square. The only one left is the Palace, still 2,800 seats strong, complete with gilded baroque ornamentation, rising orchestra pit, and a mammoth crystal chandelier.

Neighborhoods had their local theaters, too. Some, like the Eagle and the Hudson, were converted from existing buildings. Others, including the Colonial, the Delaware, and the Madison, were new buildings constructed to accommodate large neighborhood crowds.

The 1950s and '60s were difficult times for the entertainment world. The movement to the suburbs and the advent of television took their toll of the old theaters. One legitimate house, Atterbury's, survived in the former Second Presbyterian Church on Chapel Street until the 1950s. The downtown movie houses, which had provided such affordable escapism to a Depression-ridden and war-weary public, saw their demise in the 1960s. Today, in a city that once knew the attraction of a score of movie houses, only three remain not including the Palace, which serves as a municipal auditorium. While movies today are making a noticeable comeback, it is in single-feature runs held at small cluster houses on the city's edge, accessible only by vehicle.

Within this void there has sprung up a welcome addition to the city's cultural wealth. As of this writing there are nearly two dozen theater companies in Albany County. The Albany Civic Theater, housed in an old firehouse on Second Avenue, is the city's oldest group, having been on the scene for 25 years. The Egg, located in the Empire State Plaza, is home to two professionally run full-time programs: the Empire State Youth Orchestra and Empire State Youth Theater, both of which have already earned international reputations.

Musical associations have long been a part of the city's cultural life. In the second half of the 19th century they tended to center around ethnic groups, especially German, and were often offshoots of church choirs. Indeed it was often the churches that hosted celebrated performers before the existence of a "proper" hall, as in 1851 when Jenny Lind sang at a concert in the Third Presbyterian Church, to the delight of the Harmonia Society, which had been formed in 1849.

The Singing Society Cecilia, formed in 1866, was predominantly German. It numbered about 150 members who participated in songfests and balls in Albany and throughout the state. The Union Musical Association, organized in 1858, was of similar size, as was the Albany Musical Association (1868), which performed in Tweddle Hall until it burned down. The Gesangverein Eintracht, the Mozart, the Apollo and the New Harmonic were other singing societies of 100 years ago. The Liederkranz

Top left
Born in the South End in 1890, Mel Wolfgang became the first Albanian to become a member of a world champion baseball club—the Chicago White Sox.
Top right
The Palace Theater opened in 1931 as one of the jewels in the RKO chain and is one of the grand survivors of an era of theater opulence. The Albany Symphony Orchestra and contemporary rock groups have been equally at home in the 2,800-seat theater. It has been owned by the City of Albany since the late 1960s.
Bottom
Marie-Emma Lajeunesse, born near Montreal in 1847, began her singing career in Albany as soloist and choirmistress at St. Joseph's Church on Ten Broeck Street. A distinguished operatic career followed her Paris debut in 1870, during which time she was affectionately known as "Madame Albani." This portrait was painted in 1877 by Albany artist Will H. Low.

Meldon Wolfgang 3rd

Beckman Associates Advertising Agency, Inc.

Musee du Quebec

Society and German street bands were typical of Albany at the turn of the century.

Modern-day musical Albany carries on the tradition of these earlier groups. The Albany Symphony Orchestra conducted by Julius Hegyi has replaced the earlier Albany Philharmonic Society, which had its origins in 1884 at the home of George Thacher, Jr. The Monday Musical Club is comprised of active artists and has met regularly since 1904 (though no longer on Mondays). The Mendelssohn Club, a men's singing society, is equally active, as is the Capitol Hill Choral Society, whose annual *Messiah* concert, long conducted by Judson Rand, has been an Albany tradition for a generation.

A unique musical institution is the Octavo School, which has been graduating students with Regents credits applied to their own high school since the idea was brought to fruition by its originator, Alice McEneny McCullen, in 1926—decades before the "university without walls" concept became popular. Originally the school consisted of several music teachers who had studied under a common mentor, Sr. Alphonsus de Rodrigues Ferland, at the old Academy of the Holy Names on Madison Avenue opposite Washington Park. The faculty still operates out of their own homes and studios, utilizing a common standard of excellence while avoiding the encumbrance of a common campus.

From earliest times, the visual artist has had an active part in the history of the city. In the 18th century, well-to-do Albany families immortalized themselves through portraiture. Although many of these formal oil paintings have come down to us, most of them are unsigned, according to the convention of the time, and many of the artists remain unknown.

Portraiture became increasingly popular after the Revolution, as great leaders sought to leave their image to posterity. The Albany Common Council made an extensive collection of such portraits, paid for from public monies. Many of them, including most of the early governors of the state, are now on permanent loan to the Albany Institute. The most prolific artist in this collection was Albany's Ezra Ames, who maintained a gallery of fine arts until his death in 1836.

Like many of his fellow artists, Ames started his career as a coach painter, painting scenes on carriages as a practical way of supporting himself. Albany was also a major printing center throughout this period, giving many an artist the opportunity to survive as an engraver. One of Albany's best known and most popular artists maintained a livelihood much further removed from his field of painting. Joseph Eights, who drew those wonderful scenes of Albany at the beginning of the 19th century, when the city was making the final transition from Dutch to Anglo-American ways, was a prominent practicing physician.

The Hudson River School was popular in the capital city, and although its great masters are generally associated with areas further south or more rural, Albany was the subject of many paintings. Scottish-born artists Harts, William, and James were raised in the city and had also been exposed to the traditional role of coach decorator. Walter Lunt Palmer, the Buycks, David Lithgow, and the Lathrop sisters carried on the tradition of fine painting into this century.

But it was in sculpture that Albany artists excelled. Erastus Dow Palmer and his student Will Low brought the city fame with their sensitive works in marble and bronze.

One of the area's most interesting artists was a potter, Bouck White, who for a short perod in the 1920s had a studio on Chestnut Street. Shortly thereafter he built a complex of stone buildings known as Heldeberg Castle, which still stands overlooking the road to Thacher Park. Originally from Schoharie County, White was a Harvard-educated minister who wore his hair shaved in the Mohawk style of his ancestors and held a dream of Albany as the center of a World League of Cities. The radical league never materialized and the "Hermit of the Heldebergs," his castle burned by vandals, retired to the Home for Aged Men in Menands, where he maintained an active flow of creative thought until his death a quarter-century ago.

Today's artists number literally in the hundreds, and the city is experiencing a growth of private galleries as part of its widespread renewal. Talented artists/teachers such as lithographer Thom O'Conner and metal sculptor Richard Stankiewicz at SUNYA enjoy reputations that extend well beyond this region. The much-sought-after works of David Coughtry, Alice Williamson, and Betty Warren present Albany in a warm and imaginative light that would have pleased Dr. Eights.

One of the city's most diversified artists, printmaker William Schade of the Junior College of Albany, has produced pieces as unique in their orginality as they are in their execution—among them the carved birdhouse in Washington Park, the cloth sculptured Indian at the Albany Institute, and the handmade-paper-making project.

Apart from the well-maintained libraries within the academic community, the city has three significant libraries. The largest is the State Library, now housed in the Cultural Building of the Empire State Plaza, which has its antecedents in a state law of 1818. From its inception the State Library has held many of the state's major historical documents. Under the

Albany Institute of History and Art

New York State Archives

Top
Dr. James Eights (1798-1882) is shown at the age of 40, approximately when he took up drawing—the activity for which he is best remembered. Eights, also a physician and natural scientist, is responsible for a series of drawings and water-colors that meticulously depict Albany's streets and houses at the turn of the 18th century.
Above
Albany native Charles Calverly, a student of Erastus Dow Palmer, the city's premier sculptor, fashioned the Robert Burns Monument and the bas reliefs around the base that depict scenes from Burns' works. Dedicated on August 30, 1888, in Washington Park, the statue was the gift of Miss Mary MacPherson. It stands on a pedestal of Scottish granite from Aberdeen. In 1979 the St. Andrew's Society cleaned the statue as a gift to the city in conjunction with its 175th anniversary in Albany.
Facing page
Prominent Albany sculptress and early suffragette Alice Morgan Wright is shown in her studio in the early part of the 20th century. Her estate contributed generously to the Humane Society as well as providing for the over 50 cats that were her constant companions.

Smith College, Sophia Smith Collection

The Neighborhood Saloon

The role of the neighborhood saloonkeeper at the turn of the century was an important one in the sociopolitical hierarchy of any city. In a society where the average man worked 10 or 12 hours a day, six days a week, the saloonkeeper was one of the privileged few among the working classes to have virtually continuous freedom to listen to, discuss, debate, and in rare instances even read the news of the day. If he lived in an immigrant neighborhood, he was of necessity bilingual, to some extent at least, and was looked upon as an interpreter of current events by many a trusting patron of foreign extraction.

A smart saloonkeeper allowed his establishment, generally located on a corner, to become a forum for debate on a wide variety of controversial issues, from politics to the rights of labor—with himself ever present to serve graciously as the recognized judge or referee of the day's discourse. The saloon, when properly managed, became the average man's "salon" or neighborhood club. From behind his magnificent mahogany symbol of office, the proprietor presided over an endless drama of debates and pleas concerning the true grass-roots issues of day-to-day life. No problem was too great or too small to merit his sympathetic attention or patient ear.

The saloon was the gathering place of the unemployed, and the last refuge of worried family heads struggling under the pressures and uncertainties of an economy fluctuating between boom and bust. At the same time it was the mecca of the successful, whose exploits at sports, gambling, and politics could only be properly celebrated over the cool refreshment served at the local "watering hole"—or, in lieu of a personal appearance, delivered to the patron by eager neighborhood boys, sent to the saloon with tin "growlers" to be filled to the brim with sudsy brew.

Promotions were celebrated and layoffs mourned as the workingman quaffed his nickel beer and devoured his free lunch. Occasionally a toast would be raised to a beloved sweetheart, a sainted mother, or a loving wife or daughter—with the unspoken understanding that any and all of them would be thrown out into the street if they so much as set foot across the threshold of this totally male world.

It was only logical that the progressive saloon should have a back room to accommodate the more serious conversations that required a degree of privacy. Back rooms offered seclusion for union meetings, political caucuses, and serious business deals—most of which the smart saloonkeeper would be privy to.

In time the brighter and more enterprising saloonkeepers turned their wealth of diversified contacts and grass-roots information to their own advantage and that of their families. Assuming that the saloonkeeper was prudent in his life-style, he could amass at least a modest fortune; in good times and in bad, his was a business that prospered steadily. If he had children, and most did, then the proceeds of the saloon would be used to obtain an education for his sons and daughters far in excess of his own. The next generation would be filled with insurance men and lawyers who, armed with a bartender's understanding and a gentleman's education, could aspire to and achieve high positions in politics, business, education, and the church that would have been closed to their fathers. Boston's Kennedy dynasty owes at least half its makeup to such a heritage; in Albany the phenomenon was epitomized by John Augustin McCall.

Born and raised above his father's saloon on the corner of Orange and Chapel streets in lower Gander Bay, McCall rose to become state superintendent of insurance, a trusted advisor to Governor (and later President) Grover Cleveland, and president of New York Life Insurance Company, building that corporation into the largest insurance company in the world. From a townhouse still standing at State Street and Sprague Place, he moved to New York and acquired his substantial fortune. Along with Anthony N. Brady, a native of the South End's Westerlo Street, and Tom Murray of Arbor Hill's Colonie Street, he was active in that city's Albany Society, composed of ex-Albanians who had moved to the metropolis to pursue great fortunes. A few years before his death in 1906, he donated a great carved pulpit to the Cathedral of the Immaculate Conception in memory of his Irish immigrant father—who continued to run the saloon until the day he died.

John O'Connell, the Irish-American who catered to a heavily German clientele in the South End, had his opposite number on the north side of town. Glatz's Hotel, at Broadway and North Ferry Street opposite old St. Peter's Hospital, catered to the Irish of the Basin and lumber district despite the German origin of its proprietor.

From north to south, on the hills and in the hollows, and "up on the hill" as well, each neighborhood boasted of (or lamented) one or more of these establishments, where a man could tarry awhile and claim sanctuary from the real world of family and work outside.

In North Albany there was Jennings's place on Broadway. In the West End, Horan's, on the point of Livingston and Third, and Murray's, at Allen and Central, did a lively business catering to the cattlemen and railroad workers of the West Albany yards; while further west at Colvin, Schaeffer's, with a recreational pond behind, catered to the lively traffic of the Schenectady Turnpike. In Pine Hills, Chris's Klondike Hotel, sitting opposite the juncture of Madison and Western, held a near monopoly over the newly developing neighborhood. Bulgaro's and Lombardo's, names still familiar today, catered to their countrymen in Little Italy, while DeBerry's at Elk and Northern and Yanas's on Lexington served the refreshment and social needs of the city's hardworking Poles.

Like the South End, Arbor Hill was densely populated and well supplied with saloons. Flynn's stood at First and North Swan, and Flanagan and Farrell's on North Lark. A half-block away, on the corner of Livingston, was Frank and Cyril Cassidy's, where horseshoe pitching in the backyard of the saloon was a Sunday afternoon ritual.

J.F. Toohey's at 39 South Pearl Street was among the city's well-frequented saloons.

Albany Institute of History and Art

Alward's at Livingston and Northern competed with Brennan's at the same intersection, the latter establishment achieving particular fame as the traditional first stop on the way home from funeral corteges choosing the high road from the cemeteries in nearby Menands. On such occasions the men of the party would enter the welcome way station, while the ladies would be brought lemonade or toddy as they waited in their carriages outside.

North Swan Street, along with Northern Boulevard, served as Arbor Hill's neighborhood shopping district. On the upper end of the street, below Livingston, Mike's Log Cabin, whose dimly lit booths and scarred tables boasted the initials of at least two generations of young love, had its origins in the pre-World War I era as Sheehan's Saloon.

McGarry's was at Clinton and Lark, while the Irish Lords, at Monroe and Sheridan Place, served the men of lower Sheridan Hollow. O'Connor's had its start on Washington above the Capitol until development of Capitol Hill by the state forced it to move downtown to the Fireplace opposite the Albany Garage. At Central and Lark it was Bill Igo's, whose circa 1805 building is still standing, the last of a commercial row of Federal-style buildings that sprang up along the old Bowery when the Schenectady Turnpike opened. Farther up on Central, Pauley's Hotel, built on the site of the first St. John's German Lutheran Cemetery, was representative of several German-run establishments along the Avenue. It, like the present Three S's on West Hill, or the former Schramm's on Yates Street in lower Pine Hills, probably retains as much of the flavor of the early pre-Prohibition era as any establishment in the area.

The list of well-frequented saloons, as the temperance advocates were eager to point out, seemed endless. Swift Mead's White Elephant at Maiden Lane and James, and Dwyer's on Green Street near Division, offered first-class free lunches to compete with the city's better hotels and restaurants for the patronage of downtown businessmen and politicians. Along South Pearl Street were many such saloons, such as Toohey's and Farley's below Madison, and one establishment on the corner of Van Zandt which succeeded in circumventing the ethnic question by calling itself the House of All Nations.

Closer to downtown, the ever-popular McNamara's on South Pearl below Beaver served as the gathering place for a regular city dwellers' harvest rite. Each fall Happy Conroy would recruit and organize large work crews who departed by the wagon load for the hill towns of Schoharie County as hop pickers, in order that the great breweries of the capital city, along with their many hundreds of prideful workers, might never cease to produce their foaming brew. In other neighborhoods the annual hop harvest was viewed as a family ritual, with whole families taking part in the annual trip to the country as a means of supplementing their income while at the same time experiencing a welcome break in the urban routine.

Erastus Corning 2nd

The 1940s marked tense years for Albany's O'Connell organization when an ambitious Republican governor, Thomas Dewey, sought to bring about the demise of the machine through a series of sensational probes. Despite great cost and publicity, little was accomplished, except for several minor convictions on election discrepancies. O'Connell and his organization survived politically after Governor Dewey's administration had been absorbed into the history books. Corning and Dewey are shown here in a rare, joint civic appearance on the New York State Capitol steps. Their relationship was formal, with few personal contacts.

One year after Erastus Corning's election, the national career of another prominent politician affected the city of Albany. Thomas E. Dewey, who had won a reputation as a crusading, crime-busting district attorney in the city of New York, had unsuccessfully sought the governorship against Herbert Lehman four years previously. Now, in 1942, he ran his new campaign with the promise that he would make an example of the O'Connell machine in Albany. Once elected, Dewey went to work almost immediately by investigating the election process that had taken place that fall. The "Dewey Investigations," which dominated city politics for more than three years, resulted in only 38 minor convictions for subverting the election laws. These tense years saw the regular district attorney supplanted, accusations brought against the Albany County jury system, and state troopers placed at the polls at election time.

But for all his bad relations with the city of Albany, Dewey's record as governor was good. Ever since Al Smith modernized the government in the 1920s, no one had done more to streamline the bureaucracy, reform the civil service, and open up opportunities to the minorities. Yet the one thing that Dewey had aspired to achieve—a well-publicized destruction of the Albany machine—remained beyond his grasp. Unquestionably, achieving it would have greatly helped his presidential campaign of 1948.

The Democratic Party leaders in Albany have generally been conservative. They backed Al Smith instead of Franklin Roosevelt in the 1932 presidential convention, and they never quite got along with James A. Farley, Roosevelt's strong associate (who eventually broke with the President over the third-term issue). The politicos also argued with a series of New York State Democratic chairmen throughout the 1950s and

Erastus Corning 2nd

1960s. But opposition to the party in Albany during the 1950s was, by today's standards, dull and unimaginative. Probably the Party had grown complacent.

The sociopolitical turbulence of the 1960s, coupled with the aggressive governorship of Nelson A. Rockefeller, brought new challenges to the Democratic Party, and the aging Democratic organization showed a surprising degree of resilience. In 1961 the State Investigation Committee (SIC) conducted a probe of the city's purchasing operations. As with the Dewey investigation more than a decade before, the end result was negligible in terms of actions taken for long-due improvement; but the publicity was sensational and gave heart to those who sought to eliminate the domination of Chairman Dan O'Connell's organization in Albany County politics.

A series of reform movements grew up during the 1960s, spearheaded by opponents of the Democratic machine identified primarily with an independent "reform movement" and only secondarily and incidentally with the Albany Republican Party. The revolt began in 1961 with Citizens' United Reform Effort (CURE), headed by 27-year-old the Reverend Robert Hudnut, a Presbyterian minister originally from Cincinnati, and his running mate, Charles A. Liddle of Albany. Four years later the campaign was less sensational, but in 1969, and again in 1973, the efforts to take over City Hall were well organized and well financed. In each case it was a third party that took the lead, with the Republican Party endorsing the effort.

In 1966 former Attorney General Robert F. Kennedy campaigned in Albany for the position of United States Senator, an office he subsequently won and held until his death in June 1968. As the brother of the late President, who had also campaigned in the city six years earlier, Kennedy's popularity was at an unprecedented high and he attracted tremendous crowds. Local law enforcement officials struggled with security problems in crowds such as this one.

By 1966 most of the ward leaders were men who had risen to power with O'Connell decades before. Now mostly in their sixties and seventies, they chose candidates for alderman and county supervisor to represent neighborhoods that no longer existed as they had in the 1920s—modern-day "rotten boroughs," many of whose voters had long since migrated to uptown and suburban neighborhoods. As a result of population shifts, nearly one-third of the city was represented by a single ward (the 13th), while other wards such as the 4th (Dutch Hollow) and the 12th (Sheridan Hollow) held only a fraction of their former population. The election of 1966, however, was based on an entirely new structure of wards, endorsed by the League of Women Voters and imposed by the courts upon the city and county governments. From the Republican and third-party points of view, the new wards had distinct advantages. Rather than being drawn by neighborhoods, they created wide economic belts across the city that cut across traditional neighborhood lines. People living near the Crestwood Shopping Center, for example, voted in the same ward as those who lived across from the Madison Theater in Pine Hills. The people who lived across from Beverwyck Park on Washington Avenue were to vote for the same candidates as those living in the Loudon Arms Apartments far across the Tivoli hollow.

A massive shifting of candidates naturally occurred. The new county legislature that took office in 1967 included numerous new faces—young attorneys such as Thomas Brown, later assemblyman; E. David Duncan; Joseph Harris, later county judge; Paul Devane; Robert Leyden; and Harold Joyce, who alone among the group had also served on the old board of supervisors. Two years later, when aldermen were selected, they too included names and faces that were sometimes new to Albany politics, and almost invariably decades younger than their predecessors from the downtown wards that had dominated city politics for two previous generations.

During the 1960s, under Governor Rockefeller, efforts were made not only in the negative sense to bring pressure on the city's Democratic organization, but also with the positive intention of putting life into the generally disheartened Republican Party. The first major Republican candidate to be elected to office was Daniel E. Button, executive editor of the Albany *Times-Union,* which in the early 1960s had merged in general management with the *Knickerbocker News,* creating a newspaper monopoly under the Hearst Corporation while maintaining separate editorial boards. Button served two terms as congressman, defeating the popular president of the Common Council, Richard J. Conners, and Jacob Herzog, respectively. In 1970 he lost his job to neighboring Congressman Samuel S. Stratton, a former mayor of Schenectady, whose district was redrawn to include Albany County.

In 1968 the race for legislative and county offices became a debacle for the once seemingly invincible Democratic organization. The New York State senate seat was lost to Walter Langley, who had been active in the Albany Independent Movement (AIM); two years previously he had unsuccessfully sought a seat on the new Albany County legislature. Both assembly seats were lost—to Raymond Skuse, who replaced the aging Frank P. Cox, and to Fred Field, now supervisor of the town of Colonie, who replaced Albany attorney Harvey Lifset. Another Republican victory in the 1968 election went to Arnold W. Proskin, who was elected district attorney; during his career he conducted several investigations of the city administration, with few tangible results.

The State senate seat was held by the late Walter Langley, who stepped down in poor health in 1974; he was succeeded by Democrat Howard Nolan, who now holds the seat. Nolan had occasionally opposed Mayor Corning; he mounted a vigorous, if unsuccessful, primary challenge in

Erastus Corning 2nd

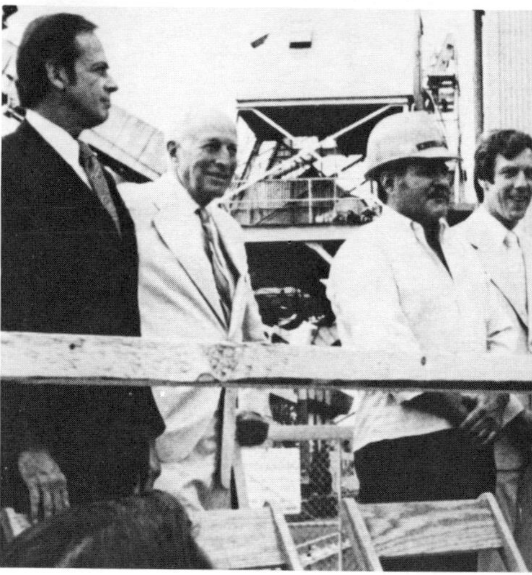

Top
The Nelson A. Rockefeller administration was marked by style and enthusiasm, as the energetic Republican governor literally changed the face of Albany. He is shown here with his wife "Happy," Lieutenant Governor Malcolm Wilson (left), who later succeeded him, and Mayor Corning (right), at one of his many receptions at the Executive Mansion.
Above
Governor Carey gives an address at the Port of Albany in 1976. Renewed interest in the economic potential of the port brought substantial state aid during the late 1970s.

1977. Ray Skuse held his assembly seat for only one term, losing in 1970 to Democrat Thomas W. Brown, but Field's seat, now held by Michael Hoblock, has remained in Republican hands ever since. (Both Field and Hoblock are from Colonie, which, like all three of the large suburban towns surrounding Albany, has been exclusively Republican for well over a century.)

City politics in the 1980s revolves to a considerable extent around neighborhood and citizens' group issues; at this writing, there are 23 neighborhood associations in the city. The Republican Party—undermined by deliberate efforts to recreate an independent third-party opposition that seeks only endorsement rather than leadership from the Republicans—has dwindled to slightly more than 2,400 registered voters, compared with more than 42,000 registered Democrats. The Republican Party itself is virtually dormant except in the towns surrounding the city, where it remains dominant.

Erastus Corning 2nd

In retrospect, the most difficult year in recent memory for the Democratic Party in Albany was 1973—probably the worst possible year for an incumbent mayor to run for office. The city's downtown area was virtually a ghost town. The new Ten Eyck Project—including a hotel, bank, office building, and parking garage—was little more than a barren landscape on the city's most prominent corner of State and Pearl. Taxes had increased more than 83 percent in one year because of the separation of the school board from the city's taxing authority. In the course of a decade the city had lost more than $10 million in revenue from areas now encompassed by the South Mall—still under construction at the time and not yet an asset to the city. The Mall, moreover, though not yet open to the public, was sufficiently completed that it no longer provided the large number of construction jobs that had been readily available throughout the previous decade.

Under these less-than-auspicious circumstances for an incumbent, a well-organized, well-financed, positive opposition campaign was launched by a prominent businessman, Carl Touhey, and citizen-activist Teresa Barbara Cooke, a relative newcomer to Albany. A strong advocate of an independent, elected school board, Cooke had also been actively involved in economic criticism of the city's purchasing and assessment practices, creating, along with Robert Stein, the Albany Taxpayers' Association. Throughout 1972, through publicity and press conferences attacking one issue or another in city government, Cooke had succeeded in maintaining a high profile.

Touhey conducted an excellent campaign, coming within slightly more than 3,200 votes of defeating the then eight-term mayor. The following year Teresa Cooke was elected Albany County treasurer for the last year that the office existed; she went on to run unsuccessfully for county executive in 1975 when the new county charter of government took effect.

With Governor Rockefeller's resignation to become Vice-President of the United States under Gerald Ford, followed by the defeat of former Lieutenant Governor Malcolm Wilson in his bid for the governorship, the situation for the city's Republicans has grown progressively worse. Whether this condition will improve with the new Republican national administration remains to be seen. It seems clear, in any case, that any effort to change the status quo enjoyed by the Democratic Party in Albany for so many years would have to be coupled with a very strong independent movement.

CHAPTER 9

THE 20TH CENTURY CITY

The turn of the century in Albany was marked by the roar of cannon, the peal of church bells—and the opening of Union Station. The mammoth Beaux Arts railroad station stood as a symbol and reflection of the gilded age of industrialization, of robber barons and labor unrest and the uniting of a great country by rail from coast to coast. That era was now drawing to a close, but in the course of the new century, Union Station would take on a patina of personal meaning for generations of Albanians. Countless journeys and adventures would have their beginnings here. Families would be separated and reunited in its cavernous waiting room. And two generations of Albany mothers would see their sons off to war, many of them never to return.

Between the opening of Union Station in 1900 and its closing in 1968, Albany's physical appearance changed only gradually—except for the intrusion of several 1920s office buildings, still standing. An Albanian of the early 1960s, when construction began on the Mall, would have felt pretty much at home in Albany of the 1910s or 1920s.

The first major change in the downtown shopping district occurred in

Dennis Holzman

Albany Public Library

Above
Just after the turn of the century this Albany baseball team posed in front of a broadside advertising Harmanus Bleecker Hall.
Left
This view of the riverfront along Hudson Avenue and Quay Street, shows the buildings as they looked before the Delaware and Hudson Plaza was built.

Albany Institute of History and Art

Beer Driver's Union No. 88 marched in this 1910 Labor Day parade. During this time Beverwyck, Dobler, Hedrick, and Amsdell brewery workers were an especially important part of the city's work force.

1906, when the old John G. Myers Company store on North Pearl Street was replaced. While construction was underway, the building collapsed; floor upon floor came crashing down, all the way to the basement. In one of the great tragedies of Albany history, 80 people were trapped in the wreckage and 13 lost their lives.

The new Myers building was ultimately completed, and soon after a number of Albany banks began to expand, tearing down older buildings that had served as theaters and hotels and putting up new skyscrapers. The resulting skyline of the city, with its great bank buildings near State and Pearl and its two big hotels, the De Witt Clinton at the head of State Street and the Ten Eyck on the corner of State and Pearl, was a skyline as familiar to people of the early '60s as it was to those of the '20s.

The turn of the century was a time of considerable labor unrest in Albany. Motormen and conductors of the United Traction Company went on strike in 1900 and again in 1901, when the National Guard was brought in to patrol the trolley routes and the city was placed under martial law. The 23rd Regiment, called in from Brooklyn as reinforcements, were greeted by a rock-throwing crowd along Broadway; they opened fire on the crowd, killing two. Other strikes involved painters and decorators, carpenters, plumbers, stonemasons, printers, and even vaudeville performers—the so-called White Rats strike that spread from New York to Albany, darkening theaters in both cities.

In April of 1917, the United States entered the war in Europe. Albany's National Guard units were called up in July, and 10,000 Albany men registered for the draft. The city responded to one Liberty Loan drive after another, as well as appeals for Armenian Relief, the Salvation Army, the Red Cross. A medical unit raised by Albany Hospital served in England as Base Hospital 33. Albanian Henry Johnson, serving with the 15th New York (Colored) Infantry Regiment, was awarded the French Croix de Guerre. Three hundred Albany men in all lost their lives in "the war to end all wars."

Prohibition

On January 16, 1920, the Eighteenth Amendment went into effect, making America the land of the dry. The Noble Experiment had begun, leaving in its wake a host of unemployed urban brewery workers, shuttered saloons, and their once-prestigious proprietors, who would now have to seek out a new life among the righteous and the saved. Or would they?

The abrupt disappearance of the saloon and inauguration of the Prohibition era were at best ill-timed, and at worst set the stage for one of the most lawless periods in American history—a period in which the average citizen became involved for the first time in wholesale disregard for the law. Many saloonkeepers did, in fact, close their establishments, seeing their premises turned into grocery stores, shops, or colorless storage facilities. Others, pursuing the only trade they knew, opened speakeasies.

The illicit "gin mills" were to be found in every neighborhood. Prohibition was held in ridicule not only by immigrant-stock Albanians, who considered alcohol a centuries-old part of their culture, integral to the family dinner table, to fellowship, mourning, and celebration, but by returning servicemen who, having seen their comrades decimated by trench warfare, mustard gas, and finally the Spanish flu, were not about to be told they could not drink to the country they loved. And drink they did—smuggled scotch from Canada, applejack from nearby farms in Albany County and the rural areas beyond, and bathtub gin made by local people in exactly the way the name implies.

Law-enforcement officials at all levels were quick to read the temper of the times, and their selective enforcement of the unpopular law was a reflection of their willing corruption. One incident, still told in West Hill, involved several barrels of whiskey confiscated from a "closed down saloon" on Judson Street and sent to the nearby 5th Precinct on Central Avenue. The following morning, a miracle was discovered: overnight, inside the police station, every barrel's contents had turned to water. Less humorous to one North Country farmer was the discovery that his cows' drinking supply had been polluted by bootleggers being pursued by Prohibition agents on their way down from Canada to Albany. The cows were intoxicated by the abandoned evidence, and their milk was unfit to drink for some time.

The most insidious aspect of the new morality, old-time saloonkeepers were quick to point out, was that Prohibition had introduced women to the bars. Unlike their predecessors, the speakeasies were used for courtship and dating. As the purveyors of forbidden fruit, with their secret buttons, signals, and passwords by which those in the know might gain entry, they provided a mystique unparalleled except by the sultry charms of Rudolf Valentino. The introduction of the automobile, the rise of movie theaters all over town, the short-bobbed hair of the flapper, the ubiquitous hip flask, and the widespread corruption of officials gave rise to the saying that America's innocent years were over. No wonder women now voted, the older generation lamented—they had sunk to the level of men.

Unlike the saloons, speakeasies are more difficult to document. Often they moved, sometimes functioning in more than one place simultaneously, and they most certainly cannot be found in the City Directory. Galogly's was in lower Sheridan Hollow. Ames O'Brien's Parody Club was on Hudson, next to the firehouse, not far from Foggy Farrell's on Green Street and the famous "Big Charley" Van Zandt at Green and Division. O'Connor's was not only on Beaver Street but also had a place in Havana, Cuba—ironically the city where Mayor Hackett died. "Mother," an Italian woman, ran her place on Market Street, while another woman, Polly Pleat, ran two establishments, on Norton below Pearl and on Broadway near the railroad station, where she competed with Brockley's, Swift Mead's White Elephant, and Johnny Mack, the gambler. Most of the downtown places had nickel slot machines, introducing a new illegal device for the patrons' amusement and the proprietor's profit.

But Albany's neighborhoods were not to see such revelry confined to downtown. Brownie Muller and Jim O'Malley ran a speakeasy at Northern and First. Eddie Cahill's was at 4 New Scotland Avenue, George Linter's was at Sherman and Quail, and Pauley's, Jennings's, and Schramm's were still doing business at their old haunts. King Brady, of baseball fame, opened a place at North Street and Broadway, not far from where Ray Curley made beer in the South Street Garage. North Albany was particularly wet, not only because of the support of the neighborhood, but also because of the convenient position of its main street, Broadway, which was the main route to Troy, Watervliet, and Cohoes. Jennings's services were augmented by those of Tom Prime on Genesee and Hugh Diamond's on Erie, as well as Jennings's son's speakeasy on South Street and Champlain, discreetly situated a block off the main road.

Illegal breweries and distilleries cropped up everywhere. Allen's was at Clinton and Quail, and Joe O'Hagan's made Black Horse Ale where the Westgate Shopping Center is today. Worst among the offenders were the druggists of the city, who dispensed "medicinal alcohol" at an alarming rate, both over the counter and out the back door. Alcohol was the marijuana of its day, symbol of a liberated counterculture firmly entrenched against the official law of the land and openly endorsed by many classes of society.

By the time Franklin Roosevelt ended the Noble Experiment in 1933, it had left in its wake an America forever different from that which existed prior to World War I. The Prohibition-based fortunes accumulated by the Dutch Schultzes, Legs Diamonds, and similar rum runners of the Roaring Twenties would found even greater crime enterprises in the years to come. It is a legacy that, while generally bypassing Albany, has plagued the nation ever since.

By the 1920s people were ready to relax and enjoy themselves—in nightclubs, speakeasies, and big-band ballrooms. Once again Albany was a crossroads of trade, this time in bootleg liquor produced in the north country and the Catskills or smuggled in from Canada. "Dutch" Schultz achieved a fame and following generally reserved for movie stars or sports heroes; "Legs" Diamond was shot to death in a Dove Street rooming house.

Albany's red-light district, notorious in the earlier days of the century, continued to thrive with its never-ending nightlife along Green, Dallius, and Liberty streets. Actually, red lights were seldom used; instead, an awning was kept out in all kinds of weather to signal the nature of the establishment. Big Charley's was only one of a whole series of establishments that offered music, booze, gambling, and women to those who sought them, catering as much to the carriage trade from up on the hill as it did to the transient, the soldier, and the gangster.

As the city moved in the early part of the century across Madison Avenue, local residents had the name Dallius Street changed to Dongan Avenue, ostensibly in the name of Irish pride. The real reason was probably to

Right
In 1918 Henry Johnson, a black resident from Sheridan Hollow, became the first American to win the Croix de Guerre in World War I. The local importance of the event is evident by the sign on this trolley car promoting the war stamp drive.
Below
Jack "Legs" Diamond is shown leaving the Rensselaer County Courthouse in Troy, New York, in this 1931 photograph. "Legs," one of the more notorious gangsters of the bootlegging era, was shot to death two years later in a Dove Street rooming house.
Below right
Albany women, such as the marchers in this 1916 War Chest parade, were very much involved in fund raising and Red Cross activities during World War I.

Albany Public Library

Capital Newspapers

Albany Public Library

City Engineer's Office

Capital Newspapers

differentiate it from the "Sin City" of Dallius Street closer to downtown. Two generations earlier the residents of Trinity Place in the South End had asked that two blocks of their street be changed to disassociate it from Broad Street and some of the goings-on there in antebellum Albany. One of the great ironies of the Pastures District is that in the end, when the area had fallen upon sad times, it was along the streets named after early ministers of the Dutch Reformed Church that many of the houses of prostitution carried on their business.

The 1920s also saw the expansion of state government under Governor Alfred E. Smith, who modernized the state bureaucracy and created a larger number of full-time jobs than had ever existed before. As a result, when the Depression hit in the 1930s, Albany was in a much better position than some of its sister cities with their aging factories and heavy dependence on industry. Not only was the Depression felt later in Albany than in cities such as Schenectady, but its effects were less severe, thanks to the "cushion" of government employment.

Efforts to combat the Depression included the Man-a-Block Program designed to employ one man on every block to do odd jobs as a means of creating work. At the same time there was a conscious effort on the part of churches to dip into their endowment funds to build church halls, schools, and other semipublic projects as a means of putting people back to work. In the long run, all of these things were in vain. The best that could be done for most families was to give them free land near the present University Heights to enable them to grow their own food.

With the election of Franklin D. Roosevelt and the advent of the New Deal, the WPA came to Albany—federally funded and federally controlled. The O'Connell organization, while welcoming the concept of job creation, was less than enthusiastic about the method. Among the WPA projects completed during this period was the building on Broadway that most Albanians still refer to as the New Post Office, which stands today as a magnificent example of Depression art. The old Bleecker Reservoir, rendered obsolete by a new system that extracted water from the foothills of the Helderbergs, was turned by WPA workers into the present Bleecker Stadium. Streets were repaved, schools were refurbished, and—of more questionable social value—most of the firehouses in the city of Albany were covered with bright yellow brick, all in an effort to put people back to work.

Above left
Albany does not appear to be too hard-hit by the Depression in this 1936 view of Hudson Avenue between Grand and Philip streets.
Above
Johnny Evers was a local baseball hero who played in several World Series with the Chicago Cubs. He also played with the Boston Braves, and later served as superintendent of Bleeker Stadium. Baseball fans may remember Evers, shown here in 1939, as pivot for the famous double play combination termed "Tinker to Evers to Chance."
Below
Temporary barrack-type homes were provided by the State of New York for returning World War II veterans and their families. The American housing market was brought to a virtual standstill by the Depression and the war.

The coming of World War II ended the massive public-works projects, as the country moved into a new era—one in which Albany would participate fully. Among the city's best-known wartime causes was a naval vessel, the U.S.S. *Albany*, the fourth ship of its kind to be subsidized by the city and to bear that name. Albany's mayor, Erastus Corning, requested that he be drafted and in fact served one year in a combat infantry regiment in Europe. Of the thousands of Albany men and women who served in Europe and the Pacific, 556 lost their lives.

Below
In April of 1944 Mayor Erastus Corning 2nd, still in his first term of office, left for service as a P.F.C. with the United States Army in Germany.
Below right
In June of 1952 buses from London were seen on Albany streets as part of a British travel promotion.

The large number of veterans returning to the city in the 1940s presented new challenges, and temporary, barrackslike housing was built near St. Mary's Park where the present Albany High School is located. After the hardships of the Depression, when many couples put off having children, and the disruption of families by World War II, the post-1945 period witnessed a "baby boom" and a corresponding boom in construction. A number of factors conspired, however, to orient this new development away from the central cities into a rapidly emerging suburban society. State funds were used to subsidize suburban schools, while the Federal Highway Act extended roads—wide and safe and federally paid for—far into areas previously thought of only as farmland. Even more important, national policy on the part of those who approved mortgages and insurance for housing clearly favored suburban development.

Erastus Corning 2nd

The automobile, whose growth and spread had been checked to some degree by the Great Depression and by wartime shortages, now burst forth in abundance. The New York State Thruway was completed in the 1950s, followed by the Adirondack Northway, rendering obsolete and impractical an interurban trolley system that up until the late 1940s enabled Albany residents to take a trolley car from downtown Albany to the Adirondacks or to Chatham in Columbia County. Trolley service within the city was discontinued in favor of buses in the 1950s, and the suburbanization of America was well on its way.

By 1959, when Nelson A. Rockefeller took office as governor, the city of Albany looked on the surface much as it had looked generations before. Downtown was still a place of prestige, dominated by banks interspersed with numerous stores and service industries—everything from clothing and furniture emporiums to hat-blocking shops and shoe-shine parlors. Grand names such as Van Heusen Charles and Lansing's offered

Arthur J. O'Keefe

Arthur J. O'Keefe

fashionable gifts, while an entire "cheap side" along lower South Pearl Street enabled families to buy shoes for growing children at Swartz and Levison's or floor coverings for the kitchen at Leonard's. Downtown was still a place where all young ladies wore gloves, a place where you "always saw someone." Mothers could be seen dragging tired children from store to store, rewarding them afterward with a trip to Peter's for a soda. The city's first shopping center, Westgate, opened in the late 1950s, followed by Stuyvesant Plaza, just outside the city limits, but the impact of the shopping center on downtown merchants had barely been felt.

Arthur J. O'Keefe

The 1960s were a different story. These were long and difficult years for the city, for reasons that were common to every Northeastern city of the period—the flight to the suburbs, the ultimate red-lining by banks and insurance companies, the subsidization of suburban schools by state governments, increasing racial tension.

Federally subsidized urban-renewal programs of the 1960s were oriented toward demolition first and new housing second; no attempt was made to rehabilitate existing neighborhoods. The first urban-renewal project in the nation took place in the area where Boardman's is located today. The historic neighborhood that had surrounded the Erie Canal basin was completely demolished in blitzlike fashion and replaced with a large shopping center and commercial properties, none of which provided a home for a single person. In the South End, under the federally funded Green Street and Morton Avenue projects, hundreds of small row houses were torn down and replaced with tall high-rises, hitherto unknown in the city of Albany. Of the 2,300 units of public housing in Albany today, the only ones that can be termed successful are those in buildings of three stories or less—as in North Albany, on Colonie Street, and along the lower end of South Pearl Street—and in the high-rises reserved for senior citizens.

Timothy Leonard

Only within the last five or six years has it become possible for cities to obtain federal aid to rehabilitate existing housing in neighborhoods built on a more human and personal scale. Under the Community Block Grant program, more than 1,000 housing units have been restored and neighborhoods have been brought back to such an extent that a major problem now, instead of abandonment and disinvestment, appears to be "gentrification"—the displacement of lower- and middle-income residents by young, educated, higher-income people seeking to move back into the city from the suburbs.

Morris Gerber

Nelson Rockefeller was a man of great vision and a man of single purpose when he put his mind to achieving a goal. Many of his accomplishments will benefit Albany and the state of New York for many years to come. Under his administration the state university system was totally revamped and the Albany State Teachers College expanded into the State University of New York at Albany. The college was moved from its modest facility in the center of the city to a huge new campus far to the west in the city's Pine Bush area, adjacent to the state office-building complex begun in the mid-1950s by Governor Thomas E. Dewey.

When it came to the question of state offices in downtown Albany, Rockefeller felt, as he had in the case of the university, that the present facilities were inadequate. The State Office Building, described in 1928 as Al Smith's folly because it would never be fully needed or utilized, was now totally inadequate, and the state had become the largest landlord in downtown Albany. Local legend has it that on the occasion of the visit of

Facing page
Top
The White Elephant Grill on Maiden Lane and James Street was once a landmark in downtown Albany. This photograph was taken in 1952.
Middle
The 119 Club opened on Dana Avenue after the repeal of Prohibition. It was owned by Eddie Cahill and former boxer John Leonard, whose brothers, Paul and Charlie, also ran the neighborhood grill. The club was popular with a generation of law school and medical students.
Bottom
The Normanskill Farm Dairy, whose route-man is shown above, had its headquarters at the Steven's Farm adjoining Normanskill. Until the 1960s Albany neighborhoods were regularly serviced by a variety of route salesmen who relied upon a lively traffic with housewives who found it convenient to patronize their street trade.
Right
The Roman Catholic Cathedral can be seen through a partially demolished building during the construction of the Nelson Rockefeller Empire State Plaza. The office building in the foreground of the cathedral was among the last buildings to be razed.

Photo by Bob Paley

Princess Beatrix of the Netherlands, Rockefeller, who acted as host for much of her visit, found it embarrassing to drive with his royal guest from the Governor's Mansion on Eagle Street up to the New York State Capitol. The city appeared to be in a state of decay, many of its downtown neighborhoods were slums, and all in all the governor considered it an unfit capital for the state of New York.

In the fall of 1962, with less than a week's notice for a consultation with the mayor of the city—something that would not be possible today—Albanians read in their local newspapers that the state, by its power of eminent domain, was seizing all the land between Lincoln Park and State Street and between Swan Street and Eagle. In addition to this parcel of nearly 100 acres, additional property would be seized for arterial highways leading into the proposed South Mall.

The Mall started slowly. There was talk in the initial stages that certain churches and other prominent buildings, such as the chancery of the Roman Catholic diocese, could be left standing and accommodated within the Mall. As time went on, however, it became apparent that a 21st-century office complex was to be imposed upon a 19th-century city and nothing could be accommodated beyond the Roman Catholic Cathedral and the Governor's Mansion itself. Everything else would have to go.

The Mall was to be placed upon a huge platform of cement with layers of parking underneath for thousands of cars. Before it was finished, it would employ thousands of workers imported from union locals stretching into neighboring states, and in one case employing artisans who only spoke French. It would utilize more than 500,000 cubic feet of marble, backing up marble orders in the states of Vermont and Georgia by more than a year. The original cost of the Mall was estimated to be in the neighborhood of $400 million; by the time it was finished, it had exceeded $2 billion in construction costs and debt service.

The Port of Albany

The Port of Albany, about to celebrate its 50th year, has a history as old as the city itself. On Albany's riverbanks the furs acquired by the early Dutch traders were gathered and shipped down the mighty Hudson by the Dutch West India Company.

The first stone docks were built at Albany in 1766—three docks 80 feet long and 30 to 40 feet wide; four more docks were added in 1770. In November of that year, the sloop *Olive Branch* cleared Albany for the West Indies; many more followed, carrying flour, lumber, and fish and returning with sugar and rum from the islands. In 1785, tradition relates, the sloop *Experiment* under Captain Stewart Dean cleared Albany for Canton—the second American ship to make the voyage. For the newly independent nation, no longer a part of the British imperial trading network, establishing commercial relations with China was an important first step toward economic independence.

Sloops, barges, and steamboats plied the Hudson throughout the 19th century, but by the end of the century oceangoing vessels were no longer reaching Albany. Silting, shoals, and sandbars rendered the last 30 miles, above the city of Hudson, too hazardous and uncertain. A particularly massive build-up located three miles south of Albany and known as the "Overslaugh" had impeded river traffic since colonial times. Unless a channel of sufficient depth could be created and maintained, Albany's days as an international port were gone forever.

On December 8, 1913, Albany Representative Peter G. Ten Eyck introduced a bill in Congress "to provide for a survey and estimate of cost of a deep water channel in the Hudson River, New York between the City of Hudson and the dam at Troy." The bill was ultimately passed as part of the Rivers and Harbors Act of 1915. Surveys, estimates, and feasibility studies followed, and at last, on March 3, 1925, President Calvin Coolidge signed a bill authorizing the expenditure of $11 million to dredge a channel 27 feet deep—deep enough to accommodate 85 percent of the world's oceangoing vessels. The cities of Albany and Rensselaer were required to commit another $10 million to provide suitable port facilities.

On March 25, 1925, New York Governor Alfred E. Smith signed a bill creating the Albany Port District—comprising about 200 acres within the city of Albany and another 35 acres across the river in Rensselaer—and a five-member Port Commission to oversee development and operation of the port. Construction of the new port was formally initiated in March 1926, and in April 1927 the process of dredging the Hudson River began. The channel was completed in June of 1931, and one year later the Port of Albany was officially dedicated.

Today the port plays an active part in the city's economy and the nation's international trade. Huge quantities of wheat and corn—stored in one of the world's largest grain elevators—are exported annually, recalling on a far grander scale the cargoes of colonial times. Once again molasses flows into Albany—not only from the West Indies, but from as far away as Brazil, Australia, and South Africa. Bananas by the ton arrive from Central America, wood pulp from Sweden, and steel products from Italy. Volkswagen of America, which recently consolidated its East Coast import operations at Albany, brings in tens of thousands of Volkswagen, Porsche, and Audi cars annually for distribution throughout New England and the Midwest. The Hudson River channel has been deepened to 32 feet and, thanks to icebreaking operations by the U.S. Coast Guard, the Port of Albany is now a thriving year-round facility.

Facing page
Top
An Albany Port District Commission vehicle loads lumber onto a freight car.
Bottom
Under construction from 1926 to 1932, the Port of Albany increased river traffic at a time when the city could boast of having the largest single-unit grain elevator in the world.

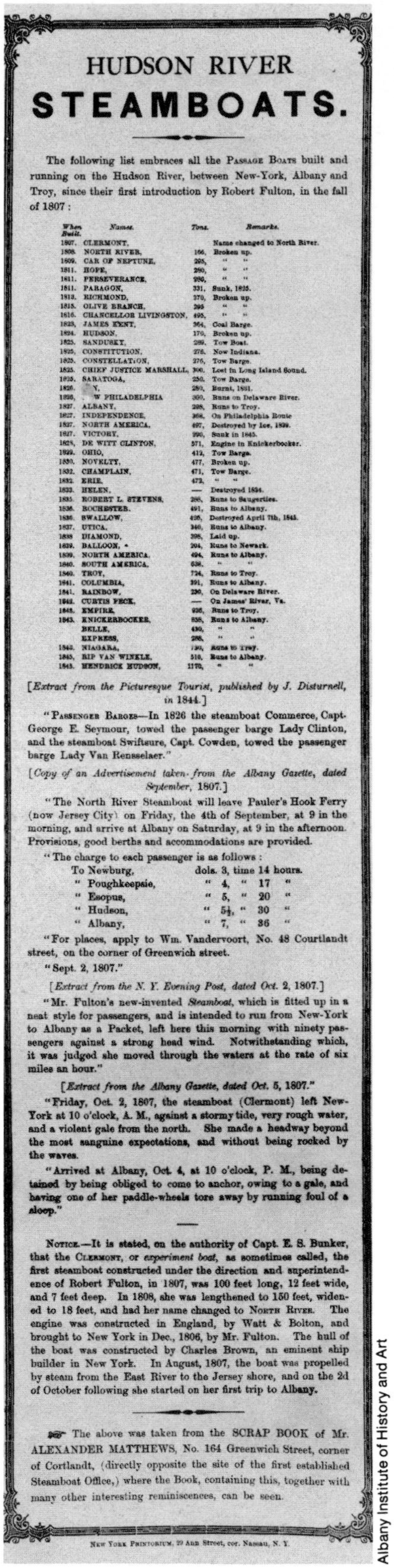

HUDSON RIVER
STEAMBOATS.

The following list embraces all the Passage Boats built and running on the Hudson River, between New-York, Albany and Troy, since their first introduction by Robert Fulton, in the fall of 1807 :

When Built.	*Names.*	*Tons.*	*Remarks.*
1807.	CLERMONT,		Name changed to North River.
1808.	NORTH RIVER,	166,	Broken up.
1809.	CAR OF NEPTUNE,	295,	" "
1811.	HOPE,	280,	" "
1811.	PERSEVERANCE,	280,	" "
1811.	PARAGON,	331,	Sunk, 1825.
1813.	RICHMOND,	370,	Broken up.
1815.	OLIVE BRANCH,	295	" "
1816.	CHANCELLOR LIVINGSTON,	495,	" "
1823,	JAMES KENT,	364,	Coal Barge.
1824.	HUDSON,	170,	Broken up.
1825.	SANDUSKY,	289.	Tow Boat.
1825,	CONSTITUTION,	276.	Now Indiana.
1825.	CONSTELLATION,	276,	Tow Barge.
1825.	CHIEF JUSTICE MARSHALL,	306.	Lost in Long Island Sound.
1825.	SARATOGA,	250.	Tow Barge.
1826.	[illegible]Y,	280,	Burnt, 1831.
1826,	[illegible]W PHILADELPHIA	300.	Runs on Delaware River.
1827.	ALBANY,	298,	Runs to Troy.
1827.	INDEPENDENCE,	368,	On Philadelphia Route
1827.	NORTH AMERICA,	497,	Destroyed by Ice, 1839.
1827.	VICTORY,	290,	Sunk in 1845.
1828,	DE WITT CLINTON,	571,	Engine in Knickerbocker.
1829.	OHIO,	412,	Tow Barge.
1830.	NOVELTY,	477,	Broken up.
1832.	CHAMPLAIN,	471,	Tow Barge.
1832.	ERIE,	472,	" "
1833.	HELEN,	—	Destroyed 1834.
1835.	ROBERT L. STEVENS,	288,	Runs to Saugerties.
1836.	ROCHESTER.	491,	Runs to Albany.
1836.	SWALLOW,	426,	Destroyed April 7th, 1845.
1837.	UTICA,	346,	Runs to Albany.
1838	DIAMOND,	398,	Laid up.
1839.	BALLOON, *	204,	Runs to Newark.
1839.	NORTH AMERICA.	494,	Runs to Albany.
1840.	SOUTH AMERICA.	638.	" "
1840.	TROY,	724,	Runs to Troy.
1841.	COLUMBIA,	391,	Runs to Albany.
1841.	RAINBOW,	230,	On Delaware River.
1842.	CURTIS PECK,	—	On James' River, Va.
1843.	EMPIRE,	936,	Runs to Troy.
1843.	KNICKERBOCKER,	858,	Runs to Albany.
	BELLE,	430,	" "
	EXPRESS,	286,	" "
1845.	NIAGARA,	730,	Runs to Troy.
1845,	RIP VAN WINKLE,	516,	Runs to Albany.
1845.	HENDRICK HUDSON,	1170,	" "

[*Extract from the Picturesque Tourist, published by J. Disturnell, in* 1844.]

"Passenger Barges—In 1826 the steamboat Commerce, Capt. George E. Seymour, towed the passenger barge Lady Clinton, and the steamboat Swiftsure, Capt. Cowden, towed the passenger barge Lady Van Rensselaer."

[*Copy of an Advertisement taken from the Albany Gazette, dated September*, 1807.]

"The North River Steamboat will leave Pauler's Hook Ferry (now Jersey City) on Friday, the 4th of September, at 9 in the morning, and arrive at Albany on Saturday, at 9 in the afternoon. Provisions, good berths and accommodations are provided.

"The charge to each passenger is as follows :

To Newburg,	dols. 3,	time 14 hours.
" Poughkeepsie,	" 4,	" 17 "
" Esopus,	" 5,	" 20 "
" Hudson,	" 5½,	" 30 "
" Albany,	" 7,	" 36 "

"For places, apply to Wm. Vandervoort, No. 48 Courtlandt street, on the corner of Greenwich street.

"Sept. 2, 1807."

[*Extract from the N. Y. Evening Post, dated Oct.* 2, 1807.]

"Mr. Fulton's new-invented *Steamboat*, which is fitted up in a neat style for passengers, and is intended to run from New-York to Albany as a Packet, left here this morning with ninety passengers against a strong head wind. Notwithstanding which, it was judged she moved through the waters at the rate of six miles an hour."

[*Extract from the Albany Gazette, dated Oct.* 5, 1807."

"Friday, Oct. 2, 1807, the steamboat (Clermont) left New-York at 10 o'clock, A. M., against a stormy tide, very rough water, and a violent gale from the north. She made a headway beyond the most sanguine expectations, and without being rocked by the waves.

"Arrived at Albany, Oct. 4, at 10 o'clock, P. M., being detained by being obliged to come to anchor, owing to a gale, and having one of her paddle-wheels tore away by running foul of a sloop."

Notice.—It is stated, on the authority of Capt. E. S. Bunker, that the Clermont, or *experiment boat*, as sometimes called, the first steamboat constructed under the direction and superintendence of Robert Fulton, in 1807, was 100 feet long, 12 feet wide, and 7 feet deep. In 1808, she was lengthened to 150 feet, widened to 18 feet, and had her name changed to North River. The engine was constructed in England, by Watt & Bolton, and brought to New York in Dec., 1806, by Mr. Fulton. The hull of the boat was constructed by Charles Brown, an eminent ship builder in New York. In August, 1807, the boat was propelled by steam from the East River to the Jersey shore, and on the 2d of October following she started on her first trip to Albany.

☞ The above was taken from the SCRAP BOOK of Mr. ALEXANDER MATTHEWS, No. 164 Greenwich Street, corner of Cortlandt, (directly opposite the site of the first established Steamboat Office,) where the Book, containing this, together with many other interesting reminiscences, can be seen.

New York Printorium, 29 Ann Street, cor. Nassau, N. Y.

Albany Institute of History and Art

Albany Public Library

New York State Library

By all accounts the Mall is a magnificent structure. Efforts have been made, at the urging of local officials including the mayor, to make it more than a 9-to-5 facility. The "I Love New York Festival," held every other fall, attracts tens of thousands of people. A grand fireworks display on the Fourth of July revives a custom of a generation ago, when such festivities were held in Lincoln Park.

Visitors to the city are almost always impressed by the Mall, but most Albanians maintain a peculiar love-hate relationship with what is known today as the Governor Nelson A. Rockefeller Empire State Plaza—and with good reason.

When Governor Rockefeller appeared before the Senate committee for confirmation as Vice President of the United States, he was challenged with the fact that more than 7,000 people had lost their homes to an office-building complex in the capital city. Rockefeller proudly answered that the area cited had been one of the worst slums in the United States, with one of the highest infant-mortality rates. The fact of the matter was that the governor was not familiar with the neighborhood at all; his knowledge of Albany was a straight line along Eagle Street from where he lived to where he worked. The area in question was a working-class neighborhood whose residents included blue-collar workers on Cathedral Hill and even some legislators who lived in rooming houses and rental properties on Capitol Hill. The infant-mortality rate for the three years prior to the Rockefeller testimony was among the lowest in the city, with a grand total of two deaths per year prior to demolition. Ironically enough, the highest infant-mortality rate in the city was in Pine Hills—a relatively well-to-do middle-class neighborhood.

To assess what really happened, one has to understand what was there originally. A time frame that goes back 10 or 15 years, when the entire city was a mass of dust and construction materials and equipment, suggests that nothing but improvement has occurred in the area. But the creation of the Mall entailed destruction of some very positive things. There was, of course, the obvious loss of buildings that had stood for more than 100 years, some of them representing the finest in 19th-century craftsmanship. Also lost to the area were four beautiful church buildings. St. Paul's Episcopal and St. Sofia's Greek Orthodox were both relocated from Lancaster Street; First Methodist and the Church of the Assumption were never replaced.

The approaches to the Mall did further damage, wiping out two small neighborhoods of particular interest. One was a street of French-Canadians opposite a French-Canadian church built shortly after the Civil War. It was an elderly community and one not known to too many people. More obvious, more flamboyant, and better known was Little Italy, centered around St. Anthony's Church. People from all over the city came to Grand Street and Madison Avenue to enjoy the annual festivals and street fairs. The residents of Little Italy were not only elderly people, as was the case with the French section, but included many younger families—many of them still speaking Italian in their homes and in the streets.

The Mall also had an effect on other urban neighborhoods. The streets that surrounded it suddenly became prey to speculators who purchased family homes at inflated prices, immediately cut them up into small apartments, and rented them out to workers at above-average prices.

Below
Generations of coal heat and city traffic have necessitated the cleaning of many landmark buildings in downtown Albany, especially during the preservation-conscious, post-South Mall era. Construction and cleaning on the facade of the New York State Education Building, shown here, took place in the 1960s.
Below right
The Van Heusen Charles and Company, established in 1843, was once a landmark in downtown Albany. During the building of the Rockefeller Empire State Plaza, there was a decline in large retail store business in the downtown area and the company established a smaller store in a renovated 19th-century commercial building on Howard Street.

On the approach to the Mall, now partially covered by the Arterial Highway, was an open-air market that had its antecedent back in Dutch times. It had been moved several times, from the center of Broadway to the center of State Street, and finally, in this century, to larger quarters in the vicinity of Hudson Avenue, Philip Street, Grand, and Market. The Market Square, as it was known, attracted farmers from truck farms outside the city who sold their produce in the early years from horse-drawn wagons, and in later years from the back of pick-up trucks. Twenty years ago it was possible for any Albanian to go to the Market Square six days a week and buy anything from live rabbits and chickens to flowers, fruits, and vegetables in season. It was a lively and wonderful place and rivaled, in many ways, Boston's Quincy Market—thought of by many people today as something new in urban development.

Perhaps the most damaging result of all, however, was the effect on downtown. Myers and Whitney's were by this time great dinosaurs in an age when only chain stores survived—and then only with difficulty—in downtown areas. They probably would have gone anyway. To the hundreds of local shopkeepers, downtown was looked upon not as a central shopping area, but primarily as a neighborhood shopping center for the 7,000 to 14,000 people who lived within the Mall area and its environs and were eventually displaced. People from Arbor Hill, Sheridan Hollow, Little Italy, the South End, and the so-called Mansions District, as well as the neighborhoods above the Mall, used downtown for everything from grocery shopping to routine clothing purchases, providing a cushion for the downtown merchants when the normal cycle of boom and bust affected the business community. Without these people, and with other families being replaced by transient workers in row houses and brownstones surrounding the construction sites, little by little downtown began to die. In time, the theaters closed—as many as five or six in the immediate downtown area. Stores closed one by one. Suburbanization continued, and downtown no longer had its local neighborhood population to support it in times of stress.

What is left is magnificent and almost unrivaled in the United States, but it is important to remember that it was built at a cost—a cost measured both in material and in human terms.

Photo by Bob Paley

Albany Institute of History and Art

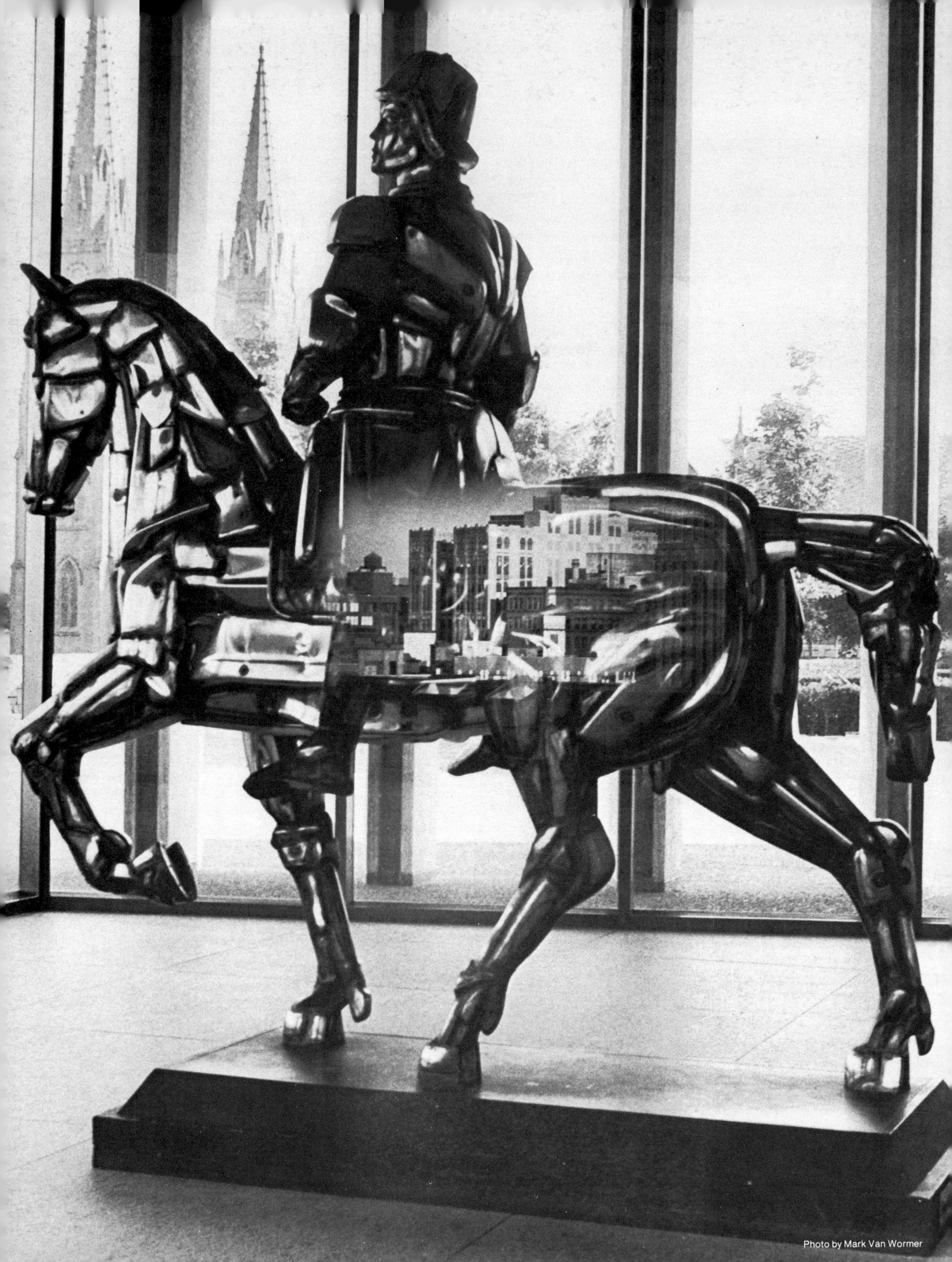
Photo by Mark Van Wormer

Albany D.H.R. Photo by Lindsey Watson

Albany D.H.R. Photo by Lindsey Watson

Photo by Rich Frutchey

Facing page
The Colleoni II, *sculpted by Jason Seley out of welded steel automobile bumpers, stands in the Tower Building of the Rockefeller Empire State Plaza.*
Top left
One may view bronze sculptures of children on the 1912 State Education Building around the lamps at the head of the stairs.
Top right
These World War I soldiers sculpted by G.K. Lathlop in 1933 appear on an Albany monument. Do you know where it stands? See the inset on the next page for the answer.
Above
The Englewood Place gardens display their colorful beauty. The Guilded Age mansions of Albany's elite held Washington Park from further expansion to Western Avenue.
Right
A panoramic view from the Tower Building looking northwest shows the Governor Nelson A. Rockefeller Empire State Plaza.

Photo by Rich Frutchey

Albany D.H.R. Photo by Lindsey Watson

Photo by Rich Frutchey

Photo by Rich Frutchey

Albany D.H.R. Photo by Lindsey Watson

Facing page, inset
The World War I Memorial Flagpole in Memorial Grove at New Scotland and South Lake avenues is flanked by bronze beavers, the city's emblem, and depicts soldiers and sailors of the "Great War" who are accompanied by horse, dog, and carrier pigeon allies.
Facing page and top left
The Normanskill Farm, recently purchased by the city, is one of several pastoral reserves that make up Albany's "green belts," separating the city from the neighboring town of Bethlehem.
Above
Can you guess which municipal building this fierce-looking stone lion appears on? See the next page, top, to find out.
Left
This view of Albany was taken from the Heldebergh escarpment at Thacher Park, a popular state facility known for its fossils, "Bear Path," and former "Indian Ladder."

Photo by Rich Frutchey

Albany D.H.R. Photo by Lindsey Watson

Albany League of the Arts

Photo by Rich Frutchey

Facing page, top
Albany City Hall, designed by H.H. Richardson, boasts elaborate stone carvings in natural, imaginary, and Classical themes on its south and west fronts as if to rival the State Capitol across the street.
Facing page, bottom and below
Pinksterfest, a spring festivity held in Washington Park in conjunction with the popular Tulip Festival, is a re-creation of an early slave celebration held on Capitol Hill. The city fathers outlawed the original Pinksterfest in 1811 and it has been revived only since the early 1970s. Below, the Poking Brook Morris Dancers perform at the festival.
Left
Lark Street, developed in the last half of the 19th century, serves as a key residential and shopping street within the "brownstone revival" neighborhoods of Center Square, Hudson Park, and Washington Park.
Right
In which of Albany's churches is this stained glass window located? See the top left picture on the next page to find out.

Albany D.H.R. Photo by Lindsey Watson

Albany League of the Arts

Albany D.H.R. Photo by Lindsey Watson

Albany League of the Arts

New York State Department of Commerce

Windsor Publications, Inc.

Albany D.H.R. Photo by Lindsey Watson

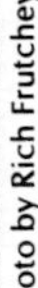

Photo by Rich Frutchey

Photo by Rich Frutchey

Facing page
Top left
The Madison Avenue window of the Cathedral of the Immaculate Conception, created in England, was originally located behind the altar when the building was constructed in 1848-1852.
Top right
Skating at the Plaza, coupled with regular festivals and fairs, demonstrates the favorable evolution of the Empire State Plaza from its original purpose as a "9 to 5" office complex into a vibrant regional attraction.
Bottom
Thomas Olcott built the Executive Mansion on Eagle Street circa 1850. It was first leased to the state in 1874 for the residence of Governor Tilden. Three years later the state purchased the building and thoroughly "Victorianized" it with trim and gingerbread decorations.
Above
The Port of Albany, relocated to the city's far South End in 1925 to 1932, bolsters the region's economy through extensive international shipping.
Top
Albany is a city of contrasts. Here the peaked roofs and dormers of Albany's early 19th-century Pastures district are overshadowed by the gleaming marble of the Empire State Plaza.
Middle
In addition to serving traffic in grain, scrap iron, oil, bananas, and paper products, the Port of Albany has several industrial firms located within its district.
Bottom
The State University of New York at Albany was transformed during the Rockefeller years into a major university center, and its main campus was relocated to the site of the Albany Country Club on the city's western edge.

Albany Institute of History and Art

Prior to World War I, the Market Square relieved congestion on State Street, where farmers had peddled their goods for generations. Many Albany housewives made daily visits to the market.

CHAPTER 10

PARTNERS IN PROGRESS: BUSINESS HISTORIES

by Robert W. Arnold III

In one respect or another it may be said that Albany has always been the capital city on the Hudson. Its often-mentioned strategic value at the head of an estuary, near the confluence of the Hudson River with the Mohawk, made the small, palisaded community important out of proportion to its size. That location, too, was important in bringing commerce to Albany.

Albany was a natural funnel for the flow of Americans moving westward, for the produce of the Old West moving east. The funnel opened wider with the building of the Erie Canal, the markets of the Great Lakes opening to Albany's manufacturers, financiers, and merchants. The people and the institutions of Albany were generally equal to the challenges of the virtually unregulated economy of 19th-century America; where they were not, the factories, banks, and companies they created were swept away.

If anything is illustrated by the business biographies in this book, it is that the business community of Albany is as adaptable, as pragmatic, and yet remains as human now as were the fur traders who started it all, on a lost island in the Hudson River, long ago. The older firms included demonstrate a great continuity, a special sort of creative endurance, the newer ones enterprise and imagination. Family-owned businesses, many of them several generations in a single family, possess a rich folklore relating to their firms and founders; a sense of familial responsibility seems to come with the obligations of management. In other corporations, without exception, the strong, the colorful, the omnicompetent, and the idiosyncratic managers, employees, and officers linger on like shades, occasional reminders of halcyon, salad days, both inspiration and example for the hectic present, the unformed future.

Albany was a center for river and canal traffic, open since its beginnings to the sea, connected by rail for nearly a century and a half to other parts of the continent, for decades by air. This city has seen all sorts of pioneers, from Dutch *boslopers* to technological and financial innovators; tradition continues in a city grown old but no less independent, vital still in ways perhaps unintelligible to the Albany of the past, in other ways most familiar. In business, as in so much else, Albanians did not lose sight of the past, kept solid grip on the present, and did not dread the future. The motto under the city's crest reads "Assiduity," which has in our case not been passive observation. In all the institutions of Albany presented here, diligence has been the key to endurance and the passage to success when coupled with vision. Because of this, Albany has been, and remains, the capital city on the Hudson.

STATE BANK OF ALBANY

"... it was one night in the fall of 1802 ..., I dreamt of the establishment of a new bank in Albany which I named at the instant State Bank. ... The moment the plan was thus matured, I started from my bed, lighted a candle, and committed the project to paper." So wrote Elkanah Watson, a transplanted Yankee omnipresent in Albany's daily affairs. The morning after he had his dream, Watson set about making it a reality. On April 6, 1803, the first board of directors of this new bank met at the Tontine Coffee House to hear Albany architect Philip Hooker hold forth on his proposed design for their building.

Before Hooker could complete the building, New York State Bank, the second chartered bank in Albany, commenced business, in September 1803. This new bank was capitalized at $460,000 and occupied Hooker's facility on May 10, 1804. Over the next 177 years, State Bank of Albany would literally grow up and around it. Since that time, it has occupied this State Street location, the oldest structure planned and continuously used as a banking house in the nation. Its classical styling and sturdy construction, combined with its landmark stature in Albany, prompted State Bank directors to carefully preserve Hooker's facade as the central architectural element of a new State Bank structure erected in 1927.

The period of State Bank's founding was promising. The industrial revolution was arriving in Albany and with it a revolution in transportation. While the Hudson River had always been the city's vital economic artery, settlement of the Northwest required construction of a web of turnpikes emanating from Albany, then a principal point in the westward movement. While still in its temporary quarters awaiting completion of Hooker's building, the directors of State Bank made their first loan, ordering their cashier "to discount a note for the sum of Four Thousand dollars for the use of the Great Western Turnpike Company." First of the big roads west through the state, this would eventually become U.S. Route 20.

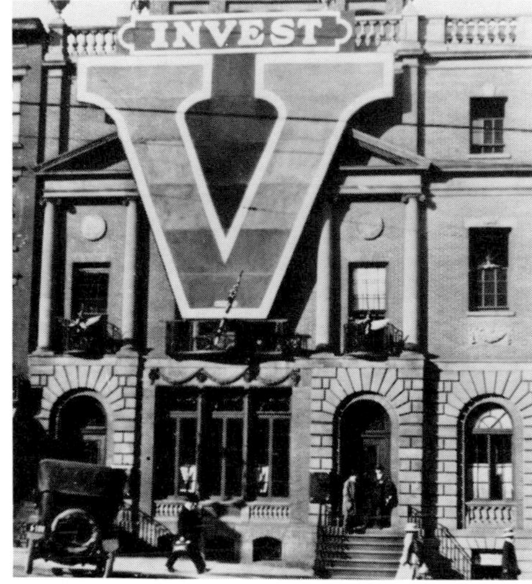

Above:
Taken during World War I, this photograph shows State Bank of Albany decorated with a large sign promoting the Fifth Liberty Loan.
Below:
Elkanah Watson, a prime mover in early 19th-century Albany society, dreamed of establishing a bank in his adopted city.

Success with the Great Western Turnpike established a precedent for State Bank's commitment to loan the Erie Canal Fund $600,000, a huge loan in 1822. In 1825, the Erie Canal became a reality, and its full length from Buffalo to New York was opened with a colorful procession of boats. Huge crowds gathered at towns and cities all along the way. Practically all of Albany turned out for this historic event. Thus, Albany became an important center of Hudson River travel and East-West trade.

Canals were soon superseded by the advent of the steam-powered railroads. In 1832, the first train passed over a route constructed between Schenectady and Gansevoort Street in Albany. A year later, New York State Bank was investing in railroads through its vice-president Erastus Corning, himself interested in the Mohawk & Hudson Railroad.

State Bank and its investments were

prudent in a time of wildcat speculation. The bank weathered the financial panic of 1837 and grew apace with Albany. The election of Rufus H. King as its president in 1840 eventually led to a new charter, a change on paper meant to bring the bank into alignment with the general banking law. By 1859, of the publicly offered stock of six banks, State Bank's commanded the highest price. In this same flourishing year, Hooker's building was remodeled and New York State Bank then "returned to its old quarters . . . the interior having been so improved that few banking rooms can be considered more commodious or better arranged."

Rufus King practiced a conservative business philosophy: even during the wartime inflation of 1861-1865, the board could pay an extra 10 percent dividend and State Bank's clerks twice received bonuses. After 62 years of operation, in July 1865, a rechartering changed State Bank to a national association, which it would remain until reverting to a state charter as a commercial bank in 1937, assuming the present name of State Bank of Albany.

The post-Civil War years saw New York State National Bank mirror the prosperity of the nation. The bank had much to do with consolidation of several independent railroads into the New York Central System. By 1869, the Central had extended its services to New York City to become the New York Central and Hudson River Railroad; it would again become the New York Central in 1914.

This photograph, taken sometime after 1859, shows the bank facade designed by Philip Hooker modified only slightly.

By 1927, the bank's growth created the necessity for a major building improvement; consequently, a 16-story building, the bank's present headquarters, was erected. The following year Frederick McDonald, an industrialist, was elected president. McDonald quickly revised bank policies, enabling the institution to outlast the stock market crash of 1929 and the ensuing Depression. In 1938, McDonald wrote, "Because of this bank's strong financial condition, many local businesses, not in the best of health, were given the assistance which enabled them to weather the recent economic difficulties."

World War II brought a return of prosperity to the Capital District. State Bank of Albany was instrumental in perfecting the wartime rationing system. State Bank was also deeply involved in massive postwar construction projects, among which were the New York State Thruway and the St. Lawrence Seaway. In 1957, after a long progressive term of leadership at State Bank, Frederick McDonald was made chairman of the board and Hollis Harrington assumed the presidency. The new president continued the progressive policies of his predecessor by extending the bank's branch facilities throughout northeastern New York State.

In January of 1972, with State Bank as its cornerstone, the United Banking Corporation of New York, a holding company, was established to take advantage of the opportunity for statewide banking. The following year, Frank Odell became president and Hollis Harrington became chairman of the board. During Odell's tenure as the current president, State Bank celebrated its 175th anniversary, at which time Odell wrote, "The strong, solid condition of our bank is best exemplified by the fact that during our 175 years of continued operation there have been only 10 presidents of this institution."

Involved since its beginning in financing landmark public and private projects intimately linked to the economy of the Albany area and New York State as a whole, State Bank has not deviated from its motto—*Officium Cum Integritate*—the Rendition of Public Service with Integrity.

ABELE TRACTOR & EQUIPMENT CO., INC.

Abele Tractor & Equipment Company, Inc. had its beginnings back in the 1870s when West Albany rivaled Chicago and Buffalo as a livestock center. It was at this time that German-born Nicholas Miller purchased land on the Everett Road less than a mile north of the stockyards at West Albany. On this site Miller established a blacksmith shop to fashion and repair farm tools and shoe the horses that worked the farms in the Colonie area.

Nicholas had four sons and four daughters. Three of the sons in time joined the family blacksmith business, John as a blacksmith, Frank as a woodworker and wheelwright, and the younger son, William F., as a machinist who served his apprenticeship in the New York Central Railroad shops that were situated in the stockyard area of West Albany. Nicholas's fourth son, Charles, was a local judge who held court on the second floor of William Miller's machine shop.

In 1904 William Miller proudly drove his handmade steam car, one of the first horseless carriages to be seen and driven in the Albany area. Miller was widely recognized for his exceptional mechanical ability and ingenuity. He was very much involved in the early days of the West Albany Volunteer Fire Company and built the first two pieces of fire apparatus that the company used, having built one on a used chassis of a Graham Bros. truck and the other on a Cadillac touring car chassis.

For several decades the Miller Shop was the principal source of repairs for the Town of Colonie Highway Department and the Latham Water District. The Albany Packing Company, now known as Tobin Packing Company, constructed its plant on Exchange Street in the 1920s, with William Miller as the chief mechanical consultant.

In January 1940 Miller hired Kenneth W. Abele to join his 2-man force as an apprentice and helper. During that first year William Miller and Ken Abele built one of the largest tow trucks on the East Coast; developed and built a ham-canning machine for the Albany Packing Company; and devised a shuttle conveyor system to move cinders from the New York Central Railroad yards, going under the tracks into a cinder block plant that was located adjacent to where I-90 now passes the West Albany community.

William F. Miller, in this photograph dated June 10, 1904, is seen at the tiller of the car he built by hand in his Everett Road shop; it was among the first automobiles in the Albany area.

In December 1940 Ken Abele married William's daughter, Thelma, and thus the third generation was now involved in the business founded by Thelma's grandfather, Nicholas Miller. In 1943 ill health forced William Miller's retirement and Ken Abele took over the business, which was at that time engaged in the repair of all kinds of essential equipment to keep it operating during World War II as new machinery was virtually impossible to obtain. Thelma, who had been a schoolteacher, was the office girl, bookkeeper, stock clerk, and machine operator.

After the war the nature of business changed from predominately repairing to selling and servicing farm, construction, and consumer outdoor power equipment. More land was acquired, new buildings built, and in 1959 the business incorporated as Abele Tractor & Equipment Company, Inc.

Abele equipment and services had a part in the major state building programs in the Albany area in the 1960s and 1970s, including the state university, state office campus complex, Empire State Plaza, and the network of arterial highways that surround the city and the New York State Thruway, as well as many other schools, churches, and commercial buildings.

The fourth generation, Warren and Rodney Abele, working with over 40 employees, assures the continued growth of this century-old business.

ADELS-LOEB INC.

It was a new item, a radical departure from American masculine tradition, when Louis Adels, founder of New York City's L. Adels Company, first introduced the wrist watch to the American market in 1917. Adels did well with the new product, once he overcame the qualms of American "he-men," and his firm, now the Winton-Nicolet Watch Company, remains in business today. Louis's brother Moe, of M. Adels and Company, was a diamond importer in New York City for more than 50 years; brother Harry settled in Troy around 1919, opening Adels Jewelers, a retail store still in operation. Louis's sister Etta and her husband, Max Segel, opened Segel's Jewelers in Schenectady. In 1923 Samuel Adels, Pearl Adels Loeb, and Pearl's husband, Martin Loeb, opened Adels-Loeb in one of the shops in the North Pearl Street facade of the once-prestigious Kenmore Hotel.

After six years at the Kenmore location, in late 1929, Adels-Loeb moved into larger and more modern quarters in the newly constructed National Savings Bank building on the southwest corner of South Pearl and State streets. The firm has remained there ever since. The refined details of the store's art deco interior largely remain—meticulously joined cabinets, and glass doors and interior windows acid-etched in floral patterns, cherished survivors of an age when even the utilitarian was made gracefully amenable. Enough remains of that original interior in Adels-Loeb to form a picture of the store as it was in 1929.

Pearl Adels Loeb alone survives of the company's three founders, and at the age of 80 works in the store each day, known to her clientele for her understanding, merchandising, and fine taste. David Loeb, son of Pearl and Martin Loeb, entered the family firm in 1949; a registered jeweler of the American Gem Society and a certified gemologist, David eventually became president of Adels-Loeb.

Adels-Loeb weathered nearly 60 years of operation by adapting to the changing times without losing sight of its tradition of friendly, scrupulous service, fine quality merchandise, and unassailable integrity. As the heyday of downtown Albany waned, as inflation, recession, and the advent of large suburban shopping centers came to pass, Adels-Loeb adjusted. Business hours were modified and Adels-Loeb, once Albany's largest retailer of sterling silver, no longer displayed even place settings. Lunch hour downtown today brings a cross section of professional people and workers of all sorts into the store, Albany's oldest credit jewelers. Appraisals, watch and jewelry repairs, and engraving mark this most versatile old-time jewelry store.

After 57 years in business at the center of downtown Albany, Adels-Loeb is intimately associated with the reawakening commercial life of the inner city. As in the interior of its store, Adels-Loeb itself preserves and employs the best elements of its past, "doing business in the old-fashioned way—with warmth, with knowledge, and with integrity."

Left:
Opening day at the new Adels-Loeb store in 1929 revealed a beautiful art deco interior and an extravagant quantity of cut flowers.
Right:
A very sophisticated display attracted window-shoppers on South Pearl Street in 1929. (Courtesy, Glen S. Cook, photographer)

ADIRONDACK STEEL CASTING COMPANY

An 1891 Watervliet map showed the land swampy and of marginal utility, which is undoubtedly why the Sherman brothers bought it when they came from northern New York State looking for a foundry site. In 1918, on 40 acres of land in the hub of the industrial Northeast, situated in a matrix of road, water, and railroad transportation, Fred W. Sherman and his brothers organized Adirondack Steel Casting Company. Fred would run the company, aided by brothers Frank and Clifton—who also operated Dominion Foundry Steel of Canada—until 1957.

Seen from the air, Adirondack's foundry could be in the Lehigh Valley or outside Birmingham. Long metal buildings stained by use and years sprawl geometrically along the railroad sidings, which ship in raw materials used by Adirondack: New Jersey sand, Wyoming bentonite clay, Florida zircon sand, and metal scrap from New England. Castings no longer go out over those sidings, but trucks move to America's industrial heartland in the Ohio River Valley and to customers farther west and south into the Texas area where oil and gas valves are now in great demand to meet America's energy needs.

Weighing from one pound to 10 tons, Adirondack's castings supply a variety of industries with components for cranes, tractors, compressors, and railroad trucks. Making railroad parts for the nearby D & H Railroad helped to bring Adirondack through the Depression, when the foundry's work force, like so many throughout the nation, was on a shortened workweek.

The outbreak of World War II saw the company immediately join the national defense effort, quadrupling its work force to turn out thousands of gun tube forgings for the army. Plant facilities doubled in 1942 as the U.S. Defense Plant Corporation built new structures to accommodate increased production, buildings later purchased by Adirondack Steel Casting Company. The Korean War brought further expansion as the plant manufactured thousands of tons of cast armor for use on fighting vehicles.

Above:
An aerial view of Adirondack Steel Casting Company's plant in Watervliet shows its essentially rural setting.
Top:
In a manner similar to that used 60 years ago, Adirondack molders "ram up," tamping the molding sand in one step toward producing a casting.

Constant technical improvement was accelerated by the demands of modern warfare and by the growing sophistication of the world market. The castings of six decades ago are crude compared to those of today, which average 500 pounds and are X-rayed, analyzed, and tested at every stage to ensure a sound, high-quality product. Nearly 400 employees—many of them second-generation Adirondack Steel Casting workers—are involved in pattern-making, molding, melting, and inspection. Adirondack's machine shop, a capital-intensive 18,000 square feet of turret lathes, boring mills, planers, and drill presses, contains one of the largest milling machines in the East to machine the locomotive "trucks."

In 1957, Consolidated Foundries and Manufacturing Company of Albany and Chicago bought Adirondack and began to broaden its market area. Adirondack manufactured subway and commuter car castings, which opened national and foreign markets in the 1960s. In the '70s, the company entered the mass market for steel castings for derricks, off-shore drilling, and scrap reclamation equipment and valves. New techniques and new technology at Adirondack Steel Casting Company answer stringent customer specifications and an ever-increasing corporate insistence on quality. Now they are just starting production of the vacuum process molded castings.

ALBANY CALCIUM LIGHT COMPANY

When founder Byron M. McCarty began lighting theaters in 1878, Albany Calcium Light Company was born in the limelight. Calcium lighting was used to create spotlights and special stage effects, burning a lime pencil to an incandescence reflected onto the stage by condensing lenses. Then headquartered at 51 Beaver Street, McCarty was providing chemically generated lighting a year before Thomas Edison successfully designed a practical incandescent bulb. McCarty also provided fireworks and display lighting for four decades of political rallies, using projectors to flash election results on a screen from one building to another.

Offices at 26 William Street, behind the Trimble Opera House, became the home of Albany Calcium Light Company in 1880. The firm continued to specialize in projection devices and stereopticons and was increasingly noted for its electrical display work as electricity came into general use. As the employment of electricity increased, so did the use of high-pressure gases for welding, a natural area of expansion for a business already using tanks of gas to fuel lighting. The growing welding trade became more important, although Albany Calcium Light continued in theater lighting, now electrically.

Louis E. Halter became a partner in Albany Calcium Light Company in 1918 and a year later the firm became area distributor for Prest-O-Lite welding equipment and batteries. Prest-O-Lite products included pressurized gas tanks, originally used in lights on motor vehicles and later with welding equipment—the smallest tanks still bear the designation "MC" for "motorcycle." The year 1924 saw a need for more space resolved with a move to 287 Hudson Avenue, where Albany Calcium Light would remain until 1972. The company became Prest-O-Lite's major distributor between Syracuse and New York City in 1927; a newspaper advertisement of the '20s proclaimed Albany Calcium Light the "Headquarters of the Oxy-Acetylene Industry."

Above:
In 1932, an Albany Calcium Light Company delivery van joined the parade celebrating the opening of the Port of Albany.
Top:
A Mack Bulldog truck owned by Albany Calcium Light Company pulls out of the shop at 287 Hudson Avenue (circa 1924).

As electrical welding grew more important to the welding industry, the company took care to remain abreast of new technology, demonstrating a marked ability to adapt to changing times. It remained a family enterprise and at one point there were three employees working—Lloyd Smith, James Wittemer, and W.B. White—who each had 50 years' service with the company. James K. Sector entered the firm as a bookkeeper in 1951 and became its president in 1969, keeping Albany Calcium Light Company on-line with the rapid development of welding techniques and technology. One of the oldest welding supply houses in the United States, dealing in electrical and gas welding equipment and safety apparatus, Albany Calcium Light Company has remained a regional firm, shipping to manufacturers in distant locations but doing the bulk of its business within 150 miles of its home at 260 Osborne Road in Loudonville. A third generation, John A. Sector, son of company president James K. Sector and great-nephew of Louis E. Halter, now serves Albany Calcium Light Company as the firm enters its second century of operation.

ALBANY INTERNATIONAL

The enterprise began modestly, with an investment of $40,000 made by the descendant of an Albany family long involved with industry, the pragmatic son of a physician, and the president of the Albany Savings Institution, for the purpose of manufacturing papermaker felts. Albany Felt Company, a closely held corporation owned by Parker Corning, James W. Cox, Jr., and Selden E. Marvin, had its organizational meeting in March 1895. The three shareholders agreed to lease 19 Thacher Street in northern Albany, and to hire Duncan Fuller, an experienced feltmaker, as superintendent. Within a year they had 30 employees making felts used to press excess water from raw paper stock and impart a finish to the sheet. Cox was president and manager of the new company, Marvin its secretary. Cox remained with the organization until 1918, Marvin until 1899. Between 1895 and 1906, the firm's paid-in capital was increased to $150,000, representing 1,500 shares of stock.

So successful was Albany Felt that by 1901 it had outgrown its facility on Thacher Street. Six acres on Broadway were acquired, north of the Albany city limits, and a new building was erected. Designed to withstand the vibrations of the heavy machinery, the Broadway plant was constructed from 275,000 bricks and 700,000 feet of lumber, spanned two acres, and contained a 100-foot chimney. About 150 employees worked there when it opened, a fivefold increase in the work force in six years.

By 1908, Albany Felt Company was marketing papermaker felts in Europe, Canada, Japan, and Mexico, and its 7-year-old Broadway plant had already become too small. Expansion was again necessary, but this time the Broadway site allowed for growth; all company manufacturing operations were conducted there until 1946, and it remained adequate as corporate headquarters until 1976.

When James W. Cox, Jr. retired in 1918, Parker Corning became president of Albany Felt Company, remaining in that post until the early 1940s. Other obligations, including service as a congressman, persuaded Corning to engage Charles P. Drumm as general manager in 1919. During Drumm's tenure, the Broadway mill was expanded several times, and when he became chairman of the board in 1945, Albany Felt was on the eve of its first venture outside Albany. This enterprise was the acquisition in 1946 of a mill in North Monmouth, Maine, in order to expand the company's production of flannel for baseball uniforms and of its other industrial fabrics.

Employees of the Albany Felt Company are shown sorting wool in this 1930 photograph.

Many years of sustained growth followed under the guidance of presidents Lewis R. Parker and John C.

Standish. In 1951, construction of the first plant outside the United States was begun at Cowansville, Quebec. As other facilities were established and foreign sales grew, Albany Felt eventually operated plants in the United States and 12 other nations: Canada, Mexico, Brazil, Australia, Great Britain, France, West Germany, Sweden, Norway, Finland, Switzerland, and Italy. This expansion into other countries brought the company closer to world markets for its products.

Albany ties remained important for Albany Felt, as the '60s proved a time to acknowledge a new and important stage in the company's development. Under the leadership of Albany Felt president Everett C. Reed, Globe Woven Belting Company of Buffalo was acquired in 1965. This was followed by the 1969 acquisition of Appleton Wire Works of Appleton, Wisconsin, the largest U.S. maker of forming fabrics for paper machines. The year 1969 also saw the acquisition of Crellin Plastics Company of Chatham, New York, manufacturer of industrial plastic products, and of a Swedish firm, Nordiska Maskinfilt of Halmstad, Scandinavia's leading supplier of papermaker felts. Large-scale expansion made Albany Felt the world's foremost supplier of paper machine fabrics; the largest maker of tennis ball cover cloth; and a major manufacturer of lightweight conveyor belts, fabric components for business machines, precision-molded industrial plastics, and filtration and pollution control fabrics.

This majestic house, called Fernbrook, was built by Senator Henry M. Sage about 1890. After painstaking remodeling, it today serves as a sophisticated, yet gracious command post for Albany International.

Recognition of the company's worldwide expansion and product diversification came in 1969 with the selection of a new name, Albany International Corp. For several years Albany International shared operational quarters with Albany Felt Company, now retitled the Felt Division. In a reaffirmation of its area ties, Albany International in 1976 moved its headquarters into the Henry Sage estate in Menands, a handsome 1890s structure sensitively renovated to guarantee its architectural integrity while meeting corporate needs.

Albany International became a public corporation in 1972, and by 1980 had approximately 2,500 shareholders who together owned over 6.7 million shares. Each of the firm's original 1,500 shares was equal to 4,620 shares by 1980, due to the many stock dividends and splits over the years. Employing a worldwide total of 6,511 people, Albany International locally maintains the Felt Division in Albany and Hoosick Falls, the Engineered Systems Division in Glens Falls, and the Molding Division in Chatham. The company's operating income for 1980 was over $49 million; net sales amounted to nearly $366 million. Albany International retains sturdy Albany roots, remaining in its Hudson River Valley birthplace while ever expanding its world trade. The company's name—Albany International—is itself a statement of its heritage.

ALBANY MEDICAL CENTER

A 1756 British Army map of Albany shows a building labeled "Hospital" near the British barracks in the vicinity of Chapel Street. One observer wrote: "It is situated on an eminence overlooking the city. It is two stories high, having a wing at each end and a piazza in front, above and below. It contains 40 wards, capable of accommodating 500 patients, besides the rooms appropriated to the use of the surgeons and other officers." This hospital did not long endure; it was, in fact, burned to salvage the iron nails used in its construction. Albany medicine then returned to a casual arrangement of home remedies, poor sanitation, superstition, and doctors educated at Edinburgh or who had "read medicine" and set up practice. Albany's 1813 city directory, lamentably, lists one man as a "cancer doctor." The Albany Medical Center itself began with one man's concern with providing competent medical care for the Albany area.

Above:
Albany Medical College opened its doors on January 2, 1839. The city government donated the empty Lancaster School building to house the fledgling college.
Left:
An imposing portrait of Albany Medical College's founder, first president, and professor of surgery, Alden March, presides over an 1890s classroom in the former Lancaster School building.

Albany Medical College

Dr. Alden March arrived in Albany in 1820 after graduating from Brown University. Within a year March was operating a tiny school, teaching anatomy and urging the establishment of an Albany school of medicine. His urging went unheeded by the community. March petitioned the state legislature, only to be stymied by the state's existing medical schools. Aided by his brother-in-law Dr. James Armsby, a persuasive public speaker, and by catastrophic cholera epidemics in 1832 and 1834, March was subsequently rewarded by a serious public interest in his efforts culminating when Albany Medical College opened on January 2, 1839.

With 57 students enrolled, Dr. March was college president and professor of surgery, Dr. Armsby professor of anatomy and physiology. The city of Albany donated the former Lancaster School building to house the fledgling institution. In 1849, March, Armsby, and their Albany supporters incorporated Albany Hospital, initiating the perpetual college-hospital clinical affiliation. March died in 1869. In 1873 Dr. Armsby brought about an affiliation of the medical school with Union University.

A faculty of more than 500 full- and part-time instructors evolved from the inaugural pair of doctors, the college remaining private, nondenominational, and coeducational. Its 1980 student body numbered about 650, the medical class of 1984 just 128 carefully selected admissions. Distinguished alumni are many: John Swinburne, 1846, Port of New York health officer and congressman, commemorated by Albany's Swinburne Park; James H. Salisbury, 1850, nutritionist for whom the Salisbury Steak was named; Theobald Smith, 1883, bacteriologist, discoverer of disease transmission by insect carrier; Thomas Salmon, 1899, National Committee for Mental Hygiene director and senior consultant in neuropsychiatry to Pershing's American expeditionary forces; and Kenneth D. Blackfan, Harvard Medical School professor of pediatrics, 1923-1941.

Faculty and staff tripled after World War II as students increased in number; Albany Medical College doubled in physical size with the 1963 construction of its $5-million, 5-story Neil Hellman Medical Research Building, housing research and student laboratories and related facilities, administrative offices, classrooms, and bookstore. Its Clinical Studies Center revolutionized medical management of trauma victims. Tremendous growth in size and medical sophistication has marked Albany Medical College's more than 140 years of progress. Growth and time have not compromised quality.

Albany Medical Center Hospital

At the persistent urging of Doctors March and Armsby, Albany Hospital was incorporated in 1849, the first private hospital in upstate New York. A fund drive three years later raised $9,000 for the purchase of the former Albany County Jail at Eagle and Daniels streets and Albany Hospital moved there from its rented home at Lydius and Dove streets. Opened to patients in 1854, the new hospital was plagued with debts, its board of governors forced to borrow $2,000 to meet them in 1855.

The Civil War required construction of hospital barracks to house wounded soldiers transported by steamboat up the Hudson River. Extra activity prompted expansion, and by 1872 additions had been built and a neighboring house acquired for use as an eye and ear infirmary and general dispensary. With a capacity of 131 beds, and a staff of 21 doctors (three of them residents), Albany Hospital's financial difficulties were unabated and in June of 1877 the sheriff padlocked its doors for unpaid debts of $5,000. It was six months before Albany Hospital reopened, obligations, except for a $24,000 mortgage, paid by "the medical gentlemen connected with the hospital."

Bottom:
In 1899 the Albany Hospital moved from a renovated county jail building on the corner of Eagle and Daniels streets to new facilities at the site of the present Albany Medical Center Hospital on New Scotland Avenue. This photograph, taken eight years later, shows a clinic setting at the hospital and the method by which medical students learned their profession around the turn of the century.
Below:
The Park Commission granted the hospital a parcel of land on New Scotland Avenue, and on this property a pavilion-type hospital was opened on May 15, 1899. The building included a wing for the nursing school which the hospital had commissioned in 1896.

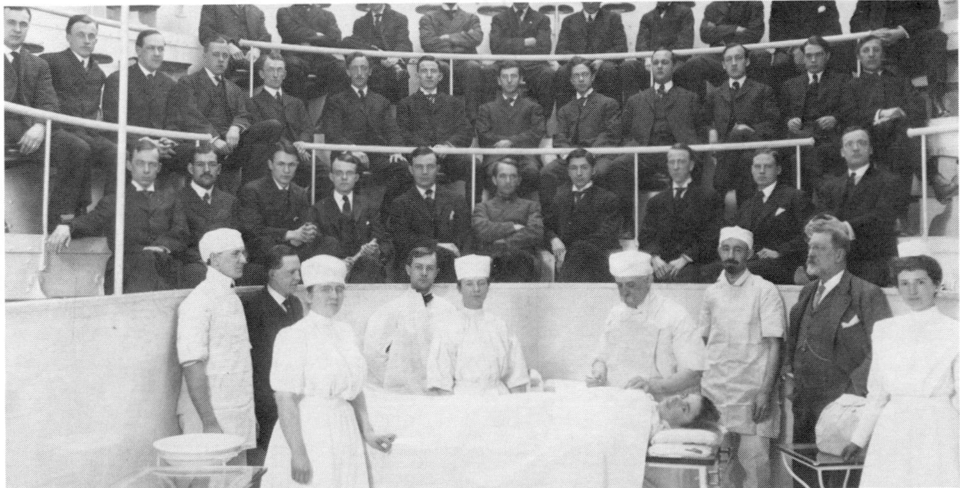

Moving to New Scotland Avenue in 1899 was costly, despite $230,000 raised by the people of Albany and an outright gift of the land by the City Park Commission. The new, pavilion-type hospital included a wing for the nursing school established three years earlier. Further facilities rapidly appeared—Mosher Memorial Pavilion, the first psychiatric unit attached to an American general hospital, in 1902; and 12 months later, Hun Memorial Tuberculosis Pavilion. Expansion weakened Albany Hospital's financial standing to the point where it had to appeal to city and county "to pay the cost of board of all patients sent to the hospital." Dismal finances were balanced by distinguished public service, including formation of Base Hospital 33 by Albany Hospital staff during World War I.

In 1928 came a fundamental step in the creation of Albany Medical Center, an agreement with Albany Medical College providing for construction of its new building at the hospital's west end. A new, main hospital wing was also then constructed. The Depression left many Albanians unable to pay medical bills during the 1930s; only a large bequest willed to the hospital saved it from insolvency. World War II ended the Depression and saw Albany Hospital medical people serving in the North African and Italian campaigns, nucleus of the 33rd General Hospital Unit.

Albany Hospital added new surgical, emergency, and outpatient facilities in 1951, increasing patient capacity by one-third. It became Albany Medical Center Hospital in 1961. Significant additions were completed in 1965 and 1973, making AMCH one of the largest private hospitals in upstate New York. From a makeshift hospital housed in a former jail has emerged a modern medical center hospital which, by virtue of its affiliation with Albany Medical College, is at the hub of a health care network that includes 50 hospitals and nearly 3,000 physicians in its 20-county service area. Today one of the top medical centers in New York State, Albany Medical Center plays a central role in medical care, teaching, and research in Albany, northeastern New York, and western New England.

ALBANY PORT DISTRICT COMMISSION

The Hudson River has been the great artery of Albany's existence. In an age when most roads were ruts full of stumps, the river was a cheap, efficient means of access to the interior of New York. In 1748, Peter Kalm wrote: "... the yachts which ply between Albany and New York ... bring from Albany boards or planks, and all sorts of timber, flour, pease, and furs. ... The situation of Albany is very advantageous in regard to trade. ... The vessels ... may come pretty near the shore in order to be laden. ..." The situation is little different today. The Port of Albany retains its geographic importance as a major facility on navigable water, readily connected by rail and highway to a market encompassing the U.S. Northeast and Atlantic Canada.

Early port facilities for Albany were stone docks constructed in 1766. Steam navigation and the opening of the Erie Canal amplified the need for dockage, and a "Great Pier" 4,400 feet long was built in 1825. The development of railroads served to extend the delivery capability of the port. When the present port opened in 1932, it was in answer to an ambition already a century old, and served, within a 250-mile radius, a third of the nation's people.

In 1931, before it officially opened, the port served 600 vessels, 71 of them international, after more than 21.5 million cubic yards of river bottom was dredged to deepen the Hudson. Over 20,000 piles were driven; initial construction alone cost $1.25 million. About 25 miles of railroad track provided transportation interface, and the world's largest single-unit grain elevator on navigable water was constructed.

The grain and corn of the Midwest continued to pass through the port until the St. Lawrence Seaway opened in 1959, a time when Albany served 200 vessels a year. Once the seaway was built, the bulk of Albany's trade gradually shifted to the industrial Northeast. Following a $19-million New York State development program, the 35 private firms leasing port district space invested $50 million of their own, demonstrating their faith in the port.

While the annual number of ships visiting the Port of Albany has declined, revenues and tonnage handled have steadily increased. Although fewer ships call, they have far greater carrying capacities, bringing in bananas, automobiles, molasses, and wood pulp, loading scrap metal and grain. Ships from Singapore, Honduras, Norway, Belgium, Italy, the Republic of China, and Great Britain dock in Albany. The old carrying trade of the Hudson River sloops has died away, but the Port of Albany maintains brisk activity as the emporium for the Northeast, handling goods worth over $862 million in 1979 and employing 1,311 persons.

A look north along the Albany side of the Port of Albany shows some of the facts of its current existence—huge oil storage tanks and a ship disgorging some of the 30,000 German automobiles that pass through the port into the U.S. market each year.

ALBANY SAVINGS BANK

A local silversmith, Joseph Rice, made the first deposit. By the end of Saturday's business, June 10, 1820, 19 other depositors had joined him, for a total of $527. These depositors were not Albany's rich and prosperous, but were instead the very people Albany Savings Bank had newly incorporated to serve, "tradesmen, laborers, miners, servants, and others. . . ." The first president of this new bank was Stephen VanRensselaer, the last area patroon; the other officers were wealthy Albanians with the particular idea of instilling working people with a sense of thrift and a means of securing their future. When Albany Savings Bank was incorporated as a mutual institution for the service of its depositors, it was only the second such savings bank in New York State. Today, it is Albany's oldest and largest.

Albany Savings Bank published its first annual report in 1821, showing a total of $19,497 in deposits, $19 deposited by slaves and more than $5,000 by women. In eight years, the bank had outgrown its original space and moved, to share quarters with the Commercial Bank of Albany. By 1844, the trustees had resolved that Albany Savings Bank would be open Wednesday afternoons exclusively to do business with the women of Albany. Five years later, the bank had deposits totaling $707,595; Albany iron manufacturer John Townsend was its president, the working people of Albany still its clientele.

Above:
Albany Savings Bank's modern headquarters, located at State and North Pearl streets, were designed by Gruen Associates as an integral part of the renovation of downtown Albany.
Right:
On the evening of June 10, 1820, a local silversmith, Joseph Rice, made the first deposit at the just-opened Albany Savings Bank.

The year 1840 had seen Albany Savings Bank's Act of Incorporation amended to allow investment of funds received "or to loan the same upon bonds and mortgages." A people-oriented move, this has remained central to bank policy. During the next 140 years thousands of mortgages made home-ownership possible for Albanians. Low- and middle-income housing projects such as Mount Hope Drive and Interfaith Homes were financed, and the bank involved itself with urban renewal and community development projects, home improvement loans, and downtown rehabilitation efforts. In 1970, without government funds, Albany Savings Bank participated in the creation of Capital Housing Rehabilitation Corporation to preserve and restore neighborhoods and help develop pride and a sense of security in their population, people for whom home-ownership was before unlikely. Evidencing this commitment to the inner city, Albany Savings Bank in 1974 moved into its ultramodern offices at the corner of State and North Pearl streets, in downtown Albany.

Savings Bank retained the trust of Albany's financially troubled depositors; and between 1929 and 1940, the bank increased its assets by $5 million. Albany Savings Bank has come a long way since silversmith Joseph Rice made his first deposit in 1820. Total assets in 1970 exceeded $350 million, and in 1981, the bank had 22 branch offices—three in Albany, one each in Guilderland and Colonie—and total assets of $1.3 billion. Albany's largest financial institution, it has paid its depositors a dividend annually for 160 years.

AMERICANA INN

At first glance the traveler would be reminded of an earlier day, a sanitary version, perhaps, of colonial Albany, an urban square in some late colonial East Coast city. This pervasive colonial ambience is not accidental, but instead the artful, considered choice of John K. Desmond, Jr., managing partner of Village Square. Village Square, Inc. is in turn a corporate general partner in the limited partnership of First Colonie Company, which does business as the Americana Inn, on Albany-Shaker Road.

When Desmond, who is president of Village Square, Inc., felt the need to seek new opportunities in the hotel field, his first choice, following considerable research, was Albany. Desmond, a self-made individual, in 1974 decided to provide deluxe accommodations in a beautiful facility. The most prominent and distinctive feature of the new hotel was to be its courtyard, mainly designed by Desmond, with a sliding dome which, in season, can be opened to admit air and light. Opening on the sides of the courtyard area are five meeting and dining rooms, their entrances camouflaged as colonial-period shops with windows displaying antique wares. The windows and French doors of some of the Americana's 178 rooms and nine suites open out onto the square, simulating Georgian row houses.

The Americana Inn maintains a healthy 83 percent occupancy rate, 56,000 room-nights annually, much of this due to the consistent flow of corporate travelers and the immediate proximity of the Albany County Airport. The Americana Inn dominates the hotel market in quality services, and its quiet cachet of luxury includes bellman and room service. Over 170 Americana employees, many in colonial-style costume, service local business meetings, an extensive banquet trade, and the conventions of Albany-based firms as well. Pool, saunas, and whirlpool are all available to guests. The courtyard's gazebo has been the site of a number of weddings, and the trademark courtyard is itself planted in season with appropriate flowers and greenery.

The Americana's decor is comfortably elegant. Reevaluation of the decor is continual and the hotel bears testimony to its meticulous upkeep, redecoration, and updating. General manager Michael Chain, a professional hotel man with Americana Inn, is treasurer of the New York State Hotel and Motel Association and is active in the Albany County Convention and Visitors Bureau. At the Americana, Chain keeps hotel rooms, meeting and banquet facilities, and a la carte dining and drinking at a high standard. The friendly staff provides gracious, unobtrusive service, adding to the overall warmth of the hotel environment.

Left:
The interior of the Americana Inn replicates a formal Georgian atmosphere through the use of carefully chosen furnishings. Several working fireplaces enhance the decor.

Right:
Sunlight spills through the dome into the Americana Inn's courtyard, its best-known feature.

ATLANTIC CEMENT COMPANY

Above:
A 420-foot ocean-going barge takes on a cargo of portland cement in the Hudson River's tradition of waterborne commerce. The Hudson was a vital determining factor when Atlantic Cement Company was searching for a site for its plant.
Top:
This recent aerial photograph of the largest portland cement plant in North America reveals the massive scale of Atlantic's facilities.

Although the Atlantic Cement Company only established its Ravena plant in 1962, in one respect it may be the Albany area's oldest business. The basis for its annual production of 1.8 million tons of portland cement is Devonian limestone, deposited 500 million years ago, when the earth's dominant life forms were mollusks. Early during the European settlement of the Hudson River Valley, this limestone was burned to make mortar for bonding bricks and stone, then the prevalent building material. While cement was employed during the height of the Roman Empire, it was not until after the Civil War that it came into general use in America. By the 1890s, portland cement was being manufactured in the United States and was in common use in the construction industry.

Establishment of the Atlantic Cement Company in Ravena was due to fortunate geological and topographical features—extensive deposits of exploitable limestone coupled with a nearby navigable river, the Hudson. Atlantic Cement's giant mining and manufacturing operation radically departed from traditional practices in the portland cement industry. Prior to the Ravena plant, 15 miles south of Albany, the industry had generally manufactured for markets within a 250-mile radius of its plants. As construction costs rose, so did the cost of this traditional marketing scheme. Atlantic Cement Company built one immense plant, then the world's largest, producing 5,000 tons per day and serving the entire East Coast through distribution centers in major port cities from Boston, Massachusetts, to Florida. The cement reaches this extensive area via Atlantic Cement's fleet of the world's largest ocean-going barges.

The Ravena plant is highly automated, with miles of conveyor belts and huge mechanical systems. All processes are equipped to safeguard the environment—10 percent of the capital investment in the Ravena plant is in pollution-control apparatus. A model operation by state and federal environmental standards, Atlantic Cement has received the Clean Air Award, the National Environmental Quality Award, and the U.S. Environmental Protection Agency's Flag of Achievement.

In addition to its commitment to environmental quality, Atlantic Cement actively participates in community life, bringing educational programs to area schools and contributing to the support of many cultural activities. Atlantic Cement Company, a direct descendant of the original Hudson Valley mining and building industries, remains dependent on river, resources, and people.

BANKERS TRUST COMPANY OF ALBANY, N.A.

Perhaps it was typical of the optimistic mood of Andrew Jackson's America that the 1838 charter for the Albany Exchange Bank, ancestor of Bankers Trust Company of Albany, was for 662 years, with option to increase its capital by 3,000 percent. Characteristic of this bank was its board of directors—community-conscious men, leading merchants, doctors, and lawyers, such as Robert Hunter, co-founder of the Albany *Daily News* in 1834, James McNaughton and Henry Green, two physicians instrumental in combating the terrible Albany cholera epidemic of 1832, and General Samuel Stephens, one of the state's most influential lawyers.

Banking then was a risky venture and the fledgling enterprise encountered all the difficulties of the age; one investment wiped out a sixth of its capital. The year 1861 saw Albany Exchange Bank solvent only due to the continual prudence exercised by its officers. During the Civil War, Albany Exchange Bank was an agent for the U.S. Treasury, distributing Union government loans. The bank shared in the war boom and the judgment of its officers proved sound. By 1865, a 54 percent profit was realized on its stock, which had been nearly non-marketable four years before. The Albany Exchange Bank became the National Exchange Bank at this time.

When the National Exchange Bank was reorganized in 1885, C.P. Williams, who had been an alderman, a candidate for Congress, and a student of European banking systems, was chosen for president. With the aid of Lansing Merchant and A.V. DeWitt, affluent Albanians, the bank earned a 20 percent surplus on its stock by 1897.

Bellwether of the 20th century was change. Mergers of the National Exchange Bank, the First National Bank of Albany, and the Albany Trust Company resulted in the formation of the First Trust Company of Albany in 1926. Throughout the expansion the officers continued to be men with community ties who gradually created a modern corporation. These men pioneered branch offices, first in Albany's largely Italian south end, recruiting Italian-speaking employees to provide trademark friendly service, and in Central Avenue's commercial center, developing special business services.

Edward S. Rooney, a lawyer who had been one of America's youngest bank directors, became president of First Trust in 1944. His talent for selecting executive talent would be largely responsible for the tremendous expansion of the bank after World War II.

Rooney and his officers pioneered in many areas that today are considered routine—small and personal loans, bank charge accounts in retail stores, personal checking, specialized services for business depositors, even Albany's first bank parking lot.

In 1966, First Trust Company of Albany participated in the organization of Bankers Trust New York Corporation, a registered bank holding company. Today, Bankers Trust Company of Albany, N.A., the largest upstate affiliate of Bankers Trust New York Corporation, remains steadfastly Albanian, continuously and progressively serving the area with which it has been proudly identified since 1838.

The "Marble Pillar Building," at the corner of State Street and Broadway, was originally the Trowbridge Museum and later used as an office for the stagecoach line of Thorpe and Sprague. Today as headquarters of Bankers Trust Company of Albany, the historic structure adds to the architectural integrity of downtown Albany.

BLUE CROSS OF NORTHEASTERN NEW YORK

In 1929 at Baylor University in Texas, Justin Ford Kimball devised a prepaid health program in which members paid a monthly sum to the University Hospital, in turn receiving health care as the need arose. During the Depression, many Americans were unable to pay hospital bills and Kimball's plan was eagerly emulated across the nation. By 1935, 11 plans existed and six more were under development. That year, a group of concerned citizens in Albany advanced a similar program for financing health care locally.

Conceived as a nonprofit community venture providing access to health care for members in the immediate Albany area, the Associated Hospital Service of the Capital District was established in July 1936 by four hospitals—Albany, St. Peter's, Memorial, and Brady Maternity. Each contributed $2,500 for start-up costs and the Plan began serving Albany, Schenectady, and Rensselaer counties from a tiny State Street office. By year's end, there were 5,000 members enrolled and 33 claims had been paid. By 1937, 10 more counties were added to comprise the 13-county area now served by Blue Cross of Northeastern New York. Two years later, the Plan officially adopted the Blue Cross emblem.

The American Hospital Association in 1938 formed the Council of Hospital Service Plans, forerunner of today's Blue Cross and Blue Shield Associations. By 1941, typical coverage included 60 days of hospitalization. Interest was growing in similar plans to cover the cost of physician care. In 1946, a nonprofit Blue Shield Plan—"the Doctors' Plan"—began, administered at first by Albany Blue Cross. At that time, the Albany Plan had 300,000 subscribers.

Growth by the Plans has been almost constant. In 1956, coverage for military dependents began under the CHAMPUS Program. Administration of the New York State Employees Health Insurance Program started in 1957, federal employees chose Blue Cross in 1960, and administration of medicare began in 1965. Such dramatic expansion required the Plans' move, first from the Rice building at 135 Washington Avenue out to 1215 Washington in 1966 and, finally, to the present building on New Scotland Avenue in 1971.

Above:
The first chief executive officer of Albany Blue Cross was Edward R. Evans, who held that position from 1936 to 1955.
Above Right:
The Standard Building, at 112 State Street, held the first small office of Blue Cross of Northeastern New York.
Below:
Blue Cross and Blue Shield of Northeastern New York moved into its new Slingerlands building in 1971.

As the '60s drew to a close, a new prescription drug program was unveiled and development of major medical, dental, and other programs commenced. A health maintenance organization, initiated by Albany Blue Cross in the 1960s, coalesced as the Capital Area Community Health Plan by 1976. An alcoholism program introduced in 1978 was a state first and a national pioneer. Concern with rising health costs contributed to the development of numerous cost-cutting procedures such as pre-admission testing, second surgical opinions, and ambulatory surgery.

Edward R. Evans was the first chief executive of Albany Blue Cross. He retired in 1955 and was replaced by Ralph Hammersley, Jr. Upon Mr. Hammersley's retirement in 1976, Dr. Clifton C. Thorne and Walter E. Owens were named presidents of Blue Cross and Blue Shield of Northeastern New York, respectively.

Dramatic enrollment gains by the Albany Plans, in poor times and prosperous, have confirmed the validity of the original Blue Cross concept. By 1980, the Plans enrolled more than 800,000 subscribers, representing nearly 80 percent of their 13-county population.

BOYD PRINTING COMPANY, INC.

William Boyd began his business with a treadle-operated printing press and a half-dozen employees in 1889. That first year, he was a job printer, but in 1890, using his unsophisticated equipment, he undertook the printing of a book for Matthew Bender & Company, beginning a close association of the two firms which has endured for more than nine decades. Since that time, "No single day has passed without some Bender publication being in that shop."

Partial interest in Boyd Printing Company was acquired in 1919 by Thomas J. Lynch, who eventually assumed ownership of the entire firm; his family continues to own and operate the company today. In 1923, Lynch moved Boyd Printing to larger quarters at 372-374 Broadway, opposite the D & H Building. In keeping with the company's family image, Lynch's son-in-law, Princeton graduate Henry Quellmalz, became his assistant in 1944, when the firm employed about 40 people. When Lynch died a decade later, control of Boyd Printing Company passed to his daughter Marion Lynch Quellmalz, the presidency to Henry Quellmalz.

Fresh management gradually brought change. In 1958 Boyd Printing Company purchased a 40,000-square-foot Sheridan Avenue building, which it outgrew just seven years later. The year 1965 saw construction of a 24,000-square-foot adjoining structure. Carl Johnson came to the firm as vice-president in charge of sales in 1969. Husband of Lynn Quellmalz, he completed his army service and joined the family business. Jane Quellmalz became vice-president of the Q Corporation in 1973, an independent firm headquartered in Boyd's Sheridan Avenue complex. The Q Corporation reflects Boyd's far-reaching interests and is United States sales representative for the World Health Organization of Geneva, Switzerland. The Q Corporation also supplies computerized subscription fulfillment services and owns Johnson Press, another old Albany printing company. In 1978, Jane Quellmalz became both Q Corporation president and assistant to the president of Boyd Printing.

Above:
The modern Sheridan Avenue complex occupied by Boyd Printing Company is many times the size of the firm's original facility.

Left:
Boyd Printing Company occupied this brick factory building at the corner of Montgomery and Columbia streets from 1889 to 1923.

Boyd Printing Company expanded rapidly during the '70s, with both long-established Albany clients, like Matthew Bender & Company, and contracted work from the United Nations. Forty-five scholarly journals, largely in the field of social work and sociology, are printed at Boyd; and in 1980, 134 employees were working there. John Carey, former Boyd apprentice and husband of Jane Quellmalz, assumed the position of plant superintendent in 1979. That same year, Lynn Quellmalz Johnson joined the Q Corporation on a part-time basis.

Boyd Printing Company reaffirmed its desire to remain in downtown Albany by purchasing additional adjacent space on Sheridan Avenue in 1979. Of two buildings on this property, one yielded to a new loading dock, parking lot, and 3,500 square feet of storage; the other was utilized as storage and is projected for operational use. Boyd Printing Company has remained an Albany firm, near its principal local customers, while printing many national professional publications.

CAPITAL NEWSPAPERS GROUP

America's first national news dispatch over Samuel F.B. Morse's revolutionary telegraph system was sent in 1847 by an *Albany Knickerbocker* reporter listening to a speech by President John Tyler in New York City, to an editor on Albany's "newspaper row," Beaver Street.

Editor Hugh J. Hastings recognized before anyone else the potential in Morse's invention, and it was his Albany readers who first benefited from a system that would shortly revolutionize communications.

Less than a decade later, the somber citizens of America's oldest incorporated city woke up to find yet another newspaper, the *Albany Morning Times,* being hawked on the streets. A hundred years ago there were as many as a dozen newspapers competing at one time, and in the course of the century, more than 60 materialized, then disappeared. But what was unique, a first among the 60, was the *Albany Morning Times*'s avowed editorial position.

Its slogan was "Independence now, independence forever," an attitude and philosophy that survived with the merger of the successful *Times* with the *Albany Evening Union* in 1891, through acquisition by William Randolph Hearst in 1924, to the present.

This same commitment to objectivity, with a continuing eye for innovation, was also the *Albany Knickerbocker*'s credo under Hugh Hastings in a day when the press was often scurrilous, and "news" was comprised of clippings from out-of-town papers.

Among the *Albany Times-Union*'s luminaries was an editor who also served as governor. He was Martin H. Glynn, a native-born Irishman, like Hastings, who wrote and managed the paper from 1895 to shortly before his death in 1924. A civic-minded man, Glynn also served as congressman, state comptroller, lieutenant governor, and governor.

In 1937, the *Times-Union* became a morning paper, which it has remained. The same year, the Gannett Company of Rochester combined the *Knickerbocker Press* and *Albany Evening News,* which they had purchased in 1928, into the *Knickerbocker News.* The new combination was and is an afternoon daily. Eventually, growth forced the *Times-Union* to a move from Beaver Street to Sheridan Avenue, where the *Knickerbocker News* also moved upon its acquisition by the Hearst Corporation in 1960.

Even before the move to Sheridan Avenue, it was the dream of the then-publisher, Gene Robb, to move his newspapers to a central location within the Capital District, reflecting a commitment both to extensive state house coverage, of which the papers were justifiably proud, and to the needs of the myriad villages, towns, and cities that together comprise the Capital District. In 1970, his dream became a reality as his Capital Newspapers Group moved to a striking facility in Colonie, the geographical center of the region.

Capital Newspapers Group covers the major news events of the day with innovation and objectivity.

Just prior to the move, Capital Newspapers expanded with the purchase of Schenectady's afternoon daily, the *Union-Star,* which became an integral part of the *Knickerbocker News.* And on July 19, 1974, the weekly *Suns* were born under the aegis of publisher Robert J. Danzig. These three regionalized editions added a new hometown dimension to the Capital Newspapers Group.

The *Times-Union* and *Knickerbocker News* continually strive to be innovative. From the days of the telegraph to the age of computers, their philosophy has been a quest for excellence and service to the public.

THE DAVID M. CAREY INTERESTS

The Albany Hyatt Billiard Ball Company

Twelve thousand elephants were slaughtered every year to provide the ivory for the world's billiard balls at the height of the mid-19th century's billiard craze. As ivory grew more costly, one billiard ball firm offered a $10,000 prize for a successful ivory substitute. Albany printer John Wesley Hyatt sought that prize in 1868; his discovery was celluloid, the world's first plastic and a cornerstone of modern technology. Hyatt became, according to the Smithsonian Institution, "one of the most important men in the development of modern chemistry in the United States." Hyatt's discovery was accidential, but experimentation led to a number of uses, celluloid eventually being used for combs, photographic film, umbrella handles, and for the detachable celluloid shirt collars that made Troy the "Collar City."

Hyatt raised $2,000 from investors and borrowed work space in the Albany machine shop of Peter Kinnear. Kinnear made the molds for casting the celluloid, a flammable plastic, and although Hyatt's early billiard balls had an alarming tendency to explode on impact, Albany Billiard Ball Company was in business, the world's first plastics manufacturer. Kinnear purchased stock in Hyatt's venture, eventually gaining control as John Hyatt, unfortunate in his investments, encountered financial difficulties. Under Kinnear's management, the firm grew rapidly. Hyatt's celluloid composition billiard ball gained universal acceptance and was used by England's King Edward VII and by Kaiser Wilhelm II. Two generations of Kinnears followed Peter into the firm, the last selling the business in 1968.

Cheaper, foreign-made billiard balls flooded the U.S. market and Albany Hyatt Billiard Ball Company fell on hard times, nearly closing down under a succession of owners. In 1977 David M. Carey acquired the troubled firm and, employing new marketing principles, adjusted prices and once again became highly competitive. By 1981, Albany Hyatt Billiard Ball Company, one of the firms composing the David M. Carey Interests, was once more in financial good health, 113 years after John Hyatt gave birth to the Age of Plastics.

Above:
John Wesley Hyatt was a journeyman printer who tinkered with various inventions in his room at Hawk Street and Washington Avenue. He invented Ice Creepers (which attached to shoes) and manufactured Dominoes and Checkers there.
Below:
Architect Charles Ogden (1858-1931) designed the Albany Billiard Ball Company building for his father-in-law, Peter Kinnear, in 1890. The Delaware Avenue site remains the firm's headquarters. Both photos courtesy the Knickerbocker Press.

Pedersen Golf Corporation

The pioneer custom golf club maker in the United States, Pedersen Golf Corporation is one of the six oldest club-making companies in the nation. The Pedersen brothers founded their company in Mount Vernon, New York, in 1926, moving it to Connecticut four years later. The golf clubs Pedersen made were, and are, used by many of history's great golfing professionals. The company always made classical, high-quality clubs and emphasized a custom fit for the average golfers, who, the Pedersens felt, needed it most to enhance their playing abilities. In 1970 Pedersen was acquired by F.O. Mossberg Corporation, and in 1979 by David M. Carey, who promptly returned it to New York State. Applying the same management techniques which revived a faltering Albany Hyatt Billiard Ball Company, Carey continued Pedersen's innovative tradition.

THE CHASE MANHATTAN BANK

Aaron Burr and Alexander Hamilton—both men with Albany connections, Burr an Albany law practice, Hamilton a marriage to General Philip Schuyler's daughter—probably agreed on only one thing, in addition to their dislike for one another. In 1799, both men served on a citizens' committee which endorsed establishment of a private company to provide New York City with clean, potable water. Chartered that year by the New York State Legislature, the president and directors of The Manhattan Company came into being, with a $2-million capital. Aaron Burr had insisted upon a proviso that the company's surplus capital could be used "in the purchase of public or other stocks, or in any other monied transactions or operations. . . ." Burr's provision was a major factor in the evolution of The Manhattan Company's banking activities.

By the 1820s, The Manhattan Company had laid 25 miles of pine water mains beneath the streets of New York City and was already heavily involved in banking. Predecessor of The Chase Manhattan Bank, The Manhattan Company played a considerable role in financing the Erie Canal, a commercial artery of enormous importance to the development of the state of New York, the nation, and to Albany in particular. In 1859, when the state legislature neglected to fund interest payments on Erie Canal bonds, The Manhattan Company provided what was then a huge loan—$385,000. Not only did this loan "save the State from the disgrace of having its obligations dishonored . . . ," but assured continual operation of the canal and the innumerable commercial interests dependent upon it.

State law allowed The Chase Manhattan Bank to open Albany offices in 1973. The Chase sought to stimulate area business by providing a wide range of banking services. During the next seven years, Chase loaned more than $300 million to businesses in the greater Albany vicinity, clients ranging from smaller family firms to major corporations. Establishing two Albany County branches among its 20 in upstate New York, Chase Manhattan continued as a partner in Albany's development, underwriting nearly $300 million in Albany city and county bonds during the 1970s, and advising the Albany Board of Education on its investments. Named New York State's transfer agent as early as 1818, Chase Manhattan Bank retains its close relationship with the state today as its fiscal agent and the bank is a leader in handling New York State's $3-billion annual Spring Note financing. Chase Manhattan supplies additional services to the New York State Tax Bureau, Department of Audit and Control, Workers' Compensation Board, and State Insurance and Common Retirement funds.

Above:
Today, The Chase Manhattan Bank in Albany occupies this building at 120 State Street.
Left:
Laborers install The Manhattan Company's wooden water mains along a New York street in this 1800 rendering.

Individual services are also extensive; checking and savings accounts, certificates of deposit, consumer loans, and residential mortgages are all available from Chase Manhattan Bank. As well as establishing a solid individual customer base, Chase has also encouraged its officers and employees to be active in the community. Continuing to work in partnership with Albany area businesses and citizens, Chase Manhattan Bank, from its upstate banking headquarters at 120 State Street, works for the continuing prosperity of the Albany area.

CHEMICAL BANK-CAPITAL REGION

The Marquis de Lafayette was due in town in two week's time when the Chemical Manufacturing Company opened its office of discount and deposit in the nation's commercial center, population 124,000. The commercial center was New York City, the year 1824, and the bank the city's 13th. In those hectic days of American banking, this new bank was immediately successful and 20 years later ceased manufacturing operations to become Chemical Bank.

Times were chaotic. Business and personal bankruptcies were frequent and financial panics of particular severity occurred in 1837, 1857, and 1873. Over 7,000 paper currencies, backed by almost as many banks, governments, and financial institutions, were in constant motion throughout the nation, a blizzard of often worthless banknotes. Through it all Chemical Bank earned a reputation for prudence and solidarity; in 1857 Chemical was the only New York City bank to redeem its notes in gold, gaining the nickname "Old Bullion."

This commemorative medallion was issued by Chemical Bank in 1954. The alchemist depicted is a symbolically apt representation of "Old Bullion."

Among the first banks to operate a national charter during the Civil War, it continued to do so until 1929, when it became state-chartered to expand its trust activities. Expansion thereafter was constant and rapid, with acquisitions, diversification in banking-related business activities, and international expansion; by 1981 Chemical had banking ties with 185 nations, branches in Belgium, Bahrain, West Germany, Great Britain, France, the Philippines, the Bahamas, South Korea, Singapore, Japan, Taiwan, Switzerland, Italy, Hong Kong, and Spain. The acquisition in 1954 of the Corn Exchange Bank and Trust Company made Chemical a large-scale retail bank. A merger in 1959 with New York Trust Company broadened trust and corporate banking capabilities.

In December 1973 Chemical Bank entered the Albany area with the purchase of a bank in Greenwich, New York. Nine months later Chemical's Albany office opened on the 10th floor of 41 State Street, symbolically far above street level, significant of Chemical's projected role in area wholesale banking. Local personnel was recruited and some staff brought up from the New York parent bank. The Albany unit operated independently until 1978, when it merged into Chemical Bank to become a district within Chemical's Metropolitan Division. Corporate customers comprise a full sample of Albany area businesses, reflecting a versatile lending policy; the average corporate client borrows $200,000. Statistical surveys commissioned by Chemical have allowed it to identify the advantages and needs of the business community.

By the end of 1980 Chemical Bank had assets of $41.3 billion and held deposits of $30.1 billion, ranking as the fifth largest bank in New York State, sixth in the United States. Chemical employs 36 persons in Albany, 18,000 worldwide. Advanced cash-management technology ties Chemical customers to the domestic and world financial picture, a tie made possible by Chem-Link, a computerized system keeping up-to-the-minute records of accounts, foreign currency exchange rates, and interest on notes, the full spectrum of corporate needs. The technology and fiscal resources of the parent bank can be rapidly harnessed to Albany's requirements; through carefully targeted, sensitive yet sensible marketing techniques, Chemical Bank is intimately linked with the financial needs of the Albany economy.

CIBRO PETROLEUM

The CIBRO story began in 1920, when Constantino Cirillo started delivering ice and coal by pushcart in Brooklyn, New York. The company has grown under family management, guided by an innovative philosophy to the point where it now is an integrated petroleum organization with sales in excess of one billion dollars that ranks with the middle range of Fortune 500 corporations.

The business grew throughout the '20s, and by 1930 there were four coal terminals in operation. One of them also supplied home heating oil, responding to the trend toward petroleum that would come to dominate the business. This trend spread not only to home heating but to business energy uses as well, and by 1950 Cirillo Brothers supplied industrial and commercial customers in the New York metropolitan area.

A turning point was evident in 1960. Coal had been phased out, and steps had been taken toward a major position in the petroleum distribution system. A deep-water terminal had been established in New York City, and a full range of products was available to customers in the metropolitan area. Negotiations had been initiated with the national oil companies then beginning to take control of developing their countries' resources, and longstanding contracts and relationships were developed.

Operations were expanded to Albany, New York, in 1965, the first major move outside the New York City market. The Albany complex began as a terminal for distributing Cirillo products and for throughput service. During the 1970s, a refinery was added, filling a capacity gap in that region and reinforcing the established reliability of oil product supplies for customers along the East Coast. The refinery was the first built in New York State in over half a century. At current full capacity, the Albany refinery can process approximately 1.5 million gallons of petroleum products per day. These products include industrial and utility-grade fuel oils, asphalt, home heating oil, jet fuel, and naphtha for petrochemical and gasoline feedstocks.

Above:
During the '70s, a refinery was added to the Albany complex of Cirillo Brothers, the first built in New York State in over 50 years. The company's name was shortened to CIBRO Petroleum at that time.
Right:
By the 1930s, when this photograph of the company fleet was taken, Cirillo Brothers operated four coal terminals. One of them also supplied home heating oil, responding to the trend toward petroleum that would come to dominate the business.

During this period, the name Cirillo Brothers was shortened to CIBRO. The CIBRO Group encompasses a variety of operating companies, each tailored to perform a specific function within the integrated organization. The substantial growth and diversification of the past six decades has been financed by internal funds coupled with major bank support, and the group remains in the hands of the Cirillo family. The third generation of Cirillo executives now is in charge of operations.

Despite its substantial size and diversity, CIBRO has retained the flexibility and sensitivity of a smaller organization. Management has been able to reach decisions and act swiftly, because it has remained close to its markets and is highly accessible to its customers.

These qualities of sensitivity and flexibility are at the core of CIBRO's innovations. Management has been able to develop an early sense of industry trends and changing customer needs and has been able to move expeditiously to deal with them.

Currently under study are plans to bring CIBRO full circle back to the coal of its origins—for example, coal transshipment centers for domestic and export needs, coal carrying vessels, and a new liquid fuel mixture of coal and oil (COM). With the advent of oil decontrol, expansion of Albany's downstream refinery processing capabilities has become a front burner consideration. Major expansion of gasoline distribution and the prospects of exploration for oil and gas is also of top priority.

Having built itself on the foundation of meeting customer needs, CIBRO will continue to strive for that goal through innovation.

FLAH'S, INC.

In 1915 brothers Albert and Paul Flah, with their cousin Joseph B. Hai, all natives of Damascus, opened their little store in Syracuse, launching Flah's. It was just a small lingerie shop then and Albert operated it while his two partners served in the U.S. Army during World War I. Upon his discharge in 1919 Joseph Hai came to Albany, which he had heard was New York's rising city. He soon opened Flah's first branch in the Ten Eyck Hotel building at 10 North Pearl Street.

Joseph Hai was able to bring his brother Paul to America to work with him in the store. Joseph also hired Mae Doling, a third-generation Albanian who persuaded him to let her buy dresses for the store, and soon expanded Flah's line of merchandise to include sportswear, millinery, coats, and accessories. Five years after he had hired her, she and Joseph Hai were married.

Flah's moved to its newly constructed 3-story building at 48 North Pearl Street in 1947, opportunity now arising to expand the store's line of quality merchandise and to handle increased numbers of customers, who typically included the wives of Governors Herbert Lehman and Thomas E. Dewey.

Mae and Joe Hai's only daughter, Barbara, grew up enamored with the world of retailing and business. Upon graduation from Cornell University, she worked in Hartford, Connecticut, for G. Fox & Company, and in 1951 married jeweler Bertram Freed of Marion, Ohio. Seven years later the Freeds and their three sons moved to Albany where their daughter was born, and Barbara and Bertram joined the family business, recently renamed Flah's of Albany, Inc., with Joseph Hai sole owner of the Albany store. Until 1956 the Syracuse and Albany stores had operated as a single company.

The death of Joseph Hai in 1959 left the Freeds and Paul Hai to operate Flah's, and Barbara and Bert Freed quickly expanded. In 1960 Flah's opened its first Albany branch at Stuyvesant Plaza, followed three years later by another in Poughkeepsie. In 1970 corporate headquarters shifted from downtown Albany to Albany-Shaker Road in Latham. By 1973, with eight Capital District and mid-Hudson region stores, the Freeds purchased the Syracuse Corporation from the heirs of Albert and Paul Flah. By 1981 a network of 10 stores—Colonie Center, Mohawk Mall, Stuyvesant Plaza, at the Atrium in Troy, Clifton Country Mall, two Syracuse stores, and three south of Albany—employed 450 regular full-time and part-time workers, operating as a family business although it became a public corporation in 1971. Now with a son of Barbara and Bert Freed in the firm, the Freeds maintain a tradition of community participation and the high standards that led *Harper's Bazaar* to cite Flah's as one of America's top 100 stores.

Above:
At a 1937 company picnic, Syracuse employees reflect on the possible agony of defeat while standing at the starting line.
Below:
Barbara Freed, president of Flah's, Inc., and Bertram Freed, chairman of the board.

FORT ORANGE PRESS, INC.

When August N. Brandow founded the Brandow Printing Company in 1883, it was during the dawn of mechanical typesetting. Brandow's shop at Maiden Lane and Dean Street had the first linotype machines in an Albany commercial shop, and later the first monotype, automatic press feeder, and other modern machinery. Brandow's bindery included the city's first automatic gold-laying stamping machine; the first quad-folding machine, folding 64 pages to the printed sheet; and the first continuous wire stitcher for pamphlets.

Brandow Printing Company's publishing phase adopted the trade name of "Fort Orange Press" in 1905 and gradually expanded its capabilities. By 1913, for example, Brandow became one of just 13 U.S. plants bonded to obtain the safety paper used in printing railroad interline passenger tickets and possessing the specialized equipment used to produce tickets.

Expansion required larger quarters and a new building was erected at State and Dean streets, linked to existing facilities at Dean Street and Hudson Avenue. Another structure at Broadway and Hudson Avenue was also leased. When the D&H Plaza was initiated in 1914, Brandow found itself forced to move its entire plant. A 5-story industrial building at Broadway and North Ferry Street was chosen.

Brandow's massive printing equipment was too much for the trucks of the day, but because the city's trolley tracks ran beneath the old plant, large openings were cut through its floors and machinery was lowered directly on to trolley cars. The trolleys carried the equipment up Broadway and over a spur line directly into the ground floor pressroom.

The Depression soon found the Brandow Printing Company with cash-flow problems, and subsequently went into receivership. A group of officers reorganized the management and, with court approval, the firm legally became the Fort Orange Press and prospered through its book, publication, and commercial business.

Fort Orange Press became noted throughout the Northeast for three significant specialties: legal, financial, and election printing, where accuracy is of paramount importance. The firm developed a 4-state reputation for excellent quality and dependable service in every phase of production. By 1975 larger, more modern facilities were again necessary if sophisticated equipment and continued growth in the commercial color market were to be accommodated. Following a move so carefully planned that no interruption of services occurred, Fort Orange Press moved to 31 Sand Creek Road in June 1975.

Below left:
In the center of this turn-of-the-century view can be seen the original site of Brandow Printing Company, later Fort Orange Press.
Below right:
Once the plant at Maiden Lane and Dean Street could no longer be used, Brandow Printing Company moved north on Broadway to the corner of North Ferry Street in 1914.
Bottom:
The move to this modern plant on Sand Creek Road in 1975 is indicative of the progressive attitude of current management toward the exciting technological advances in the printing industry.

THE GRIFFIN AGENCY

Since 1868 Massachusetts Mutual Life Insurance Company of Springfield, Massachusetts, has had only six general agents in Albany, and three of those were named Griffin. Originally established in Albany by Dr. H.P. Waterbury, the agency then had a modest office at 31 North Pearl Street, in the city's financial heart, according to an equally modest advertisement published in the 1869 Albany City Directory. Waterbury remained general agent until 1882, when he became president of the Albany Normal School, progenitor of the State University of New York at Albany.

Waterbury was succeeded by William F. Winship, who would be general agent for the next 47 years. Winship was a company legend, an almost Dickensian figure always seen dressed in cutaway coat, string tie, and striped trousers. Winship made his home in Slingerlands and was known as the "grand old man of the suburbs," commuting then not so common a practice as it would later become. For a long time an unofficial advisor to the New York State Insurance Department, Winship also authored a plan still widely used in mutual life insurance policies, wherein dividends may be accumulated to shorten the premium paying period or mature the policy as an endowment. Winship died in 1919, to be followed as general agent by William A. Baker, who had been Winship's cashier. Baker served Massachusetts Mutual as Albany general agent until 1944, when Gerald L. Griffin came to Albany from the company's Springfield office.

Griffin would prove a pacesetter. In 1944 the Griffin Agency would do a million-dollar business, with only two sales representatives. One of the life insurance industry's early chartered life underwriters, licensed in 1927, Griffin's office was at 11 North Pearl Street. As his business volume climbed, he moved his offices uptown, first to the corner of State and Lodge streets, then to Lark Street, and finally, in 1971, to 6,000 square feet of ultramodern space at 50 Wolf Road, its current location. The Wolf Road move reflected an agency philosophy of availability to the public and the site offered the ultimate in ease of access, growth potential, and ready physical coverage of the local market area.

Gerald Griffin's sons, G. Barton and Robert C. Griffin, entered the agency, eventually in their turn succeeding their father as general agent, G. Barton in 1971 (then moving up as a vice-president of the company's home office) and Robert in 1977. The Griffin Agency is the only insurance agency in New York State to have had a father and two sons as general agents. With professionalism on the increase in the insurance business, Griffin has more CLUs than any other area insurance agency, and the Griffin Agency's 32 sales representatives cover a 17-county area from Wolf Road and six satellite offices, with the firm's annual payroll alone now equaling 1944's business gross.

Robert C. Griffin, CLU general agent, stands with his father, Gerald L. Griffin, CLU, in the lobby of the Griffin Agency at 50 Wolf Road, Albany.

HARRY W. LININDOLL PEST CONTROL INC.

It was the worst of times. A promising future vaporized for Harry W. Linindoll, Sr., who had arrived in Albany as district manager of Service Appliance Company, seller of Eureka Vacuum Cleaners. When the stock market crash of 1929 shattered an unstable American economy, Service Appliance Company folded early and Harry W. Linindoll was out of a job by November 1929.

In desperation Linindoll took every job he could, full- or part-time, nights, days, or weekends. Despite his efforts there was no steady employment for the former white-collar man, although he managed during this period to earn a livelihood while completing an associate's degree in business management at Albany Business College.

By chance, in February 1931, Harry's wife Elizabeth had a friend whose cellar was infested by a rat that defied the best-laid traps. Harry agreed to deal with it, bought a pound of rat poison at a feed store, read the instructions on the box, and set out the bait. Later the bait was gone, the rat was dead, and Harry five dollars richer. He began to think immediately about a new profession and moved to 806 Washington Avenue in March 1931.

He continued odd jobs and solicited business. Friend Victor Sullivan, in charge of City and County Savings Bank's mortgage repossessions, brought Linindoll in to deal with bank properties that had pest infestation problems. These jobs established Linindoll to a point where he was able to share an office and secretary with several other small businesses at 11 North Pearl Street. By 1936 he was able to employ himself full-time, becoming a founding member and director of the National Pest Control Association; with wife Elizabeth to keep records and answer the phone, the business moved into the Linindolls' Washington Avenue home.

Harry Linindoll operated this way until 1941, when he hired a full-time serviceman. By 1943 he was able to purchase 228 Broad Street, now a portion of the firm's present site at 509 South Pearl Street. The following year he hired a second full-time man and moved the warehouse and service operations to Broad Street; two years later a third man was hired.

This 1958 photograph of Harry W. Linindoll, Sr. (seated) and Harry W. Linindoll, Jr. was taken about the time that the younger man was beginning to assume greater management responsibility.

After receiving degrees from Bard College, then part of Columbia University, Harry W. Linindoll, Jr. became the fourth serviceman in the family firm in 1954. When Harry Sr., for medical reasons, took a less active role in the business, his son became general manager. Under this arrangement the present South Pearl Street complex took form. Harry Sr. retired in 1966 and his son purchased the business.

Since the age of 16, Harry W. Linindoll III had worked summers and holidays in the business; after graduation from Clarkson in 1979 he became a serviceman and in January 1981, vice-president. By this time Harry W. Linindoll Pest Control's 32 employees served the Capital District and a wide territory beyond, and the firm was involved in professional education and advisement in a field growing ever more technical, retaining a 3-generation management tradition of excellent service at a fair price.

HUDSON RIVER CONSTRUCTION COMPANY

At the beginning of 1937, there were two asphalt plants within 15 miles of the center of Albany, one located at Feura Bush and owned by a Rochester-based company, and the other at Watervliet under the control of a Troy contracting family. Albany streets had been paved from a city-owned asphalt plant which closed in the early '30s, and concrete, granite block, and red brick were standard street pavements. Driveways, if finished at all, were usually composed of loose stone or gravel.

That same year Hudson River Construction Company was formed in Buffalo by two lifelong friends, Eugene D. Hallock, Jr. and Frederic H. Stutzman, and opened in the Capital District as the first company specializing in bituminous concrete paving. Stutzman was 24 then, a recent Amherst College graduate, and Hallock at 20 had already been involved with the construction trade. With six employees and the front wheel of an old steamroller as a hand roller, they did a total of $8,000 worth of business that first year. By 1981 the company's total annual revenue had increased one thousand times to just under $8 million.

The start of the fledgling company was interrupted by World War II, when the partners joined the U.S. Navy, Stutzman as a line officer and Hallock as a Seabee. Then, in 1947, the company won its first municipal contracts, for the paving of Dove and Swan streets in the city of Albany, and early in 1948 the firm landed its first New York State Highway contract in Rensselaer County.

To secure a source for excellent paving materials, the first subsidiary, Albany Asphalt & Aggregates Corporation, was formed that year. Built in the Port of Albany on the newest section of dock on the Albany side, the asphalt plant has been renewed and updated to maintain the latest improvement in pavements and to meet environmental safeguards, not least of which is the new $200,000 bag-house being installed at this writing for greater dust control.

To break the local stone monopoly, this new plant was able to capitalize on the cheap transportation afforded by the Hudson River and shipped all of its aggregates from just south of Poughkeepsie 70 miles up the river until 1971. Since 1948 it has stood on this same site, to supply asphalt paving materials for the city and county of Albany and Rensselaer and numerous other customers.

In 1961 the partners opened the third of their subsidiaries, Port Concrete, which eventually furnished 25 percent of all the concrete used in building the vast Empire State Plaza. The new Dunn Memorial Bridge between Albany and Rensselaer is Port's concrete from the river-bottom caissons to its highest columns and was the site of around-the-clock pours that totaled up to 2,700 cubic yards of concrete in a 24-hour period.

Hudson River Construction Company is a joint family enterprise and plans to remain so; each of the founders has two sons in the firm and present and future transference of leadership will preserve the status quo. Forty-three years of experience have made Hudson River Construction Company an enterprise with a steady and productive past and a viable and prosperous future.

Left:
In June 1952 Hudson River Construction Company crews lay blacktop on Broadway at Steuben Street, near Union Station.
Right:
Flanked by crew and equipment in this 1949 photograph are company founders Eugene D. Hallock, Jr. and Frederic H. Stutzman (standing fourth and third from right, respectively). They are cutting the ribbon to open a Department of Transportation job—the paving of 6.31 miles of Route 66 in Columbia County.

KEY BANK N.A.

The founding of Key Bank—originally known as "Commercial Bank"—stemmed from the opening of the Erie Canal and the resultant vast markets made available for Albany's merchants. Four banks, all owned by local plutocrats, then existed in Albany. The increase in commerce caused by the Erie Canal forced the realization of a need for a "people's bank" for Albany, and in 1826 the state legislature chartered Commercial Bank. Since this was the first such bill to legally define the functions of a bank, it became a national model for subsequent bank chartering legislation.

By 1830 the bank was circulating $413,700 in its bank notes, and by the following year it had become a depository for New York State funds, which it remains to this day. As Albany's economy burgeoned, Commercial Bank's assets topped $1.4 million by 1845. Its officers were also early investors in railroads and provided determined economic leadership—during the financial panic of 1837 they were the first bankers in the state to resume specie payments.

In 1862, when the state of New York found itself with no money to support the Union Army's recruiting drive, Commercial Bank advanced $3.5 million, enabling it to raise required military units. At the end of the Civil War the bank was chartered as "National Commercial Bank of Albany." Politically active—one bank officer, Robert H. Pruyn, was Lincoln's Ambassador to Japan, and president Daniel Manning became Grover Cleveland's Secretary of the Treasury—the bank attained national stature.

Merging in 1901 with Merchants National Bank of Albany and Albany City National Bank, National Commercial constructed a new building at 60 State Street. Designed by York and Sawyer and constructed in 1902, it remains a distinguished element of the downtown area. Later consolidation with Union Trust Company in 1920 formed "The National Commercial Bank and Trust Company of Albany" with a branch at Lark and Washington. Consumer services, such as auto and appliance loans, were developed in the '20s and '30s. The Northern branch opened at Broadway and Pleasant Street in 1939 and rural branches in Altamont, Ravena, and Delmar opened after mergers in 1936-37.

Derived from classical Greek architecture, the stately bank was erected in 1920. Keeler's Restaurant is on the left; Boyce and Milwain, Clothiers, on the right.

During the national bank holiday in 1933, National Commercial was the only bank which continued to cash state paychecks. It was also instrumental in testing World War II's ration banking system and raised $238.4 million in war bond subscriptions, financing the heavy cruiser USS *Albany*. Postwar prosperity saw growth to nine branches with 19 more added by 1960.

In 1971, an affiliation with Syracuse's First Trust Deposit Company formed the multi-bank holding company First Commercial Banks. The name of the holding company subsequently was changed to Key Banks, Inc., and National Commercial became known as "Key Bank N.A." in January 1980. A new 10-story building next to 60 State Street now headquarters Key Bank's billion dollars in assets and controls a network of 65 branches, just one block from where the bank started in 1825.

LANGE-FINN CONSTRUCTION CO., INC.

James F. Finn was something of a pioneer. Born in 1875 in Toledo, Ohio, of transplanted Albany parents, his family two years later returned to Albany to stay. Young James attended Albany schools, eventually becoming a carpenter for several years. In 1903 he joined the general contracting business of his father, James J. Finn, and specialized in what was then an innovative method of building with reinforced concrete, subsequently a cornerstone of most modern American construction. By 1923 Finn was "one of Albany's busiest men,'' his firm known for its reinforced concrete buildings.

The projects James J. Finn and Son tackled were not small ones, given the scale of Albany's architecture then and the technology available. The Wellington Hotel rose in 1914, a Finn endeavor, followed by Hackett Junior High School, St. James Church on Delaware Avenue, the Albany Garage, the gymnasium of the former Vincentian Institute, and Philip Livingston Junior High School, built as a WPA project during the Depression. Many of Albany's large public buildings constructed before World War II were built by James J. Finn & Son, General Contractors.

In 1934, an unfortunate year to be an American businessman, Lange-Finn was optimistically incorporated. The Lange was Victor Lange, an Albany mason, and the Finn was Joseph F. Finn, Sr., who remained president of the firm until 1961. In those years Lange-Finn established its strong reputation in eastern New York State's construction business, the jobs undertaken gradually increasing in complexity and importance.

Most Albanians at one time or another come into contact with facilities built by Lange-Finn Construction Company. The firm has since 1903 built all sorts of structures and was the first general contractor to work in the Empire State Plaza, constructing the first five floors of the New York State Motor Vehicle Building. Lange-Finn built the North Albany Wastewater Treatment Plant, a 23-million-gallon per day facility purifying fully one-half of Albany County's wastewater. Deteriorating sheds and docks at the Port of Albany were replaced by Lange-Finn, part of the port's renaissance as a major facility. It was Lange-Finn which built the Westgate and Colonie shopping centers, dormitories for Siena College and Albany Law School, an addition for Albany Medical Center, the Thruway Authority Building on Southern Boulevard, the parish house of St. Vincent's Church, and St. Joseph's Provincial House in Latham.

Above:
The American Flag flutters at the top of the concrete hoist at the Wellington Hotel addition in this 1914 photograph taken from Eagle and Howard streets.
Below:
J.J. Finn & Son, Contractors, predecessors of Lange-Finn, constructed the Albany Parking Garage at Lodge and Howard streets in 1929.

Now in its fifth generation of family ownership, Lange-Finn has increasingly moved into the specialization in reinforced concrete construction, in flat and folded plate, single and 2-way pan systems, precast and post-tensioned concrete, and more conventional beam and girder systems. Bridges have been an important challenge and those completed by Lange-Finn include the Broadway Bridge in Rensselaer and bridges in Little Falls, and on the final leg of Route I-88 between the Capital District and Binghamton. The corporate structure now consists of James W. Finn, chairman of the board; Joseph F. Finn, president; William M. Linnan, Jr., vice-president; E.M. Finn, secretary; and James W. Finn, Jr., treasurer.

JOHN W. McGRATH CORPORATION

Strong men and big machines are the stock in trade of John W. McGrath Corporation, stevedores and terminal operators. The company was founded in New York City by Captain John W. McGrath, an Atlantic coast sailor, in 1932. Convinced that the Port of Albany offered great potential for his firm, Captain McGrath established an operation which became a leading force in Albany's emergence as a major port. In years following, facilities were opened in all major Atlantic and Gulf ports and several in the Pacific.

McGrath's heavy equipment and practice of competitive bidding encouraged consignment of cargo via Albany. His investment in machinery and feeling for the port itself were leading inducements when such international firms as Volkswagen of North America and United Brands sought port facilities in the Northeast—United Brands ships 180,000 boxes of bananas through the port each week, all handled by McGrath's stevedores. McGrath's stevedoring operation, equipped with five cranes, paper machines, and huge forklifts, can move any cargo—foodstuffs, grain, scrap metal, lumber, heavy machinery. It was McGrath Corporation which loaded the Port of Albany's first outbound cargo, Schenectady-built locomotives, in 1932.

The Great Depression was a traumatic experience for Albany. McGrath's vice-president, John J. McGahay, recalled that the port was a source of employment which steadfastly aided many Albanians through the difficult 1930s. When World War II caused the closing of the Port of Albany—U.S. strategists knew that the sabotaged hulk of a single ship could block the Hudson River—other stevedoring firms left the port, but McGrath elected to stay. The U.S. Army Corps of Engineers administered the port during the war years, with McGrath men maintaining and operating the equipment, including the giant grain elevator.

Above:
John J. McGahay, vice-president of John J. McGrath Corporation, has worked as manager of the firm's Albany operation for 27 years.

Below:
McGrath stevedores move a cargo of lumber at the Port of Albany in this photograph taken during the 1930s. (Courtesy New York State Library Manuscripts and Special Collections)

Change was rapid after World War II. The nation's highways made truck traffic preeminent, contributing to the decline of both railroads and the New York State Barge Canal, both of which had been of considerable importance to the Port of Albany. John McGahay, veteran of 50 years in the port, 27 of those with McGrath Corporation, noted many of these changes. Large oil tankers among the river's ships serve as icebreakers and keep Albany a year-round competitive port. Ships are now three or four times bigger than when McGahay first came to the port as a crane operator, and handling techniques for cargo are now radically different.

A third generation of the McGrath family now participates in the operation of the corporation. More than 300 men may be employed at Albany at a time, depending on the requirements of ships and cargoes in port; these men are drawn from a reserve of manpower that helps keep the Port of Albany a gateway to Canada and the northeastern United States. Capital improvements in the port to develop its facilities and a steady annual growth in total incoming cargo justify the faith that Captain McGrath had in the Port of Albany in 1932.

THE McVEIGH FUNERAL HOME INC.

JOHN HARRIGAN,

General Furnishing Undertaker,

WAREROOMS:—21 & 22 CANAL STREET,

ALBANY, N. Y.

The McVeigh Funeral Home began as John Harrigan, General Furnishing Undertaker, in 1852 in business at the corner of Sheridan Avenue (then Canal Street) and Chapel Street. John Harrigan joined New York's National Guard in 1858, then a social activity popular throughout the nation. With the outbreak of the Civil War, Harrigan's militia unit became part of New York's 25th Regiment, serving two tours of federal service and aiding in the control of an Albany strike in 1863. John Harrigan was mustered out in 1865.

Harrigan's family was well-known and prosperous, owning considerable Albany property. John's sons, Harvey, Daniel, and Joseph F. Harrigan, lived at 22 Sheridan Avenue until 1936 when the last, Joseph, died, like his brothers a bachelor. The brothers were local *bons vivants,* fanciers of fine horseflesh racing trotters on a course that later became Academy Road; Joseph's tastes later turned to luxury automobiles, especially a 5-speed custom-made Cunningham.

When ex-President Ulysses S. Grant died at Mount McGregor in 1885, the Harrigans handled the arrangements, in which the President, one of the first modern embalmings, was laid out in the Albany State Capitol. The artifacts of a Victorian state funeral were negotiated, including the black buggy whips (at 60 cents apiece). Instructions from the Adjutant General specified carriages drawn by black horses to bring General Sherman and Albany-born General Sheridan from Broadway's Delavan House uphill to the capitol. Entombment took place in New York City.

As the Harrigan brothers aged, they cast about for trustworthy help. William C. McVeigh was a young man from Saratoga who in 1901 passed the state embalming exam in Albany's City Hall. McVeigh went to work in Schenectady for the firm of Gleason and Bernardi and in 1908, endorsed by his employers, was recruited by the Harrigans, who he also helped to manage their real estate holdings; McVeigh subsequently earned a real estate license as well. In McVeigh's time change came to John Harrigan Sons, change that included the purchase of a Cadillac hearse with an Albany-built Kingsbury custom chassis to replace Harrigan's horse-drawn hearses.

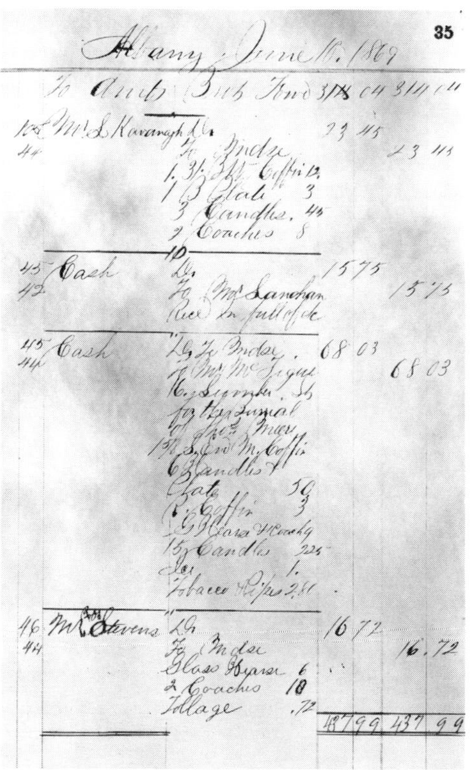

Above:
This John Harrigan business card dates from the 1880s.
Left:
A ledger page from the McVeigh collection illustrates both the completeness of funeral arrangements in the third quarter of the 19th century and their relative inexpensiveness in modern terms.

McVeigh remained in business on Sheridan Avenue until 1940, when he moved to 208 North Allen Street, off Central Avenue. He lived upstairs from his business and by this time had been joined at work by his son William J. McVeigh, licensed in 1938. William C. McVeigh survived Joseph Harrigan by just 11 years and died in 1947. McVeigh's son William J. then succeeded to operation of the family firm. He was aided in turn by his son William E. McVeigh, who entered the business in 1958 and was licensed in 1960.

JAMES H. MALOY, INC.

James H. Maloy began heaving coal into the red-hot fireboxes of locomotives on the Boston & Maine Railroad. One night in 1910, as his train burrowed through the Hoosick Tunnel, it occurred to the 24-year-old fireman that to be working so hard for someone else was not for the ambitious. After a brief stint operating a derrick on construction of the State Education Building Maloy struck out for himself. By 1918, with his own truck, Maloy was hauling meat from Newark to Philadelphia—probably quickly—without refrigeration. During World War I he drove for the Aluminum Corporation of America in Philadelphia, then returned to Albany, his wife's hometown, where Maloy owned the city's first dump truck, hauling for the Van Rensselaer pit. Once it found a little traction, the dump truck easily outdrew the teams of horses then used and James H. Maloy became well established.

The prosperity of the 1920s was reflected by Albany's building boom, James H. Maloy hauling many of the tons of river sand for making concrete. In 1926 he incorporated and purchased a farm on Albany-Shaker Road, encouraged by the presence of a gravel pit on the property. Three years later his company moved from its Green Street headquarters to the Albany-Shaker Road site, where it has remained. Maloy at that early date envisioned his property at the crossroads of Albany, Troy, and Schenectady. He proved correct, and gravel from his pit there was used to build part of this focal point—the Albany County Airport.

During the dismal 1930s, the firm stayed busy hauling coal, delivering from dealers to buildings all over Albany. James H. Maloy, Inc. had coal haulage contracts with the city, county, and New York State. Maloy equipment also worked on construction of Albany's Arch Street sewer in 1936. In the late '30s Maloy's sons, James Jr. and John, began working for him when Christian Brothers Academy built its New Scotland Avenue campus in 1938. At the same time Maloy, Inc. moved earth for housing developments along New Scotland Avenue.

Top:
On a snowy day in 1938, Maloy equipment is seen in operation off New Scotland Avenue.
Above:
James H. Maloy, Inc. grades state parking lots on the south hillside of Sheridan Hollow in 1948. On the horizon is the Alfred E. Smith Building.

James H. Maloy, Sr. died in 1944, leaving his sons in charge of the company—James Jr. president, John vice-president. Their first postwar opportunity came with the construction of Siena College's Loudonville campus. Maloy, Dugan & Maloy was formed for the job.

Building the State Office Campus in 1957 found Maloy, Inc. on the job. The first contract for the Empire State Plaza was awarded to James H. Maloy, Inc. in 1964, as was work on the Saratoga Performing Arts Center. Maloy now owns a large fleet of equipment. Jobs were fewer but their volume much greater, the public sector growing increasingly important. Recent projects—the Albany County Airport, Troy's Uncle Sam Mall, major construction of Route 9W, and the building of Interstate 88—point the direction for James H. Maloy, Inc.

MANPOWER INC.

Manpower Inc., the nation's leading temporary help firm, opened its first office in Albany in January 1958. Alexander Courtney, an alumnus of the Harvard Business School trained in sales and marketing by Proctor and Gamble and the Coleman Company of Wichita, Kansas, pioneered the concept of temporary help service in the Capital District. His franchise in Albany, covering the tri-city area, was born just 10 years after Manpower Inc. was founded in Milwaukee, Wisconsin.

The first office division, located at 119 State Street (now the "new" IBM Building) shared space with the Cluett Music Company and the IBM office products division. In rapid succession, an industrial office was opened at 14 Grand Street, followed by offices in Schenectady and Troy.

Acceptance by the business community was immediate, and the company enjoyed steady growth. Even the second headquarters location at 50 State Street was rapidly outgrown; in 1965 the firm acquired the building at 132 State Street, which has been its administrative headquarters since that date. In earlier days this facility had considerable historic significance. It was known as Benson's Tubs, a combination residence and athletic club incorporating steam baths and one of the earliest swimming pools in the area. It was the Albany residence of Alfred E. Smith during the years he served as a legislator prior to becoming governor. Later, the building would become known as the Chatham Apartments. The present facade was constructed in the 1930s.

Almost a quarter of a century after its founding, Manpower Temporary Services in the Capital District has grown to a full-time staff of 22, has an active customer list exceeding 1,500, and provides employment to 4,000 temporary workers. The fourth and most recent Manpower office is in the Environmental Conservation Building at 50 Wolf Road in Colonie. Alexander Courtney, Jr., representing the second generation of the Courtney family in association with Manpower, is the operations manager of the company.

Above:
Alexander Courtney, Sr. (right), founder of the local franchise of Manpower Inc., was joined in the business by his son, Alexander Courtney, Jr., in 1978, two decades after the enterprise began in Albany.
Left:
"The Chatham," as conceived by architect H.F. Andrews, was the Albany residence of Alfred E. Smith—later governor and presidential candidate—when he was a state assemblyman prior to 1951. Today the facility houses Manpower Temporary Services.

In the early days of temporary help the delivery of service to the business community combined the mechanical testing of skills with careful checking of references, comparable to any well-organized personnel department. In the 25 years intervening, Manpower has, in addition, developed a sophisticated testing system, scientifically validated with thousands of working temporaries, which permits the company to identify clearly those workers capable of superior job performance in a variety of working conditions.

Similarly, work environment surveys and quality performance checks with Manpower customers provide the information necessary for the closest possible match of the skills of the temporary worker to the needs of the customer. Continued concentration on high service standards, coupled with the most advanced computer techniques, gives company management the confidence that the next 25 years will witness similar growth for Manpower Temporary Services in the Capital District.

MARINE MIDLAND BANK, N.A.

Nineteenth-century bank tellers had to be good shots. At the Catskill office of what later became Marine Midland Bank, tellers were armed with "Remington frontier model pistols" and as late as 1926 tellers contested with bookkeepers in a competition held on the rifle range maintained in the basement of the Franklin Square branch office in Troy. Female employees competed for annual pistol prizes until 1936; during the Depression brass plaques were substituted for gold ones. Marine Midland employees, evidently, were ready for anything.

Marine Midland Bank, N.A., had its origins in 1852, when the Manufacturers Bank of Troy was organized under New York State law, opening for business in May of that year, and occupying its own building by October. In 1856, having already outgrown that building at 13 First Street, the bank moved to a 3-story brick structure at the juncture of King and River streets in Troy, described in one account as "towering" over neighboring buildings. Nine years later, the bank received its national charter and became Manufacturers National Bank of Troy. While no branch office was opened until 1923, by 1979 this small bank had joined with the most extensive banking system in the state of New York, serving 201 communities through 296 offices, the 12th largest bank in the entire United States.

A 1921 merger with Security Trust Company and Security Safe Deposit Company led the way for future growth. A new building was erected and occupied in 1923, the year that Peoples Bank of Lansingburgh was acquired, becoming the first branch bank in the city of Troy. A merger with the National State Bank of Troy followed in 1927, and finally, in the inauspicious year of 1929, Manufacturers National Bank of Troy, in conjunction with 16 other New York banks, became Marine Midland Banks, Inc. The system thus created would merge into one statewide bank in 1976. Net earnings of $21,535 in the first half of 1866 would grow to a net income in 1979 of almost $40 million. Assets in 1929, following Marine Midland's creation, rose from $524 million to almost $16 billion a half century later.

Above:
Frank E. Howe was president of Marine Midland Bank from 1907 to 1925. This candid photograph, capturing a moment of repose, quietly seems to say quite a bit about him.
Left:
The "bank with a clock" in Troy was patriotically adorned for the Hudson Fulton celebration in 1909. The ship is Hendrick Hudson's Half Moon, *lit up with dozens of electric bulbs.*

Marine Midland Bank by 1980 operated 24 branches in the 13-county Capital Region, a third of those in Albany County. Instead of equipping branch offices with six-guns, Marine Midland now employs the area banking industry's only truly electronic bank outlet—the MoneyMatic—one in which no teller is needed. Headquarters for Marine Midland-Capital were constructed on Wolf Road in Colonie, in 1971. "The most modern bank operations facility in the Northeast," it houses technologically advanced electronic equipment capable of handling Marine Midland's burgeoning branch system. The 5-story building—which in its location does qualify as "towering"—contains its own branch office, Personal Credit and Master Charge departments, Trust and Mortgage departments' bookkeeping operations, and a number of the bank's other principal functions. Appreciative of its local origins, Marine Midland constructed its nerve center in Albany County.

MATTHEW BENDER & COMPANY

A 2-room walk-up office at the corner of State Street and Broadway was the location of Matthew Bender, "law bookseller," in 1887. At that time, Bender sold other firms' publications but quickly emerged as a publisher of quality New York State lawbooks. Matthew Jr. ("Max") was already working for his father when younger brother John joined the business. The family concern soon moved around the corner, to 36 State Street, and then to a Broadway storefront in 1892, when the city directory first listed Bender as "law bookseller and publisher." That year, Matthew Bender began issuing an annual "Lawyers' Diary," a desk book successful for the next 56 years. Issuance of William M. Collier's treatise on bankruptcy in 1898 marked the advent of Bender's most long-lived series. Abreast of the times, Bender published early books on streetcar and automobile laws.

Matthew Bender became partners with his sons, Max and John T. Bender, in 1905, and within a year they had three salesmen on the road. In 1910 the firm consumed 108 tons of paper and employed seven salesmen, with gross sales exceeding $188,000. By 1915 Bender had a nationwide clientele, with customers in Paris, London, Havana, and Berlin; the company established a New York City office at that time.

Matthew Bender, Sr. died in 1920; his son Max succeeded him as president of the company, a position he held for 21 years. During his tenure, Matthew Bender & Company prospered with the 1920s and successfully weathered the Great Depression. His son, Matthew Bender III, and his nephew, John T. Bender, Jr., entered the firm during the '30s. Nephew John took charge of the New York City operation, displaying considerable ability in recruiting writers. It was John Jr. who pioneered loose-leaf binding for ease in updating Bender's publications, a system employed thereafter.

Although World War II inhibited the growth of Matthew Bender & Company, the postwar years were ones of continual growth. If as late as 1950 the State Street offices were "straight out of Dickens," the company was seeking improved facilities; the firm relocated in 1952 to modern offices at 255 Orange Street. In 1963 Matthew Bender & Company became a subsidiary of the Times-Mirror Company and shortly thereafter occupied its 1275 Broadway headquarters. By 1980, Bender employed 1,000 persons, 300 of them in its Albany operation, and had offices in San Francisco, New York, and Washington, D.C. Printing its first international catalogue in 1980 to serve customers throughout the world, Matthew Bender & Company has continually increased its international market. The overall picture of this old Albany firm is one of dynamic growth in a highly competitive and specialized field.

In 1892, the Benders—Matthew, Matthew Jr., John, and Melvin—were photographed standing in front of their store at 511-513 Broadway. Fred Bender, far right, was no relation.

NEW YORK STATE CONFERENCE OF MAYORS AND OTHER MUNICIPAL OFFICIALS

In August 1910, *Life & Health* magazine published an article entitled "Echoes of the Conference of Mayors." There, the secretary of the National Housing Association wrote, "A new era has dawned when the mayors of 40 cities of one State come together. . . ." The mayors had met two months earlier in Schenectady, at the invitation of Mayor Charles C. Duryee, to discuss municipal health problems.

Buoyed by the conference's positive tone, they met again in 1911 and formed a permanent association. Interested in municipal home rule, health and welfare programs, city planning, and housing conditions, the New York State Conference of Mayors typified the Progressive era, seeking standardized municipal procedures and legislation for socio-governmental improvements. Groundwork laid in the years from 1910 to 1920 set the pace for the next seven decades. The Conference pioneered in regional planning, water pollution abatement, and national building codes. The association designed pertinent legislation and conducted training programs for municipal officials throughout New York State.

In 1915, a full-time director was chosen. He was William P. Capes, editor of the Schenectady *Evening Star*. Capes had been secretary of the Conference since the first meeting in 1910. Under his leadership enrollment grew to 59 in 1920, and membership was offered to mayors of villages in the state in 1924. In time, the membership requirements changed so that it was the city or village government itself that became the primary member. By 1980, 493 cities and villages had joined.

The Conference of Mayors formulated its first legislative program in 1920 and its legislative committee reviewed and commented on 115 bills before the state legislature. During the 1979-1980 session, when the legislature churned out 20,000 bills for review, the Conference expressed support for or opposition to over 1,000 bills which affected local governments. Its own legislative program included almost 100 bills.

Since the initial meeting in Schenectady, educational programs for municipal officials have multiplied. In 1930, the Conference established its first training schools. Supported from 1931 to 1936 by a grant from the Spelman Fund, these programs have since become self-supporting. In cooperation with Cornell University, annual classes are held for public works personnel. Annual sessions are conducted for new municipal officials and for fiscal officers and clerks in conjunction with the state comptroller's office. The Conference publishes and distributes regular bulletins: *Across the Table,* the *Legal Bulletin,* and the *Municipal Bulletin.* And the Conference continues to conduct an annual meeting to promote interaction among local, state, and federal officials.

At first, the Conference of Mayors was run from the Schenectady mayor's office. As the association and its staff grew, the Conference moved its offices to Albany, first to 25 Washington Street, then to the old Municipal Building at Howard and South Pearl streets, and then to the top floor of Albany's City Hall. In 1940, the Conference purchased the building at 6 Elk Street and remained there until 1979, when it relocated to 119 Washington Avenue.

"City Healthful" was the theme of the inaugural meeting of the New York Conference of Mayors, when mayors, city officials, and public health officers from throughout the state gathered for two days of discussions on municipal health issues.

NEW YORK STATE UNITED TEACHERS

In the United States, the 1840s were a time of fraternities, medical and bar associations, and lodges and clubs of all sorts. Americans had a passion for joining societies and movements, from Masons, Redmen, and Oddfellows to the many temperance and abolitionist organizations of the time. In this fraternal atmosphere Thomas W. Valentine, president of the Albany County Teachers Association, and John W. Bulkley, another Albanian, founded the New York State Teachers Association in Syracuse on July 30, 1845. Although initially opposed by the New York State secretary of state, the organization eventually became the New York State United Teachers, with a 1981 strength of 230,000 members, the largest public employee union in the state.

Since the start, the history of New York State United Teachers has been synonymous with the history of education in New York State. When New York's first superintendent of public instruction was appointed in 1854, it was Victor Rice, eighth president of the New York State Teachers Association, who was chosen. United Teachers has had a major voice in drafting, developing, and passing legislation which in the aggregate formed the state's public education system. The influence of United Teachers over the years has been pervasive, supporting compulsory free public education, teachers' tenure, state aid to local schools, minimum salary requirements, and the establishment of the New York State Education Department and the Teachers Retirement System. Through an extensive program of legislation, research, workshops, and conferences, United Teachers works for the upgrading of professional standards, teaching competence, curriculum, and instructional techniques. This involvement with the educational future of New York State has kept Albany the natural home of United Teachers.

In 1923 United Teachers established headquarters at 212 State Street, in 1934 erecting its building on Washington Avenue at Dove Street. That same year the organization elected its first woman president, Mabel E. Simpson. Today more than 800 affiliated locals in 44 election districts choose 2,000 representatives who meet annually to establish policy—one early delegate to the annual meetings was Susan B. Anthony.

New York State United Teachers includes public and private elementary and secondary school teachers; college and university faculty; state professional, scientific, and technical employees; personnel from public health care agencies; and school-related employees such as cafeteria and secretarial workers, teachers' aides, custodians, and school bus drivers. To better serve its constituency, United Teachers in 1963 established its first regional office at Jericho, Long Island. Today there are 16 regional offices, including one in Albany. The staff of United Teachers grew from 12 in about 1945 to nearly 280 in 1981, and it was following World War II that the organization came of age as a militant teacher advocate engaging in collective bargaining, legislative lobbying, and equal educational opportunity. United Teachers has indeed become "the front line of defense for every teacher in the state."

Left:
This dignified structure at the corner of Washington Avenue and Dove Street housed the New York State Teachers Association from 1934 until 1972. An annex, at the right, was built in 1937.
Right:
The building at 80 Wolf Road has housed New York State United Teachers since the 1972 merger of its two parent organizations, the New York State Teachers Association and the United Teachers of New York.

PICOTTE REAL ESTATE

The year 1933 was an inauspicious one to enter the real estate business. John D. Picotte and his sons Bernard and Clifford had built small houses in Schenectady but found selling them difficult in a city hard-hit by the Great Depression. The Picottes relocated in Albany, to construct single-family homes on Maple Avenue off Albany-Schenectady Road. The first 10 of these 5-room houses sold for about $3,500 each; other houses soon followed, constructed on Homestead and Winthrop avenues and Van Buren and VerPlanck streets.

"Golden Acres" was Picotte Building Company's next venture, on 25 acres of land on New Scotland Avenue west of Krumkill Road. Pavement, water, and sewer lines were added on Crescent Drive, Home Avenue, and Berncliffe Avenue (named for Bernard and Clifford Picotte). One hundred homes and six 4-family apartments were built in 1937.

John D. Picotte retired in 1938, the year his son Bernard married Kathleen McManus. Brothers Bernard and Clifford continued to build apartments and homes on Homestead and Western avenues and Eileen Street, until the shortage of building materials caused by U.S. involvement in World War II halted their construction activities. After the war Clifford Picotte built residential homes, while Bernard developed apartments and commercial buildings. The year 1946 saw development of Crestwood—250 homes, 150 apartments, and Crestwood Shopping Center on 50 acres near Whitehall Road.

Bernard Picotte erected his first office building, at 324 State Street in 1950. Three years later, he renovated the facility at 135 Ontario Street and began a series of commercial projects in Schenectady. Clifford Picotte died in 1961, soon after Bernard began construction at 111 Washington Avenue, the first office building measuring over 100,000 square feet built in downtown Albany since 1930. In 1962 Bernard constructed offices at 130 Ontario Street, the first effort of Picotte & Sons. (Bernard's eldest son, John, had joined him in the business.) The Picottes then constructed buildings at 1 and 2 University Place in 1965, and at 44 Holland Avenue in 1968. When Bernard's son Michael joined the enterprise in 1969, they erected a building at 50 Wolf Road. After Bernard F. Picotte retired in 1975, his sons developed office buildings at 80 Wolf Road and One Park Place. William Picotte, Clifford's son, became vice-president of Picotte Real Estate at that time.

Picotte Real Estate owns, operates, and manages over 600,000 square feet of downtown space, an important factor in downtown Albany's revival, and sells more than 250 homes each year. Picotte Real Estate has donated buildings to the College of St. Rose and to the Albany Episcopal Diocese, a scholarship at Siena College. The company has demonstrated its commitment to Albany's downtown area through continued renovation and rehabilitation of residential, commercial, and industrial buildings there. Now under the direction of John and Michael Picotte, it remains a community-oriented, family business, its future a pursuit of the same goals and prosperity that have made it one of the Capital District's largest developers.

This storefront at 1040 Madison Avenue was the site of Clifford and Bernard Picotte's first real estate office.

PRICE CHOPPER SUPERMARKETS

Fifty-four supermarkets, 13 gas stations, and a drugstore had their genesis in 1932, in a windowless Green Island Warehouse. Bernard and William Golub, wholesale grocers, entered the supermarket business with an entirely new concept—a market where shoppers could serve themselves with wholesale-priced merchandise. Crude wooden tables held goods that customers could place in wicker baskets slung from their arms. Groceries chosen, shoppers carried them to checkers at a large square counter at the store's center, where the bill was totaled on an adding machine. The tape was taken to a cashier, the bill paid, the tape stamped, and the groceries reclaimed from the checkers. With coffee 27 cents a pound and butter 24 cents, a five-dollar grocery order was too much for one person to carry out.

The Golubs were enterprising men, sons of Lewis Golub, since 1908 himself a wholesale grocer, who started them in his business delivering goods to grocery stores in a horse-drawn wagon. Bernard and William Golub graduated from college, entering the family business full-time. After Lewis's death in 1930, his sons merged with wholesaler Joseph E. Grosberg, immediately doubling the volume of business, although the total was less than one-tenth the volume done by a single modern Price Chopper Supermarket. "The central idea . . . is to provide a selling mart for all kinds of retail items, reducing overhead and trouble for the shoppers," wrote the *Troy Record* in 1932. Following its success with the Green Island "Public Service Market" and a store in Watervliet, the company opened its first Central Market in a former automobile dealership in Schenectady. Stores soon opened in North Troy and Glens Falls, enabling the company to leave the wholesale trade entirely.

GOLUB'S CASH AND CARRY
Schenectady, N. Y.
47-49 Van Guysling Avenue
Overlooking The Market Square
2-0755 PHONES 2-0756
ALL PRICES NET CASH F. O. B. WAREHOUSE

SPECIALS WEEK DECEMBER 2-7

SUGAR 100lbs.	5.05 bg
CAMPBELL BEANS 48s	3.75 cs
5 Case lots	3.70 cs
CAMPBELL SOUP 48s	4.03 cs

These prices strictly cash warehouse

GOLD CRUST FLOUR 1-8s	7.35 bbl
Golden Tree Syrup Maple Flavor 24pts.	3.85 cs
Fisher's Salted in Shell Peanuts	.17 lb
Minute Tapioca 36s	3.50 cs
BABO 48s	4.75 cs
Emerald WALNUTS 100 lbs	.22 lb
Machine Oil Ever Ready Handy Cans	1.10 dz
LIBBY'S Saur Kraut 15 gal. kegs	7.00 keg

Above:
The Golubs were still in the wholesale grocery business when this advertisement was printed on a penny postcard, to be mailed to customers in the early 1930s.
Above right:
Ben Golub (left) and Bill Golub look over congratulatory telegrams on their company's 25th anniversary in 1957.
Right:
This photograph of a typical Central Market was taken in Schenectady in the late '30s. The Golubs were in business with Joseph Grosberg at that time.

In 1943, the Golub Corporation pioneered numerous industry firsts in the Capital District. Central Markets introduced the sale of nonfood items in the mid 1940s, trading stamps in 1952, 24-hour shopping in 1972, and the first in-store bakery in 1975.

After the death of Bernard Golub, the chain undertook some major policy changes. A third generation of Golubs took the helm under the guidance of William Golub, who became chairman of the board. In 1975, Lewis Golub, son of Bernard, became president with Neil Golub, son of William, assuming the responsibilities of executive vice-president.

Renamed Price Chopper in 1973, the company dropped trading stamps and became a low-cost operator. It further emphasized its long-standing position as a good corporate citizen through participation in community events and charitable gifts.

The company embarked on a major building campaign and a series of remodels. By 1980, replacements and acquisitions brought the number of supermarkets to 54 located in upstate New York, western Massachusetts, and Vermont.

When the Golub brothers opened that primordial market in Green Island during the Great Depression, they had that same flexible, aggressive spirit which is still in evidence two generations later.

QUACKENBUSH, WAGONER & REYNOLDS, ARCHITECTS

Except for those who designed steeples and towers, Marcus T. Reynolds was the first architect to make fundamental alterations in Albany's horizon. His 10-story City and County Savings Bank building, constructed in 1902, towered over downtown. That year Reynolds also restructured the old Trowbridge Museum into the building now occupied by Bankers Trust Company. His concerns were consistently urban, from the 1893 publication of his prize-winning essay, "Housing of the Poor in American Cities," to his last job, the renovation of an Englewood Place carriage house in 1937. Along the way, Reynolds created warehouses, row houses, the Broadway building of United Traction Company, the Dutch Revival firehouse on Delaware Avenue, Hackett Junior High School, the Niagara Mohawk Building at 126 State Street, the Albany Academy, and his best-known project, the D & H and Albany *Journal* complex at the foot of State Street hill.

The D & H Plaza was part and parcel of Marcus Reynolds's concern with developing a then-decaying riverfront portion of Albany and the buildings were themselves inspired by the Flemish High Gothic Great Cloth Hall in Ypres, Belgium. Typical of his designs, the building used tall towers and was richly medieval in exterior appointments. Reynolds received this commission in 1915, a year after he brought his nephew, Kenneth Reynolds, into the firm. While Marcus Reynolds worked on large projects up until his death in 1937, it was Kenneth who would carry on after him.

Upon completion of additions to the City and County Savings Bank building in 1927, Marcus Reynolds moved his offices into the 10th floor; Kenneth Reynolds would remain there until 1946. After the death of Kenneth Reynolds in 1955, the firm was purchased from Kenneth's estate by longtime associate August Lux. In 1956 Lux became partners with John J. Quackenbush, who had joined Reynolds in 1942, with August Lux and Associates, retitled in 1965 as Lux and Quackenbush. Lux died in 1972 and Quackenbush retained the firm's name until he formed a new partnership with architects Frederick A. Wagoner and Kenneth G. Reynolds, great-nephew of Marcus Reynolds, in 1980.

Quackenbush, Wagoner & Reynolds, Architects, and its lineal forebears have designed millions of dollars worth of projects, including offices, corporate headquarters, firehouses, anti-pollution devices, medical facilities, nursing homes, schools, and colleges. The firm's clients are from a broad spectrum of the region's educational, medical, commercial, and industrial leaders: the City of Albany, U.S. Navy, Memorial Hospital, St. Peter's Hospital, Williams College, United Traction Company, and the Albany Roman Catholic Diocese. Capitalizing on a core of architects and draftsmen who have long worked together, Quackenbush, Wagoner & Reynolds, Architects, and its predecessors have designed many outstanding projects which have altered the appearance of and improved the quality of life in Albany. When Marcus T. Reynolds opened his practice in 1895, he could not have envisioned the continuity that practice would assume.

Top left:
The 10-story City and County Savings Bank building was designed by Marcus T. Reynolds in 1927, and erected at a cost of just under $1.25 million. Reynolds's own offices were on the 10th floor from 1928 until his death in 1937.
Above:
Taken in 1917, this photograph shows the D & H Plaza, probably Reynolds's most striking creation. The Albany Journal *building, at right, is nearing completion.*
Bottom left:
The addition to St. Peter's Hospital, completed in 1975, provides facilities for ambulatory care, an emergency room, pharmacy, laboratory, critical care beds, pediatric beds, and medical-surgical beds.

RTA CORPORATION

In 1939 the Federal Communications Commission was involved in pioneer television testing in the Newburgh-New York area. Assisting with these tests was a young University of Pennsylvania student and a New York University graduate named Harold Gabrilove who had been involved in television marketing since 1936 through his association with Shapiro Distributors of Newburgh, an RCA franchise. Later, during World War II, Gabrilove rose to lieutenant commander as navy assistant senior electronics supply officer.

After the war, in 1946, Gabrilove incorporated RTA Distributors, named after its principal products—radios, televisions, and appliances. This Albany firm, a new eastern New York franchise for Radio Corporation of America, was an entirely independent offshoot of Shapiro Distributors, an appliance business founded in 1907 by Hyman Shapiro. RTA Distributors occupied quarters on Hudson Avenue until 1951, then moved to its own building at 36 Broadway, in Menands.

As RTA expanded its market, developing new sales territory from scratch, it began to attract franchises from other lines of appliances additional to televisions. By 1980, RTA Corporation's RCA line had captured a 20 percent share of the regional market, Whirlpool 24 percent, and other products 30 percent. In its first 12 years of operation alone, the number of employees increased from six to 75 persons.

Growth, especially boom sales in color television, required more space. In 1957 RTA Corporation purchased the former Albany plant of the American Meter Company at 991 Broadway, commissioning an extensive remodeling of the building. Over 125,000 square feet of useable space held offices, a service and parts department, the Northeast's largest showroom, and an auditorium used for dealer meetings.

Interest in new growth areas and increasingly sophisticated products, whose marketability was thoroughly researched by First Ideas, a unit of RTA Corporation, necessitated equally sophisticated technical training for dealers and service personnel. Dealers in a territory stretching from Westchester County to the Canadian border in New York, Berkshire County in Massachusetts, and the state of Vermont, are today buttressed by RTA's commitment to the independent dealer system. This involvement with independent dealers, the backbone of the industry, has included ongoing service and management training programs, financial and personnel management, advertising, merchandising, and technology.

RTA Corporation now deals in "white" appliances and "brown" wares, stereo and electronic gear, and a wide range of other products: bicycles; two-way telephone systems for police, fire, and civil defense departments; time clocks; CB scanners; electronic games; calculators and watches; and automobile stereos. In its white-ware line, RTA Corporation particularly addresses the building industry, annual consumer of one-third of total major appliance production. All of this has resulted in steady growth, with RTA Corporation carefully watching future opportunities, in the enterprising spirit Harold Gabrilove displayed when he began to sell the first little 10-inch mass production television sets from Hudson Avenue in 1946.

Left:
Harold Gabrilove began selling television sets when a 10-inch black and white TV cost $375. Within 10 years, RTA Distributors was serving a 35-county market.
Center:
Annapolis graduate A. Maxon became president of RTA Corporation in 1979 after serving as executive vice-president and sales director.
Right:
In 1970, Ronald Richardson, a University of Bridgeport business administration graduate, became president, and later, vice-chairman of RTA.

SANO-RUBIN CONSTRUCTION COMPANY

Sometime before World War I Louis Rubin arrived in this country and became an Albany carpenter. By 1912 his 2-man operation at 81 Elm Street set a personal tone that made him well-liked by his employees until his death in 1975. He established a hands-on reputation in his early years in business, and a tradition of high-quality workmanship that would endure in the company he had founded.

Louis Rubin formed a partnership with Angelo and Ben Sano in 1934. The Sanos had emigrated from Italy and shared Rubin's hands-on philosophy and respect for good workmanship. Sano-Rubin Construction Company did business from a Myrtle Avenue address, but about 1941 acquired a site on Delaware Avenue; shortly thereafter the partnership reorganized, its principals Louis Rubin and Angelo Sano. Rubin's son, Donald S. Rubin, graduated from Rensselaer Polytechnic Institute with a degree in civil engineering in 1943 and after service in the U.S. Navy during World War I earned a RPI degree in architecture in 1947, then entering his father's firm.

Donald S. Rubin was licensed as a professional engineer in 1944 and later taught in RPI's Department of Architecture, coming to Sano-Rubin especially well-qualified. The postwar years witnessed a nationwide building spurt; pressures from the accompanying "baby boom" necessitated new schools and Sano-Rubin built many of them—South Colonie and Shaker Junior-Senior high schools, Bethlehem Central Senior High School, Albany's School 24 in Lincoln Park, even Altamont's LaSallette Seminary. Also constructed in Albany were Temple Israel, the Albany Medical College building, an addition to Albany Medical Center's nurses' residence, the Labor Temple, SUNYA's downtown dormitories, office buildings at 877 and 881 Madison Avenue and 162 Washington Avenue—the list reflects Albany's postwar prosperity.

In 1958 Sano-Rubin Construction Company incorporated. Known for flexibility and efficiency, professionalism and proficiency, Sano-Rubin increasingly involved itself with construction management, during the 1960s and 1970s supervising the building of numerous area health-related facilities, a particularly involved and demanding sort of construction. Projects included Daughters of Sarah Nursing Home, Cohoes Memorial Hospital, portions of Albany Medical Center, the Capital Area Community Health Plan Building, and additions and modifications to Memorial Hospital. In the same period, projects were undertaken for Adirondack Trust Company, New York State Thruway Authority, Bankers Trust, and the Farm Bureau Insurance Company.

During 1974 Sano-Rubin Construction Company, building to architect Donald J. Stephens' design, erected a cleanly functional structure on its Delaware Avenue site, indicating the firm's stature and professionalism. When Louis Rubin died in 1975 and Angelo Sano two years later, David M. Rubin, Donald's son, was preparing himself at Brown University and MIT to enter the business as the third generation, heir to a record of competent versatility and anticipating Albany's future building needs.

Above Left:
The sort of rough-and-ready ambience of Sano-Rubin Construction Company's early years is reflected in this job-site photograph taken about 1920.

Left:
The 1974 building now occupied by Sano-Rubin at 624 Delaware Avenue is the essence of modern professionalism, presenting considerable contrast to the earlier photograph.

M. SCHER & SON INC.

Michael Scher was a tailor. When he came from Russia at the beginning of the 20th century, Scher opened a small tailor shop on Albany's Green Street, later moving to Clinton Avenue below North Pearl Street. Michael's son, Samuel S. Scher, was born in the south end and came of age at the same time as did the use of electricity in America. Samuel preferred work to Public School 15 and found a job as soon as he could with the Madison Electrical Company, a firm responding to post-World War I Albany's demand for electrification. The use of electric lights, radios, refrigerators, and small appliances continued to increase with the waxing American prosperity of the early 1920s. The relatively small number of local electrical contractors meant that the demand for electrical work exceeded the supply of skilled labor.

In 1924 Samuel Scher opened his electrical contracting business at 138 Hamilton Street, where his father Michael lived above his tailor shop, overlooking the future location of the Empire State Plaza. Michael Scher discovered that he preferred the electrician's trade to the tailor's and left the latter for the former. The Schers and their two to four employees concentrated on south end residential jobs and new-home wiring done along New Scotland Avenue during the '20s and '30s. The largest project undertaken was the newly erected Mayflower apartment complex at South Lake and Western avenues. Among Albany's earliest licensed electrical contractors, M. Scher & Son still holds city of Albany License 13.

Downtown commercial and residential work led to M. Scher's 1951 move to 59 Westerlo Street, the former Decker Saw Works. Until the mid-1960s, M. Scher & Son remained essentially a small electrical contractor doing household, commercial, and maintenance work, including the Palace Theater. Michael Scher died in 1954, a year after grandson Paul began to work in the family business; Paul's brother Martin H. Scher came aboard in 1963.

Above:
An M. Scher & Son crew, at Central Avenue and Northern Boulevard, installs new traffic signals. In the background is the Townsend Park apartment complex, wired by M. Scher & Son in 1976.
Below:
An M. Scher crew works on an addition to the 34.5-KV electric station at the Seaboard Allied Milling Company in the Port of Albany, part of a major expansion of facilities there.

Construction of the Empire State Plaza eliminated much of M. Scher's market and the company quickly adapted to change. In 1966 Samuel S. Scher semiretired and sons Martin and Paul jointly took over the business. They entered the heavy industrial and commercial electrical contracting field, undertaking utility construction specializing in high-voltage power systems. M. Scher & Son was awarded contracts at the Albany Institute of History and Art, Empire State Plaza, the Albany State Capitol, the Alfred E. Smith building, Albany traffic signal and street lighting systems, and Albany Housing Authority. A move in 1967 to 136 North Lake Avenue relocated the firm near Central Avenue's business district, providing room for 75 year-round employees and some of the company's 30 heavy trucks. With Paul Scher's son Mark now employed by the company, M. Scher & Son is a fourth-generation family enterprise, one of the three oldest electrical contracting firms under continual one-family ownership in the Albany area.

ST. MARY'S ROMAN CATHOLIC CHURCH OF ALBANY

New York State's second parish (after St. Peter's, Barclay Street in New York City) and the first parish in the nation's oldest incorporated city, St. Mary's stands as a historical monument and a living spiritual center. Incorporated in 1794 (four years before Albany was officially designated the state's capital), St. Mary's was founded in a time when the new nation had but one diocese and one bishop—John Carroll, whose brother, Charles, signed the Declaration of Independence.

Now listed in the National Register of Historic Places, the church has been connected with four North American saints: Jesuit missionary Isaac Jogues, who, in 1643, escaped from Indian captors holding him in a barn on the very spot where the present church is located; Mother Elizabeth Seton, whose order of nuns taught at St. Mary's beginning in 1828 and who was herself received into the Catholic faith by a priest who previously had been pastor to Albany's Catholics; Philadelphia Archbishop John Neumann, who celebrated Mass at St. Mary's; and Indian maiden Kateri Tekakwitha, whose cause for sainthood was first advanced and strongly backed by St. Mary's pastor Father Clarence Walworth.

Albany's few Roman Catholics worshipped in private homes until St. Mary's was built in 1797 on land given by what was then the governing commune, and through contributions from Protestants as well as Catholics. This early ecumenical dimension to the parish was stressed again when, in 1828, a Sunday school was founded through the urging of a Protestant woman. She was then invited to be one of the school's teachers.

Noted architect Philip Hooker designed a second church for St. Mary's growing congregation, expanding the original cubical building into a federal-style structure completed in 1830. But poor or hurried workmanship left the new building unsound. The force behind a third, permanent, and appropriately distinctive church was Father Walworth. The son of the state's last chancellor (governor), a lawyer, and an Anglican seminarian, Walworth converted to Catholicism in 1845 and was ordained a priest four years later. The cornerstone for the third (and present) St. Mary's was laid in 1867 after his meticulous planning and irrepressible campaigning had raised funds.

Walworth left an impression not only on St. Mary's but also on Catholicism, the state, and the city through his championing of Kateri Tekakwitha's cause, his advocacy of Indian rights, his support for cultural movements, his charitable activities, his eloquent writing and preaching, and his leadership of the Oxford movement in America.

In 1895 a now-familiar landmark was added to the Albany skyline when the statue of St. Gabriel the Archangel, blowing his trumpet of judgement, was hoisted to the peak of St. Mary's bell tower—a final touch by Walworth.

Through the decades, St. Mary's has been an Albany institution, from a time when the city had but 100 Catholics to the current day when, it is estimated, as much as 50 percent of the Albany population is Catholic. St. Mary's has endured while the city has grown up, flourished, and recommitted itself.

A center of historical and spiritual significance, St. Mary's is one of the most distinguished of American churches and a central chapter in the story of New York's capital city.

Above Left:
The third church building on the same site, the current St. Mary's Church was erected in 1867, replacing the Philip Hooker-designed church built in 1830. (Etching by Ruth Rhoads Lepper Gardner)

Left:
Father Clarence Walworth (1820-1900) was pastor at St. Mary's for 34 years, a crusader for the rights of labor, a protector of foundlings and deserted women, as well as a noted scholar and pamphleteer.

ST. PETER'S HOSPITAL

In 1869, a hospital could be established for $15,000. In memory of Peter Cagger, an Albany lawyer who had dreamed of endowing a hospital, his wife and daughters donated the money for St. Peter's. A building at the corner of Broadway and North Ferry Street, formerly housing a signer of the Declaration of Independence, a governor of New York, and an orphanage, was purchased.

Staffed by four Sisters of Mercy, St. Peter's Hospital opened on November 1, 1869, with 33 general-ward beds, two private rooms, and an outpatient dispensary. "The accommodations were limited and imperfect, but the well-directed zeal of the Sisters in charge made up for all deficiencies, and the institution soon acquired public confidence and favor." That much, at least, remains the same.

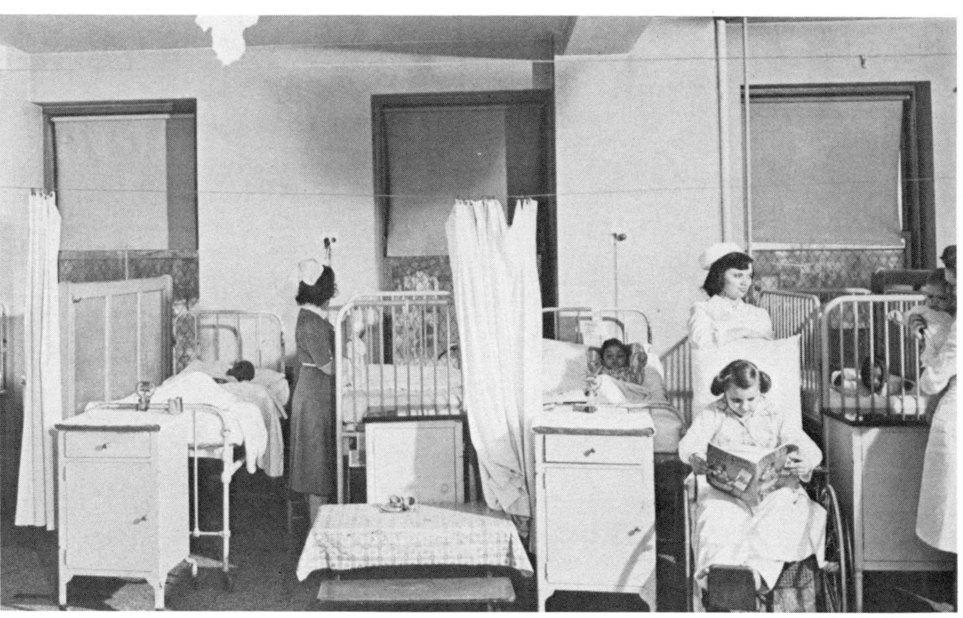

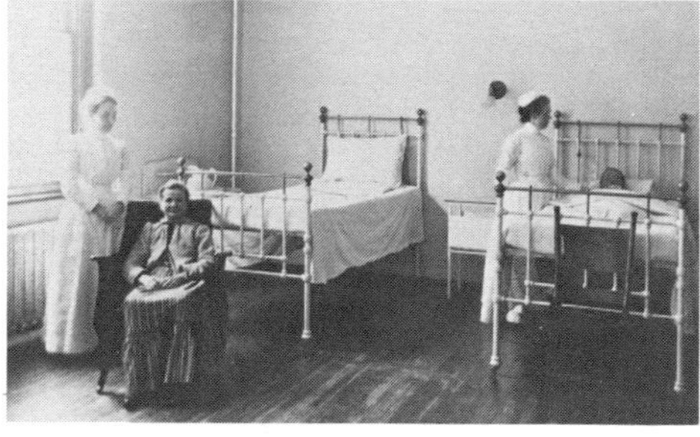

Above:
In 1948, St. Peter's pediatric unit exhibited a high nurse-to-patient ratio.
Left:
A typical St. Peter's interior view of 1875; the rooms were spartan by today's standards. Water was provided in ceramic pitchers like the one behind the bed at center.

Any account of St. Peter's Hospital is of necessity one of constant progress, change, and ceaseless reevaluation. In 1871, having in its first two years treated 600 hospital patients and 4,000 outpatients, St. Peter's was incorporated, receiving a grant of $10,000 from the New York State Legislature. A fourth story was added to the big building on Broadway and a new addition, also fronting on Broadway, brought the hospital to a 100-patient capability. The year 1873 saw St. Peter's patients attended by many of Albany's most skilled physicians, and 30 or 40 persons were daily provided with free prescriptions at the hospital dispensary. The high costs of the recent construction were a dangerous burden to the young hospital and a bazaar was held at the Martin Opera House to raise funds to reduce the hospital's indebtedness. Among the items donated were a milk cow, a plot of real estate, a piano, and "a handsome pony."

By 1895 rising prices of all sorts had increased the daily cost of a stay at St. Peter's Hospital to 75 cents; the payroll was then only 16 percent of the budget. The State Board of Charities licensed the hospital's dispensary in 1899. A year later, St. Peter's School of Nursing opened, graduating its first class of three nurses in 1903; the School of Nursing was chartered by the State Board of Regents two years later and would continue to graduate nurses until phased out in 1970, when Maria College commenced its 2-year nursing program. In 1901 and 1904, new wings were added, which increased St. Peter's capacity to 129 beds and the religious staff to 15 sisters. The year 1904 also witnessed the formation of St. Peter's Hospital Auxiliary, which subsequently grew to 400 members who helped to raise money for the purchase of land adjacent to the hospital. Over the next 75 years, the auxiliary would raise nearly a million dollars for St. Peter's.

World War I slowed the growth of St. Peter's as wartime prices increased dramatically. The Spanish flu epidemic of 1918, a national disaster, found this Albany hospital—provided with $2,000 from Mrs. Margaret Brady Farrell—able to cope with it locally. Care for the returning veterans of World War I necessitated the opening of a 24-bed ward devoted to medical and surgical cases. All this deprived the nurses of their residence in 1920, as the requirements of the hospital forced it to employ that area. It was now obvious: there was no more room and St. Peter's had to move.

Bishop Edward F. Gibbons initiated a major program for constructing a new facility, providing for future growth. A site at the intersection of New Scotland

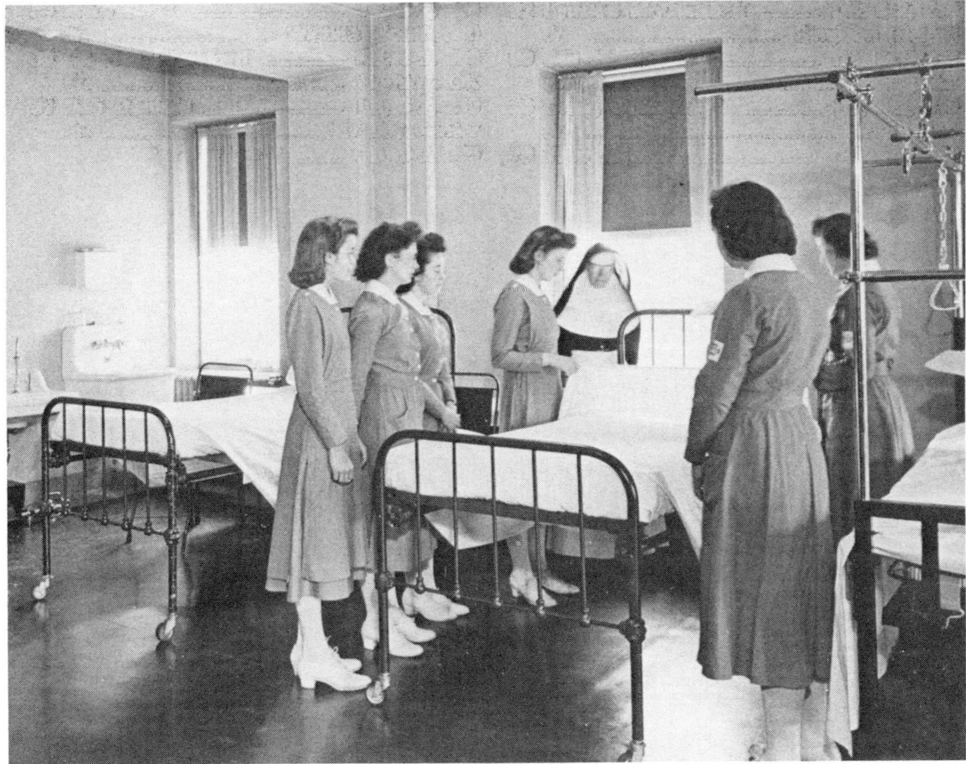

Above:
A Sister of Mercy instructs student nurses in the fundamentals of the "hospital career," circa 1948.
Top:
The original St. Peter's Hospital, at Broadway and North Ferry Street, its original building dating from 1783, served St. Peter's for more than six decades.

Avenue and Allen Street was selected and a campaign to raise $250,000 launched, supported by former governor and editor of the *Times-Union* Martin H. Glynn. Glynn wrote, "Albany needs St. Peter's Hospital and St. Peter's Hospital requires a new building to render the measure of service it is called upon to perform. . . ." Mrs. Margaret Brady Farrell was again generous, financing the Cusack Pavilion, in memory of the late Bishop of Albany Thomas F. Cusack, as a nurses' residence. Actual construction began in 1928.

Opening in 1930, the new hospital transferred 44 patients from the old one. Its new X-ray department was "one of the finest in the Eastern United States." A year later Mrs. Farrell provided a deep therapy X-ray machine, then one of just five such in the nation. The pediatrics department was inaugurated in 1931.

Sixteen years after opening on New Scotland Avenue, St. Peter's needed more room. The bishop granted permission for expansion, with actual construction commencing in 1946. The bishop, persons in the community, and 4,600 volunteers raised the needed money, and the Nolan-Riddle Pavilion was dedicated in 1948. By 1954, the nursing school was overcrowded to a point where students were living on a floor of the hospital wing (or at home) and classes met in unsuitable areas. An addition to the School of Nursing was built to rectify this, housing 92 students and four housemothers. One year later a physical therapy department opened, a social service department in 1957.

The early '60s again found need for expansion; the $6-million Brady Farrell Pavilion opened in 1966, beginning a new era in Albany hospital care. That year the obstetrics department opened, assuming the functions of the A.N. Brady Maternity Hospital, which was closing; during the 1970s, 28,894 babies were born at St. Peter's Hospital. A department of nuclear medicine began in 1967, a coronary care unit in 1968. In 1969, the home care program came into being, the first such endeavor in upstate New York. In the '70s other services were added—the South End Health Center, alcoholism services, rehabilitation medicine center, and ambulatory surgery. More new buildings were constructed: a new major wing and a professional building.

New times demanded new philosophies to manage St. Peter's 427 beds, 154,000 annual patient days, and 18,000 yearly patient discharges. A remarkable continuity has benefited St. Peter's, which has had only seven administrators since 1869. Ambitious holistic programs serve the patient, providing comprehensive health care services encompassing the physical, emotional, and spiritual needs of the patient, the goals Peter Cagger must have considered so long ago.

SMITH AND MAHONEY, CONSULTING ENGINEERS

The Progressive spirit bloomed in early 20th-century America, expressing a common awareness of American problems, professionalizing and standardizing certain occupations and procedures to assuage them. Population pressures, emergence of uptown residential areas, and resulting demands on existing water facilities were one Albany manifestation of this trend. When Whitman, Requardt and Smith of Baltimore opened an Albany branch of their engineering concern in 1927, it soon dealt with Albany's fresh water supply.

Albany's Board of Water Supply engaged Benjamin L. Smith in 1928 to plan and supervise construction of a new water supply. Smith designed an $11-million system, then the nation's largest public works project. Its 20-mile flow of water, from Alcove Reservoir, provided a daily 30 million gallons of water when completed in 1932. Whitman, Requardt and Smith's Albany office, in the Home Savings Bank building, conducted large public works projects throughout the Northeast during the 1930s, continuing to monitor Albany's new water supply system and constructing an additional 100-million-gallon storage basin in Loudonville as a depression-era WPA project.

In 1945, Smith established Benjamin L. Smith & Associates, municipal engineering consultant to communities in New York, Massachusetts, and Ohio. Smith concentrated on designing hydraulic projects—filter plants, water mains, water supply and distribution systems, sanitary and storm sewer networks, and sewage disposal and sludge treatment plants. Benjamin L. Smith & Associates during the decade after World War II planned land subdivisions and street and utility designs for private residential developments.

As Smith's staff grew from five persons to 20 in the late '50s and '60s, it met an emerging need for community redevelopment in the cities of America. Urban renewal programs became increasingly important to Benjamin L. Smith & Associates, the firm serving as engineer for some of the country's first urban renewal projects and developing many upstate New York community master plans.

Top left:
In 1936, Works Progress Administration employees worked on Benjamin L. Smith's design for the Albany Board of Water Supply's Loudonville distribution reservoir.
Above:
Patrick F. Mahoney is now managing partner at Smith and Mahoney, Consulting Engineers.
Bottom left:
The late Benjamin L. Smith's Albany-based engineering career spanned more than four decades. This photograph was taken in the 1940s, in front of one of Mr. Smith's water supply projects.

Patrick F. Mahoney, a young Rensselaer Polytechnic Institute graduate, came to Benjamin L. Smith & Associates in 1965 as a design engineer. In May 1970 he became Smith's partner, the firm's name becoming Smith & Mahoney, Consulting Engineers. Benjamin L. Smith soon retired from his long, distinguished career and passed away in 1978 at the age of 88.

Under Mahoney's direction, the firm retained its ties to the city of Albany, while increasing involvement in land surveying and solid waste management. Its design for the Albany, New York, Solid Waste Energy Recovery System (ANSWERS) is a unique regional facility converting solid waste to fuel for generating steam while recovering all recyclable materials. Deeply committed to the redevelopment of Albany's downtown, Smith and Mahoney is restoring and rehabilitating numerous structures of historical value—the Brewster Building (once Albany Business College), Kenmore Hotel, Albany Energy Store, and the YMCA on Steuben Street. Now located in the Brewster Building, Smith and Mahoney will occupy offices in Steuben Place, the renovated YMCA building, continuing to offer upstate New York its finest in engineering project design systems.

L.A. SWYER COMPANY

The skyline of Albany has only been radically altered by two 20th-century men: Nelson Rockefeller and Lewis A. Swyer. Governor Rockefeller's contribution is concentrated in the massive plateau of the Empire State Plaza named for him. L.A. Swyer's is less centralized, but more directly connected to the pulse of the city and to its economic lifelines. An unshakeable symbiotic relationship with the Capital District, the product of specializations in development, general construction, and construction management, has made L.A. Swyer Company a distinguished prime mover in Albany's urban environment. Since its founding in 1948, the Swyer Company has come to perform an annual average volume of over $25 million worth of construction projects, with the company's president, Lewis A. Swyer, and vice-president, John J. Foley, closely involved with each from start to finish. A dedicated staff of office and field personnel has established a record for high quality, attention to detail, and a corporate commitment to meet exacting time restraints with an abiding concern for economy.

The Ten Eyck Project, one of L.A. Swyer's most important undertakings, is in the center of Albany's historic downtown district and includes a bank, a 400-room hotel, a 1,000-seat banquet facility, 300,000 square feet of office space, a 675-car parking garage, and a tree-lined plaza.

To fly above the Capital District is to see Swyer-built structures throughout the region: in Schenectady, major buildings for the General Electric Company, the Unitarian Church designed by Edward Durrell Stone, and the 22-story Summit Towers building for senior citizens; in Saratoga, the world-renowned Performing Arts Center, and a high-rise dormitory at Skidmore College; in Troy, major buildings for Russell Sage College and the landmark building of the RPI campus, the Richard Gilman Folsom Library; and in Albany County, a large collection of Swyer projects. Among them the new headquarters of the United Bank Corporation at 1450 Western Avenue; the Swyer-built Stuyvesant Plaza, the area's bellwether shopping center; Northway and Mohawk malls; 50 Wolf Road, central headquarters of New York State's Department of Environmental Conservation; and much of the other high-rise construction along Colonie's Wolf Road, itself a look at the future of the area.

Within Albany city limits, Swyer has constructed housing, schools, offices, banks, and hospitals. Among them, the 8-story headquarters for the Department of Mental Hygiene on Holland Avenue; the 13-story B'nai B'rith senior citizen residence, the 9-story Thurlow Terrace senior citizen building, and the 12-story Ohav Sholom; the 24-story Central Towers; temple and school for historic Beth Emeth; Albany Academy for Girls and Child's Hospital in the Academy Road area; and the Mechanics and Farmers Bank on Madison Avenue (now the Bank of New York).

Walking east along Washington Avenue and State Street, from Lark Street to Broadway, an Albany pedestrian would pass some of L.A. Swyer's most ambitious undertakings: Twin Towers, the largest office complex in the state outside of New York City; the Ten Eyck Project, a multi-use complex in the heart of downtown Albany, covering a 4-block area and including the new Albany Hilton, the Albany Savings Bank, a 675-car parking facility, and the 14-story headquarters for the New York State Department of Social Services; and the new 10-story National Commercial Bank & Trust Company (now Key Bank) building at State and Green streets. The list is lengthier, the impact pervasive.

It may be fairly said that in one way or another, sooner or later, every Albanian will be affected by an L.A. Swyer Company project—through working in some of the over seven million square feet of offices, shopping in stores, attending classes in schools, enjoying the performing arts, or transacting business in banks built by Swyer.

With its current focus on downtown Albany, L.A. Swyer Company continues to be "a conduit for change" and the quickening pace of a once moribund downtown is being advanced by Swyer's commitment to make Albany "the most pleasant, exciting, small city in the United States."

L.A. Swyer Company, through new construction, restoration, and rehabilitation, has dotted the map of modern Albany with structures now a part of the daily lives of thousands of Albany's citizens—making this area a more exciting place in which to live and work.

UNITED BANK NEW YORK

Hollis Harrington, chairman and president of State Bank of Albany, had become concerned about the influx of large, New York City banks into upstate New York. In early 1972, Harrington's State Bank, founded in 1803, merged with an old-line Buffalo bank—Liberty National Bank and Trust Company, founded in 1882—to form the United Bank Corporation of New York, in an effort to counter the growing New York City banking presence.

Harrington became the first chairman of this new holding company and targeted its expansion south through the Hudson River Valley and Long Island. With this intent, UBNY acquired Newburgh's second largest bank, Highland National, later in 1972.

In 1974, Peter D. Kiernan became president of the holding company. Harrington remained chairman until 1975, when Kiernan was elected to that position. Kiernan maintained a conservative financial course and also continued the acquisition of sound, well-run banks. In 1975, the National Bank of Orange and Ulster counties and First National Bank & Trust Company of Ellenville were made part of Highland National. In 1977, Long Island's second largest commercial bank, the Hempstead Bank, was acquired. Three years later, the acquisition of Peninsula National Bank in Cedarhurst, Long Island, was completed.

The pace of acquisitions accelerated in 1980 as agreements in principle were reached to acquire Sullivan County National Bank in Liberty, the Island State Bank in Patchogue, and the Rondout National Bank in Kingston. An agreement to acquire The Oneida National Bank and Trust Company in Utica was announced early in 1981.

As 1980 drew to a close, UBNY ranked among the largest upstate bank holding companies with assets of $2.2 billion. State Bank remained the flagship of UBNY but important positions had been achieved in the mid-Hudson and Long Island market areas to broaden the holding company's original presence in the northeastern and western parts of the state. Including the four banks for which agreements in principle have been reached, there will be 185 New York State banking offices under the UBNY banner.

United Bank New York occupies its own modern office building at 1450 Western Avenue, near Stuyvesant Plaza.

United Bank New York's return on average assets has been better than twice the norm for comparably sized northeastern holding companies. At the end of 1980, UBNY ranked 111th nationally in size among banks with more than $2 billion in assets, 63rd in earnings, and 2nd in return on its assets. In New York State, UBNY ranked at the top in most quantifiable measurements of relative financial performance, with all of its bank members earning over one percent on their assets.

UBNY has since its founding followed a prudent and efficient financial policy directed toward an ambition to become "the strongest and most profitable holding company in upstate New York.'' Aggressive marketing, conservative operation, and disciplined and responsible decision-making all contributed to the corporate philosophy aiming toward this goal.

"A merger often means a bank loses its name and its identity,'' said Robert F. Macfarland, president of Highland National Bank, "but this is not the case here.'' UBNY's member banks retain a large degree of operating autonomy, working within broad guidelines from the holding company. Member banks retain their names, their boards of directors, and their officers and employees. The acquisition of well-established banks allows United Bank New York, through retention of its members' existing facilities, to avoid the high expense of constructing and publicizing new branches. UBNY and its constituent banks are thus already a visible part of the community.

THE UNIVERSITY CLUB IN THE CITY OF ALBANY

A notice board proclaims the salient facts of membership: name, college, class, and date of membership. Generations follow one another into the University Club and many have been members for a half century or more. One—Dartmouth, 1911—joined when Woodrow Wilson was first inaugurated President. Approximately 20 of the 1,800 members live in the ivy-covered clubhouse at 141 Washington Avenue, the embodiment of continuity.

It began one March night in 1901, when 135 Albany graduates from various colleges met to establish a University Club which would "cultivate and maintain university spirit" and promote social exchange between themselves. Their constitution had the object, also, of maintaining library, reading, and assembly rooms, rooms initially rented at 99 Washington Avenue for $125 a month. Later, in 1901, men who had attended but not graduated from college were made eligible for the club, and by late that year there were 193 members.

In 1907, the club purchased the George Amsdell house at 141 Washington Avenue for $34,000 and spent $10,000 in renovations. It soon was a Saturday night ritual for members to congregate at the club for singing, billiards, "whiskey poker," and the "Amen Corner," where members engaged in lively topical discussion. The all-male "Duck Dinner," now annual tradition, originated in 1908, when the members gathered at a tobacconist's and crossed the Hudson to Kapp's in Rensselaer. "Club Shows" were annual events for many years and the New Year's Day "Wassail Bowl" tradition still endures. University dinners, held from 1907 to 1914, had such keynote speakers as President Taft, Canadian Governor-General Earl Grey, Charles Evans Hughes, and Andrew Carnegie.

As early as 1901, a "ladies' night" was offered by the University Club, and a ladies' dining room created. In November 1923, a regular weekly ladies' night was instituted.

Late in 1923, the original clubhouse burned. Only seven months later, construction of a new brick building was under way at the same site. This new structure, with main lounge, foyer, 27 sleeping rooms, billiard and card rooms, men's lounge, cocktail lounge (the Bayotte Room), main and three private dining rooms, and a 4-lane bowling alley, was ready for occupancy in May 1925. Two squash courts were eventually constructed in the club's annex at the north end of the property. As in the earlier clubhouse, a frieze of college and university seals and the club's coat of arms decorate the foyer.

The Great Depression saw the University Club in dire financial straits. By late 1935, the club owed more than $7,000 to tradesmen and its property taxes were in arrears. Two years later its mortgage was in foreclosure. To save the University Club, the constitution was amended to admit wives to privileged membership and to admit, on a limited basis, men who had not attended college. By mid-June 1938, a new $170,000-mortgage was obtained, and was subsequently burned with elaborate ceremony in 1957. Renovation and modification went on, at a gradual pace thereafter, as membership continued to grow as well.

The University Club itself comprises a dynamic monument to its past members, remaining paradoxically the same while always changing. Perhaps 125 new members enter annually, becoming a part of a stable institution which still promotes the spirit its founders had in mind that winter night in 1901.

Left:
The University Club's facility at 141 Washington Street is of brick and stone construction. Hanging in its Remington Room is Frederic Remington's painting, "The Lone Scout," donated by Mrs. John D. Parsons.
Right:
A university dinner held on March 19, 1910, featured President William Howard Taft (seated fourth from the left, under the presidential banner) as the principal speaker.

URBACH, KAHN & WERLIN, P.C.

"We began in 1951 with a handshake and zero clients." The handshake sufficed, and Urbach, Kahn & Werlin's word is still its bond. Only the highest professional and ethical standards were acceptable to the partners—Eli Werlin and Howard M. Kahn, young Siena College graduates. In 1963, they joined with Sidney Urbach, their teacher at Siena, establishing the firm of certified public accountants that bears their name today. The new partnership conducted a major audit for the city of Cohoes; then, in 1964, merged with three other area CPAs. After the Cohoes audit, Urbach, Kahn & Werlin became involved with special investigative audits for Albany city and county governments, the U.S. Department of Labor, the state of Vermont, several local school districts, the Port of Albany, and the Albany County Sewer District. In 1970, Urbach, Kahn & Werlin began to audit grants for the federal government and soon gained considerable experience, auditing billions of federal dollars in hundreds of municipalities across the nation. Today Urbach, Kahn & Werlin is one of the nation's top CPA firms.

The partnership, incorporated in 1974, has experienced growth during every year of its existence. The precepts of Urbach, Kahn & Werlin are integrity, unity of the firm, ongoing education, and individualism. Early in its existence, the firm realized that its growth was linked to that of its clients and strived to develop the most proficient staff possible, well-rounded professionals able to meet the specialized needs of every client.

Memberships in major professional societies such as the American Institute of Certified Public Accountants; the New York State Society of CPAs; and CPA Associates, a multi-country group providing sophisticated national and international service, are taken seriously. Participation by Urbach, Kahn & Werlin is evidenced by dozens of framed certificates in the company's headquarters at State Street, and by a *de jure* acceptance of the firm's excellence with four of its officers chairing senior committees of the New York State Society of CPAs.

Also prominently displayed in the State Street building are plaques and awards for civic participation. Shareholders and employees are encouraged in such involvement and serve on the boards of St. Peter's Hospital, Junior Achievement, Albany Symphony Orchestra, Chamber of Commerce, and Hospitality House, among others. A general philanthropic commitment became specific in 1979 with incorporation of the Urbach, Kahn & Werlin Foundation, funded by the shareholders to aid scientific, charitable, religious, and educational endeavors.

The company's clients run the gamut from colleges to movie houses, lumber yards to governments, newspapers to banks. Structured for auditing, accounting, taxation, and management services, Urbach, Kahn & Werlin in 1979 prepared 1,600 personal income tax returns; and in 1980 served 1,200 commercial clients nationwide, a far cry from that handshake almost three decades ago.

Top:
Headquarters of Urbach, Kahn & Werlin is located at 66 State Street, in a dignified turn-of-the century structure.
Left:
Founding partners of Urbach, Kahn & Werlin are (left to right) Eli Werlin, Howard M. Kahn, and the late Sidney Urbach.

WOLBERG ELECTRICAL SUPPLY CO., INC.

The 1920s marked America's first flirtation with electrified consumer products—appliances, tools, and household conveniences powered by small electric motors. Rural electrification was underway and inventors of every stripe were pouring out all sorts of electrically powered items. The electrified homes of America became a jumble of exposed wires and few of the nation's older buildings were equipped for this increased consumption.

Albany electrical contractor Samuel Wolberg foresaw this new demand and in 1925 founded Wolberg Electrical Supply Company at 68 Beaver Street. In just 12 months the business swelled to the point where Wolberg had to purchase and largely remodel a building at 47 Hudson Avenue, moving into it in 1927. Later, in 1939, RPI graduate Louis Wolberg joined his brother Sam, providing the business with what would become more than 35 years' expertise in electrical engineering. Further expansion was required after World War II ended, Wolberg Electrical Supply Company acquiring an additional facility at 86 Alexander Street. Another period of inflation and consumerism brought with it prosperity and a construction boom, reflecting in Wolberg's greatly expanded operations.

The interior of Wolberg's Hudson Avenue store in the late 1920s displayed a variety of household appliances—efficient then, bulbous and primitive by today's standards.

Burgeoning demand and an ever-increasing volume of business necessitated a final company relocation in 1967. At 35 Industrial Park Road, Wolberg Electrical Supply Company constructed a modern complex including 43,000 square feet of warehouse, 5,000 square feet of showroom, and 5,000 square feet of office and counter space. In the warehouse were built two fully enclosed tractor-trailer bays equipped with electric dock-levelers to facilitate loading and unloading operations.

Although Samuel Wolberg died in 1968, his company continued to grow, expanding its lines of merchandise and its services to industrial accounts receivable, stock control, and price maintenance. In 1975 a second Wolberg facility opened to serve the Schenectady market; 22,000 square feet in the Rotterdam Industrial Park followed the successful formula developed in Albany, becoming known for dependable, efficient service.

Under chairman of the board Milton Bindell and president Ralph LaPorta, Wolberg made a dramatic response to the changing times, launching their company into the retail market for electrical products and design services. World of Light, the Wolberg showroom, was redecorated to optimize customer choice. An IBM System 38 computer was installed and programmed to handle Wolberg's needs for maximum information flow, response to customer demand, inventory management, and accurate forecast of future needs. From 20 employees in 1927, Wolberg Electrical Supply Company's staff reached a level of 62 skilled workers by 1981. That growth, and the company's as a whole, is directly traceable to Sam Wolberg's initial insistence on excellence in service, the keystone of Wolberg's business philosophy.

THE WOODWARD CO.

"A passing fancy'' nearly put The Woodward Co. out of business after a century of successful operation. As a manufacturer of carriage and harness mountings, it was natural that The Woodward Co. would refuse to buy a truck for its own use until after World War I.

The Woodward Co. was founded in 1819 by Nathaniel Wright, who manufactured and sold his wares from his shop in Albany's south end. He marketed his high-quality closed silver plating as far away as Cuba and Latin America. Wright sometimes bartered for his goods, exchanging them for barrels of tobacco, beans, or wine.

In the early 1850s, Wright hired John Woodward, Jr. and William Hill as clerks. These men, who were related to one another, became Wright's partners in early 1854. Six years later, the company had moved to Broadway, where it would remain, at various addresses, for more than six decades. Upon Wright's death in 1860, the surviving partners soon reorganized as Woodward & Hill Co., offering "inducements to purchasers of harness and carriage trimming equaled by but few houses in the line.'' By the end of the 1870s, Woodward & Hill made, stocked, and sold all sorts of related products—woodwork; trimmings; varnishes; coach colors; iron and steel axles; oak and hickory felloes; elm hubs; springs; wheels; enameled leather, wolf, fox, bear, and buffalo robes; trunks; traveling bags; and buggy tops. A typical shipment, to storekeeper J.L. Rice of Rensselaerville, included 20 horse blankets and three lap robes and cost him just $25.70 in 1884.

Woodward & Hill became well-known suppliers of carriage and saddlery hardware, blacksmith's supplies, and similar items. In 1900 the firm incorporated and two years later became The Woodward Co. With the advent of the automobile—that "passing fancy,'' according to then-president Walter Woodward—it became vital for the firm to develop new products and new services to market. In 1926, warehouse and store were consolidated at a single site on Tivoli Street in north Albany; it remains there today. Once at the new site, The Woodward Co. expanded its heavy hardware lines, added other metals to the stock it offered, and became a leading source of fasteners and ferrous and nonferrous metals. As this expansion occurred, adjacent structures on Tivoli Street were acquired, many of them 19th-century industrial buildings.

The fifth generation of The Woodward Co. is now active in the company's operation, and its steel and metal warehousing has expanded into the fabrication of a wide variety of industrial components. Between 1970 and 1980 Woodward more than doubled its facilities, and plans further expansion and continuation of its local tradition of conscientious, individualized service.

Below:
Woodward Co. employees pose on one of the firm's wagons in this photograph taken in 1912. The company's headquarters behind them, on the southwest corner of Broadway and Hudson, has since been restored.
Bottom:
This typical 19th-century letterhead shows Woodward & Hill as it appeared in 1884, while located at 324 Broadway. The horse-drawn car is at the intersection of Broadway and Hamilton.

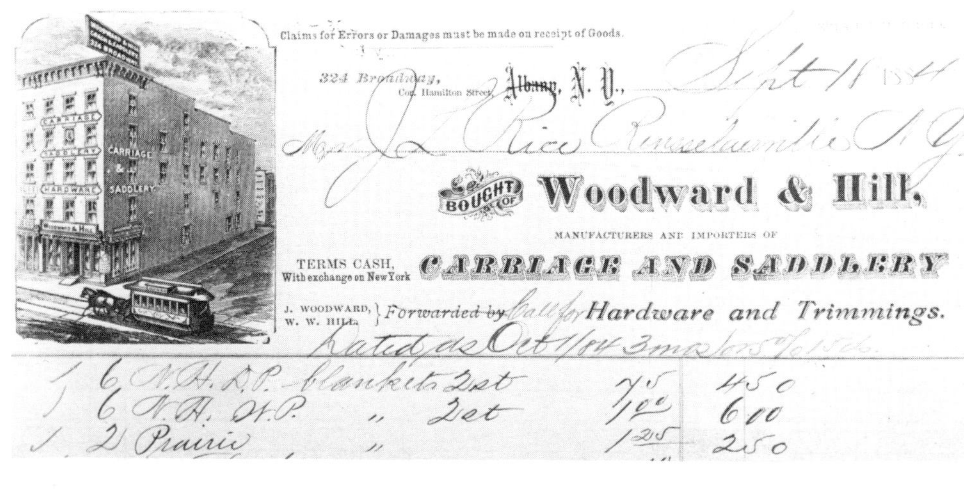

Claims for Errors or Damages must be made on receipt of Goods.

324 Broadway, Cor. Hamilton Street, Albany, N. Y., Sept 11 1884

Mr J. L. Rice Rensselaerville N.Y.

BOUGHT OF Woodward & Hill,

MANUFACTURERS AND IMPORTERS OF

TERMS CASH, With exchange on New York

CARRIAGE AND SADDLERY

J. WOODWARD, W. W. HILL. Forwarded by Call for Hardware and Trimmings.

Dated as Oct 1/84 3 mos

1	6 N.H. D.P. blankets 2st	75	450
1	6 N.H. H.P. " 2st	100	600
1	2 Prairie "	125	250

MAYORS OF ALBANY

1686-93	Pieter Schuyler
1694	Johannes Abeel
1695	Evert Bancker
1696-97	Dirck Wesselse ten Broeck
1698	Hendrick Hansen
1699	Pieter Van Brugh
1700	Jan Jansen Bleecker
1701	Johannes Bleecker, Jr.
1702	Albert Janse Ryckman
1703-05	Johannes Schuyler
1706	David Davidse Schuyler
1707	Evert Bancker
1709	Johannes Abeel
1710-18	Robert Livingston, Jr.
1719-20	Myndert Schuyler
1721-22	Pieter Van Brugh
1723-24	Myndert Schuyler
1725	Johannes Cuyler
1726-28	Rutger Bleecker
1729-30	Johannes De Peyster
1731	Johannes ("Hans") Hansen
1732	Johannes De Peyster
1733-40	Edward Holland
1741	Johannes Schuyler
1742-45	Cornelis Cuyler
1746-47	Dirck Ten Broeck
1748-49	Jacob C. Ten Eyck
1750-53	Robert Sanders
1754-55	Johannes ("Hans") Hansen
1756-60	Sybrant G. Van Schaick
1761-69	Volckert P. Douw
1770-77	Abraham Cornelis Cuyler
1778	John Barclay
1779-82	Abraham Ten Broeck
1783-85	Johannes Jacobse Beeckman
1786-89	John Lansing, Jr.
1790-95	Abraham Yates, Jr.
1796-98	Abraham Ten Broeck
1799-1815	Philip S. Van Rensselaer
1816-18	Elisha Jenkins
1819-20	Philip S. Van Rensselaer
1821-23	Charles E. Dudley
1824-25	Ambrose Spencer
1826-27	James Stevenson
1828	Charles E. Dudley
1829-30	John Townsend
1831	Francis Bloodgood
1832	John Townsend
1833	Francis Bloodgood
1834-36	Erastus Corning
1837	Teunis Van Vechten
1838-40	Jared L. Rathbone
1841	Teunis Van Vechten
1842	Barent P. Staats
1843-44	Friend Humphrey
1845	John K. Paige
1846-47	William Parmelee
1849	Friend Humphrey
1850	Franklin Townsend
1851-53	Eli Perry
1854-55	William Parmelee (died in office)
1855	Charles W. Godard
1856-59	Eli Perry
1860-61	George H. Thacher
1862-65	Eli Perry
1866-67	George H. Thacher
1868-69	Charles E. Bleecker
1870-73	George H. Thacher
1874	George H. Thacher (resg. Jan. 28)
1874	John G. Burch, ex-officio
1874-75	Edmund L. Judson
1876-77	A. Bleecker Banks
1878-83	Michael N. Nolan
1883	John Swinburne
1884-85	A. Bleecker Banks
1886-87	John Boyd Thacher
1888-89	Edward A. Maher
1890-93	James H. Manning
1894-95	Oren E. Wilson
1896-97	John Boyd Thacher
1898-99	Thomas J. Van Alstyne
1900-01	James H. Blessing
1902-08	Charles H. Gaus
1909	Henry F. Snyder
1910-13	James B. McEwan
1914-16	Joseph W. Stevens
1917	Joseph W. Stevens
1918-21	James R. Watt
1922-25	William S. Hackett
1926-40	John Boyd Thacher 2nd
1942-44	Erastus Corning 2nd
1944-45	Frank S. Harris (temporary, while Mayor Corning left for military service)
1945-	Erastus Corning 2nd

GOVERNORS OF NEW YORK

1777-95	George Clinton
1795-1801	John Jay
1801-04	George Clinton
1804-07	Morgan Lewis
1807-17	Daniel D. Thompkins
1817	John Taylor
1817-23	DeWitt Clinton
1823-25	Joseph C. Yates
1825-28	DeWitt Clinton
1828	Nathaniel Pitcher
1828-29	Martin Van Buren
1829-33	Enos J. Throop
1833-39	William L. Marcy
1839-43	William H. Seward
1843-45	William C. Bouck
1845-47	Silas Wright
1847-49	John Young
1849-51	Hamilton Fish
1851-53	Washington Hunt
1853-55	Horatio Seymour
1855-57	Myron H. Clark
1857-59	John A. King
1859-63	Edwin D. Morgan
1863-65	Horatio Seymour
1865-69	Reuben E. Fenton
1869-73	John T. Hoffman
1873-75	John A. Dix
1875-77	Samuel J. Tilden
1877-79	Lucius Robinson
1879-83	Alonzo B. Cornell
1883-85	Grover Cleveland
1885-92	David P. Hill
1892-95	Roswell P. Flower
1895-97	Levi P. Morton
1897-99	Frank S. Black
1899-1901	Theodore Roosevelt
1901-05	Benjamin B. Odell, Jr.
1905-07	Frank W. Higgins
1907-11	Charles Evans Hughes
1911-13	John Alden Dix
1913	William Sulzer
1913-15	Martin H. Glynn
1915-19	Charles S. Whitman
1919-21	Alfred E. Smith
1921-23	Nathan L. Miller
1923-29	Alfred E. Smith
1929-33	Franklin Delano Roosevelt
1933-43	Herbert H. Lehman
1943-55	Thomas E. Dewey
1955-59	Averell Harriman
1959-73	Nelson A. Rockefeller
1973-75	Malcolm Wilson
1975-	Hugh L. Carey

Albany, City of. *Albany's Tercentenary, 1624–1924: Historical Narrative Souvenir.* Albany: City of Albany, 1924.

Albany, N.Y. City Directory. 1813–1980. (Several publishers.)

Albany, N.Y., City of. *Dongan Charter, July 22, 1686.* Reprinted from Book of City Laws 1842. Albany: 1964.

Barnard, Daniel D. *A Discourse on the Life of Stephen Van Rensselaer.* Albany: Hoffman and White, 1839.

Barnes, Thurlow Weed, ed. *Souvenir of the Albany Bicentennial Celebration, July 1886: containing the Official Program . . . lithographs of the Great Historical Pageant.* Albany: The Journal Co., 1886.

Bennett, Allison P. *The People's Choice: A History of Albany County in Art and Architecture.* Albany: Albany County Historical Assoc., 1980.

Bielinski, Stefan. *Abraham Yates, Jr., and the New Political Order in Revolutionary New York.* Albany: New York State American Revolution Bicentennial Commission, 1975.

Blackburn, Roderic H. and Piwonka, Ruth. *A Remnant in the Wilderness: New York Dutch Scripture History Paintings of the Early Eighteenth Century.* Albany: Albany Institute of History and Art, 1980.

Blackburn, Roderic H. *Cherry Hill: The History and Collections of a Van Rensselaer Family.* Albany: Historic Cherry Hill, 1976.

Blayney, Rev. J. McClusky. *History of the First Presbyterian Church of Albany.* Albany: Jenkins & Johnston, 1877.

Blessing, Charles W., comp., ed. *Albany Schools and Colleges, Yesterday and Today: An Anniversary Volume, 1686–1936.* Albany: Ft. Orange Press, 1936.

Bolton, Theodore and Cortelyou, Irwin F. *Ezra Ames of Albany: Portrait Painter . . . , 1768–1836.* New York: New York Historical Society, 1955.

Bonney, Catharina V.R., comp. *Legacy of Historical Gleanings.* 2 vols. Albany: J. Munsell, 1875.

Boos, John E. *Rambling With Jerry.* 1931. Reprint. Albany: Privately Printed, 1972.

———. *Roaming Near the Fireplace.* 1944. Reprint. Albany: Privately Printed, 1972.

Bush, Martin H. *Revolutionary Enigma; A Re-appraisal of General Philip Schuyler of New York.* Port Washington, N.Y.: Ira J. Friedman, Inc., 1969.

Christman, Henry. *Tin Horns and Calico.* 1945. Reprint. Cornwallville, N.Y.: Hope Farm Press, 1975.

City of Albany, Dept. of Human Resources & Federation of Historical Services. *Handbook to Historic Resources of the Upper Hudson Valley.* Martha D. Noble and Shelby Marshall, comps. Old Chatham, N.Y.: Federation of Historical Services, 1980.

Coulson, Thomas. *Joseph Henry: His Life and Work.* Princeton, N.J.: Princeton University Press, 1950.

Crowley, James A. *The Old Albany County and the American Revolution.* Troy, N.Y.: The Historian Publishing Co., 1979.

Danckaerts, Jasper. *Journal of Jasper Danckaerts, 1679–1680: Original Narratives of Early American History.* Edited by Bartlett Burleigh James and J. Franklin Jameson. New York: Charles Scribner's Sons, 1913.

DeMille, George F. *Pioneer Cathedral: A Brief History of the Cathedral of All Saints, Albany.* Albany: Cathedral of All Saints, 1967.

Dillon, Rev. John J. *The Historic Story of St. Mary's, Albany, N.Y. . . .* New York: P.J. Kennedy & Sons, 1933.

Dutch Settlers Society of Albany Yearbook. 1924–1979. 46 vols. Albany: The Dutch Settlers Society of Albany.

Edelstein, David S. *Joel Munsell: Printer and Antiquarian.* New York: Columbia University Press, 1950.

Federal Writers' Project, comp. *Albany - Past and Present.* Albany: Works Progress Administration, The State of New York, n.d.

Filley, Dorothy M. *Recapturing Wisdom's Valley: The Watervliet Shaker Heritage, 1775–1975.* Albany: Albany Institute of History and Art & Town of Colonie, 1975.

Gerber, Morris, comp. *Old Albany.* 4 vols. Albany: Privately Printed, 1961–1979.

Gerlach, Don R. *Philip Schuyler and the American Revolution in New York, 1733–1777.* Lincoln: University of Nebraska Press, 1964.

———. *Philip Schuyler and the Growth of New York.* Albany: The University of the State of New York, 1968.

Gilman, William G. *Melville's Early Life and Redburn.* New York: New York University Press, 1951.

Grant, Ann McVicar. *Memoirs of an American Lady . . . . 1808.* 2 vols. Reprint. New York: Dodd, Mead & Co., 1901.

Gregg, Arthur B. *Old Hellebergh.* 1936. Reprint. Guilderland, N.Y.: Guilderland Historical Society, 1975.

Groft, Tammis Kane. *Cast With Style: 19th Century Cast-iron Stoves from the Albany Area.* Albany: Albany Institute of History and Art, 1981.

———. *The Folk Spirit of Albany.* Albany: Albany Institute of History and Art, 1978.

Hamilton, Milton W. *Henry Hudson and the Dutch in New York.* Albany: The University of the State of New York, 1959.

———. *Sir William Johnson: Colonial American, 1715–1763.* Port Washington, N.Y.: Kennikat Press, 1976.

Hamilton, Milton W., et al. *The Papers of Sir William Johnson.* 14 vols. Albany: The University of the State of New York, 1921–1965.

Heins, Henry H. *Swan of Albany: A History of the Oldest Congregation of the Lutheran Church in America.* Albany: First Lutheran Church, 1976.

Hislop, Codman. *Albany: Dutch, English, and American.* Albany: The Argus Press, 1936.

Historic Albany Foundation. *Albany Architects: The Present Looks at the Past.* Albany: Historic Albany Foundation, 1978.

———. *Plaza Row.* Albany: Historic Albany Foundation, 1979.

Hooper, Rev. Joseph. *A History of Saint Peter's Church in the City of Albany.* Albany: Fort Orange Press. 1900.

Hotchkiss, Jacob T. *Diverse Backgrounds of Old Albany: A Concise History of Nationality Groups.* Unpublished. Albany: Research study for Albany Institute of History and Art, 1964.

Howell, George R. and Tenney, Jonathan, eds. *Bi-Centennial History of Albany: History of the County of Albany, N.Y. from 1609 to 1886.* 3 vols. New York: W.W. Munsell & Co., 1886.

Jameson, J. Franklin, ed. *Narratives of New Netherland, 1609–1664.* New York: Charles Scribner's Sons, 1909.

Kalm, Peter. *Peter Kalm's Travels in North America: The English Version of 1770.* Edited by Adolph P. Benson. 2 vols. 1937. Reprint. New York: Dover Publications, Inc., 1966.

Kennedy, William. *Legs: A Novel.* New York: Coward, McCann & Geoghegan, Inc., 1975.

Kenney, Alice P. *Albany: Crossroads of Liberty.* Albany: City and County of Albany American Revolution Bicentennial Commission, 1976.

———. *Stubborn For Liberty: the Dutch in New York.* Syracuse: Syracuse University Press, 1975.

———. *The Gansevoorts of Albany: Dutch Patricians in the Upper Valley.* Syracuse, N.Y.: Syracuse University Press, 1969.

Kim, Sung Bok. *Landlord and Tenant in Colonial New York; Manorial Society, 1664–1775.* Chapel Hill: University of North Carolina Press, 1978.

Kimball, Francis P. *Albany—A Cradle of America, 1609–1959.* Albany: Albany County Hudson-Champlain Celebration Committee, n.d.

———. comp. *Albany: Birthplace of the Union.* Albany: The National Savings Bank, 1940.

———. *The Capital Region of New York State: Crossroads of Empire.* 3 vols. New York: Lewis Historical Publishing Co., 1942.

Louden, M. J., ed. *Catholic Albany . . .* Albany: Peter Donnelly, 1895.

Mendel, Mesick, Cohen—Architects. *The Ten Broeck Mansion: A Historic Structure Report.* Albany: The Albany County Historical Association, 1975.

Munsell, Joel, ed. *Annals of Albany.* 10 vols. Albany: Joel Munsell, 1850–1859. Vols. 1–4, expanded 2nd edition, 1869–1871.

———. *Collections on the History of Albany from Its Discovery to the Present Time.* 4 vols. Albany: J. Munsell, 1865–1871.

Neu, Irene D. *Erastus Corning: Merchant and Financier, 1794–1872.* Ithaca, N.Y.: Cornell University Press, 1960.

New York State Division for Historic Preservation, Bureau of Historic Sites. *Schuyler Mansion: A Historic Structure Report.* Albany: New York State Parks and Recreation, 1977.

Nissenson, S.G. *The Patroon's Domain.* 1937. Reprint. New York: Octagon Books, 1973.

O'Callaghan, Edmund Bailey, ed. *Documents Relative to the Colonial History of the State of New York.* 13 vols. vols. 12, 13 edited by Berthold Fernow. Albany: The State of New York, 1853–1881.

———. *The Documentary History of the State of New York.* 4 vols. Albany: The State of New York, 1850–1851.

Our Two Hundred and Fifty Years: A Historical Sketch of the First Reformed Church, Albany, N.Y. Albany: Officers of the Church, 1899.

Paltsits, Victor H., ed. *Minutes of the Commissioners for Detecting and Defeating Conspiracies in the State of New York: Albany County Sessions, 1778–1781.* 1909, 1910. 3 vols. Reprint. New York: DaCapo Press, 1972.

Parker, Amasa J. *Landmarks of Albany County.* Syracuse, N.Y.: D. Mason & Co., 1897.

Pearson, Jonathan. *Contributions for the Genealogies of the First Settlers of the Ancient County of Albany, 1630–1800.* 1872. Reprint. Baltimore, Md.: Genealogical Publishing Co., Inc., 1976.

———. *Contributions for the Genealogies of the Descendants of the First Settlers of the Patent and City of Schenectady, 1662–1800.* 1873. Reprint. Baltimore, Md. Genealogical Publishing Co., Inc., 1976.

———, trans., ed. *Early Records of the City and County of Albany and Colony of Rensselaerswyck, 1656–1675.* 4 vols., vols. 2–4 revised and edited by A.J.F. Van Laer. Albany: The University of the State of New York, 1869, 1916–1919.

Reynolds, Cuyler, comp. *Albany Chronicles: A History of the City Arranged Chronologically, From the Earliest Settlement to the Present Time.* Albany: J.B. Lyon Co., 1906.

———, ed. *Hudson-Mohawk Genealogical and Family Memoirs.* 4 vols. New York: Lewis Historical Publishing Co., 1911.

Reynolds, Helen Wilkinson. *Dutch Houses in the Hudson Valley Before 1776.* 1929. Reprint. New York: Dover Publications, Inc., 1965.

Rice, Harriet Langdon Pruyn. *Harmanus Bleecker: An Albany Dutchman, 1779–1849.* Albany: Privately printed, 1924.

Rice, Norman S. *Albany Silver, 1652–1825.* Albany: Albany Institute of History and Art, 1964.

Rittner, Don, comp. *Pine Bush: Albany's Last Frontier, April 1976.* Albany: Pine Bush Historic Preservation Project, 1976.

Robinson, Frank S. *Albany's O'Connell Machine: An American Political Relic.* Albany: The Washington Park Spirit, Inc., 1973.

Root, Edward W. *Philip Hooker: A Contribution to the Study of the Renaissance in America.* New York: Charles Scribner's Sons, 1929.

Roseberry, Cecil R. *Capitol Story.* Albany: State of New York, 1964.

Rowley, William Esmond. *Albany: A Tale of Two Cities, 1820–1880.* Unpublished Ph.D. thesis presented to Com. on the History of American Civilization . . . Cambridge: Harvard University, 1967.

Rubinger, Rabbi Naphtali J. *Albany Jewry of the Nineteenth Century: Historic Roots and Communal Evolution.* Unpublished Ph.D thesis, Yeshiva University, 1970.

Sears, Mary Hun. *Hudson Crossroads.* New York: Exposition Press, 1954.

Sevier, Christine. *History of the Albany Cathedral of the Immaculate Conception 1852–1927.* Albany: Cathedral of the Immaculate Conception, 1927.

Sheridan, Philip H. *General Philip H. Sheridan's Personal Memoirs.* 2 vols. New York: Charles L. Webster & Co., 1888.

Skinner, Christine, comp. *Albany Churches: Brief History of Some Protestant Churches in Albany Prior to 1800, up to 1947.* 2 vols. Unpublished manuscript in Coll. Albany Institute of History and Art Library, n.d.

Sullivan, James and Flick, Alexander C., eds. *Minutes of the Albany Committee of Correspondence, 1775–1779.* 2 vols. Albany: The University of the State of New York, 1923, 1925.

Trelease, Allen W. *Indian Affairs in Colonial New York in the 17th Century.* Ithaca: Cornell University Press, 1960.

Van der Donck, Adriaen. *A Description of the New Netherlands.* Edited by Thomas F. O'Donnell. Syracuse: Syracuse University Press, 1968.

Van Deusen, Glyndon G. *Thurlow Weed: Wizard of the Lobby.* 1947. Reprint. New York: DaCapo Press, 1969.

Van Laer, Arnold J.F., trans., ed. *Correspondence of Jeremias Van Rensselaer, 1651–1674.* Albany: The University of the State of New York, 1932.

———. *Correspondence of Maria Van Rensselaer, 1669–1689.* Albany: The University of the State of New York, 1935.

———. *Minutes of the Court of Albany, Rensselaerswyck and Schenectady, 1668–1685.* 3 vols. Albany: The University of the State of New York, 1926, 1928, 1932.

———. *Minutes of the Court of Fort Orange and Beverwyck, 1652–1660.* 2 vols. Albany: The University of the State of New York, 1920, 1923.

———. *Minutes of the Court of Rensselaerswyck, 1648–1652.* Albany: The University of the State of New York, 1922.

———. *Van Rensselaer Bowier Manuscripts, 1630–1643.* Albany: The University of the State of New York, 1908.

Watson, Winslow C., ed. *Men and Times of The Revolution; or Memoirs of Elkanah Watson Including Journals of Travels in Europe and America, 1777–1842.* New York: Dana & Co., 1856.

Weed, Harriet A., ed. *Autobiography of Thurlow Weed.* Boston: Houghton Mifflin Co., 1883.

Weise, Arthur James. *History of the City of Albany.* Albany: E.H. Bender, 1884.

Wilcoxen, Charlotte. *Albany in the Seventeenth Century: A Dutch Profile.* Albany: Albany Institute of History and Art, 1981.

Worth, Gorham A. *Random Recollections of Albany from 1800 to 1808.* Albany: J. Munsell, 1866.

For the completion of this book—the first overall view of the city's history since Codman Hislop's fine work of 1936—credit belongs to many people, most of whose names do not appear on the title page.

Before all others, I am indebted to that unique group of Albany scholars who over the generations have undertaken tedious efforts to preserve and pass on the city's heritage at a time when it was in its most vulnerable state: chiefly E.B. O'Callaghan, Cuyler Reynolds, and, above all, Joel Munsell.

Within the past decade, Albany has been blessed with a renewed interest in her rich past. I have drawn upon the contemporary scholarship and encouragement of Margaret Conners Harrigan, Stefan Bielinski, Charles Gehring, and Don Rittner, as well as Alice Kenney, Tammis Kane Groft, Dorothy Filley, Roderic Blackburn, and Alison Bennett, who with Charlotte Wilcoxen have shown us that the city's history has not all been written, and that our understanding of our roots is an ever-evolving process.

It takes a special gift to create an atmosphere in which an entire community will come to know and value its past. Much of our most fascinating history is contained in folklore and oral tradition, quoted from the keen minds of average people in the twilight of their years. My thanks goes to the late Edgar Van Olinda and Bill Schirving, as well as to their fellow columnists Charles Mooney, Cecil Roseberry, and my long-time friend Raymond Joyce, Sr., whose widely read newspaper columns have done much to bring the city's history and traditions into all our homes over the years.

William Kennedy, the late John Boos, and, of course, Morris Gerber deserve special mention for their welcome dissemination of Albany memories.

In addition to the many citations credited within the book, several people deserve special recognition for their dedicated assistance given to either myself or Dennis Holzman in our two-year search for rare photographs and information. Kathleen Roe of the N.Y. State Archives and James Corsaro of the State Library, Manuscripts and Special Collections, were invaluable in their aid. Marguerite Mullenneaux of the Albany Public Library has been my standby for many years. The staff of McKinney Library of the Albany Institute of History and Art—James Hobin, Kenneth MacFarland, Suzanne Roberson, Christine Ward, Daryl Severson, and others mentioned above—showed a degree of cooperation far beyond the call of obligation.

For their contributions to the photographic aspects of the book we are further indebted to Joseph McCormick, Arthur O'Keefe, Lindsay Watson, and the wonderful expertise of Lou Carol Lecce.

I extend my gratitude to Martha Noble, who spent innumerable hours in proofreading as well as preparing the comprehensive reading list contained in this work; to Robert Arnold for his detailed compilation of the business biographies and his updating of the city's chronology, a task of great value that has long needed doing; and to Emerson Moran for his condensing and writing of several "sidebar" sections in the text.

Some have helped in this endeavor far more than they realize. To Brother Conrad and the late Brother Alfred of CBA, James Magee and Robert Flacke of Fort William Henry, as well as to the late Fr. Michael McCloskey and the excellent history department of Siena College, belongs the credit for giving me what ability and confidence I needed to commence this work.

The genesis of these thoughts and facts about Albany as a published work belongs entirely with Windsor Publications, whose series of American urban histories have made major contributions to this country's historical resources. Overall credit belongs to Windsor vice-president John M. Phillips for his decision to stay with the Albany book through its completion; to sales representatives Clive and Christine Bates, who enlisted support for this ambitious and costly publishing venture from Albany's business community; to Margaret C. Tropp for her editing and arrangement of a rambling manuscript into a readable book with chapters of a common theme; to Phyllis Gray for patiently retyping my rough copy as well as transcribing innumerable tapes made from notes of lectures given by me over the years; to administrator Katherine Cooper for capably handling many details all along the way; to Karen Story, business-biography editor; to Phyllis Rifkin for overseeing the book's evolution from typescript to printed page; to proofreader Andrew Christie; to Teri Greenberg and her assistants, Judith Zauner and Jana Wernor, for making the difficult choices associated with evaluating over 400 illustrations; to designer John Fish for his flexibility, patience, and artistic ability in laying out the book. And above all, both I and my family are especially indebted to editor-in-chief Barbara Marinacci, whose perseverance, troubleshooting, and fine editorial skill are the main factors which have enabled this book to see the light of day.

Additionally, I want to thank the many Albany business concerns and institutions who helped to underwrite the book's manufacturing costs and whose own histories are briefly recounted by Robert Arnold in the last chapter.

Encouragement is a quality of inestimable value without which I could not have started, much less completed, this task. In addition to much helpful advice rendered, I am especially indebted to Mayor Erastus Corning and Albany Institute Director Norman Rice for unselfishly helping me at every juncture of the long and often trying journey.

I express gratitude to those who have remained close to me over the years: Dick Conners, Jane McNally, Mel Wolfgang, George Marguin, and the dedicated staff in City Hall and the Department of Human Resources; also to my students in Old Albany for the constant input of information which they continue to provide, years after our formal relationship has ceased.

I am immeasurably grateful to my family: to my parents, John and Margaret Gaffie McEneny, for the love and education they imparted to me; to my brother Terry, who has never failed to support me in anything I have ever attempted to do; and to my Aunts Alice McCullen and Josephine Belser, who are my constant mentors.

Finally, this book could never have been written without the irreplaceable support of my best friend, Barbara Leonard McEneny, whom I had the good sense to marry 13 years ago.

——John J. McEneny

Italic numbers indicate illustrations.

Published Books in Windsor Local History Series

St. Paul: Saga of an American City, by Virginia Brainard Kunz (1977)

The Heritage of Lancaster, by John Ward Willson Loose (1978)

A Panoramic History of Rochester and Monroe County, New York, by Blake McKelvey (1979)

Syracuse: From Salt to Satellite, by William Roseboom and Henry Schramm (1979)

Columbia, South Carolina, History of a City, by John A. Montgomery (1979)

Kitchener: Yesterday Revisited, by Bill Moyer (1979)

Erie: Chronicle of a Great Lakes City, by Edward Wellejus (1980)

Montgomery: An Illustrated History, by Wayne Flynt (1980)

Charleston: Crossroads of History, by Isabella Leland (1980)

Baltimore: An Illustrated History, by Suzanne E. Greene (1980)

The Fort Wayne Story: A Pictorial History, by John Ankenbruck (1980)

City at the Pass: An Illustrated History of El Paso, by Leon Metz (1980)

Tucson: Portrait of a Desert Pueblo, by John Bret Harte (1980)

Salt Lake City: The Gathering Place, by John McCormick (1980)

Saginaw: A History of the Land and the City, by Stuart D. Gross (1980)

Cedar Rapids: Tall Corn and High Technology, by Ernie Danek (1980)

Los Angeles: A City Apart, by David L. Clark (1981)

Heart of the Commonwealth: Worcester, by Margaret Erskine (1981)

Out of a Wilderness: An Illustrated History of Greater Lansing, by Justin Kestenbaum (1981)

The Valley and the Hills: An Illustrated History of Birmingham and Jefferson County, by Leah Rawls Atkins (1981)

River Capital: An Illustrated History of Baton Rouge, by Mark T. Carleton (1981)

Chattanooga: An Illustrated History, by James Livingood (1981)

New Haven: An Illustrated History, edited by Richard Hegel and Floyd M. Shumway (1981)

Kalamazoo: The Place Behind the Products, by Larry Massie and Peter Schmitt (1981)

Mobile: The Life and Times of a Great Southern City, by Melton McLaurin (1981)

New Orleans, by John Kemp (1981)

Regina: From Pile O' Bones to Queen City of the Plains, by W.A. Riddell (1981)

King County and Its Queen City, Seattle: A Pictorial History, by James Warren (1981)

To the Setting of the Sun: The Story of York, Pennsylvania, by Georg Sheets (1981)

Buffalo: Lake City in Niagara Land, by Richard C. Brown and Bob Watson (1981)

Springfield of the Ozarks, by Harris and Phyllis Dark (1981)

Charleston and the Kanawha Valley, by Otis K. Rice (1981)

Selected Works-in-Progress

Dallas: Portrait in Pride, by Darwin Payne (1982)

Heart of the Promised Land: An Illustrated History of Oklahoma County, by Bob L. Blackburn (1982)

Winnipeg: Gateway to the New West, by Eric Wells (1982)

City of Lakes: An Illustrated History of Minneapolis, by Joseph Stipanovich (1982)

Rhode Island: The Independent State, by George H. Kellner and J. Stanley Lemons (1982)

Calgary: Canada's Frontier Metropolis, by Max Foran and Heather MacEwan Foran (1982)

Evanston: An Illustrated History, by Patrick Quinn (1982)

Norfolk's Waters: An Illustrated Maritime History of Hampton Roads, by William L. Tazewell (1982)

Windsor Publications, Inc.
History Books Division
Editorial Offices:
21220 Erwin Street
Woodland Hills, California 91365
(213) 884-4050

THIS BOOK WAS SET IN
CENTURY AND CENTURY BOLD EXTENDED
AND GENEVA ITALIC TYPES,
PRINTED ON
70 POUND WARRENFLO
AND BOUND BY
WALSWORTH PUBLISHING COMPANY.
COVER AND TEXT DESIGNED BY
JOHN FISH
LAYOUT BY
SANDRA LEE BELL
CONSTANCE BLAISDELL
E. SHANNON STRULL
JEAN MALONEY-HAGERMAN
AND MELINDA WADE

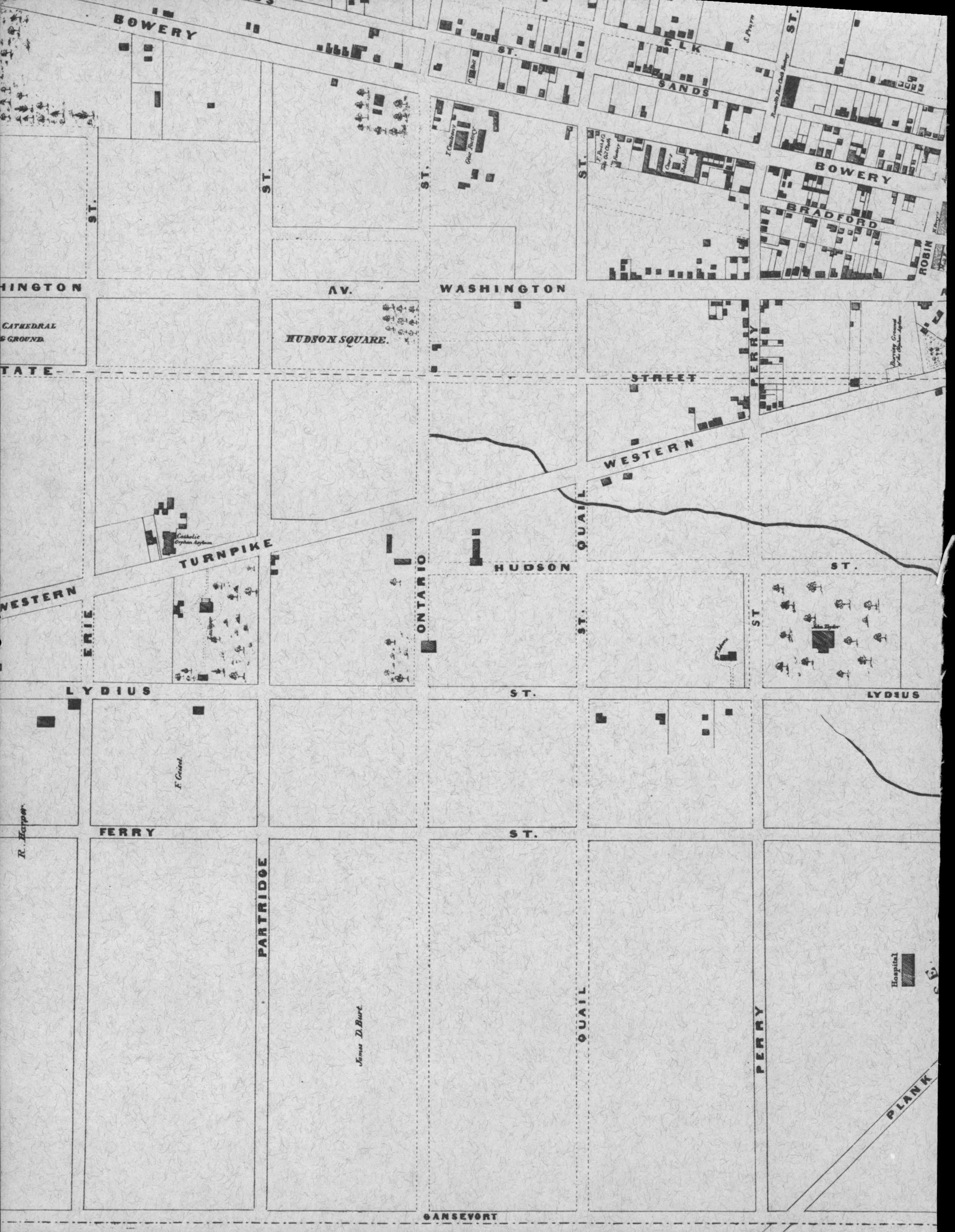

BOWERY
ELK
ST.
SANDS
BOWERY
BRADFORD
ROBIN
ST.
WASHINGTON
AV.
WASHINGTON
CATHEDRAL
GROUND
HUDSON SQUARE.
STATE
STREET
PERRY
WESTERN
TURNPIKE
WESTERN
Catholic Orphan Asylum
QUAIL
ONTARIO
HUDSON
ST.
ERIE
John Taylor
LYDIUS
ST.
LYDIUS
F. Geisel
R. Harper
FERRY
ST.
PARTRIDGE
James D. Burt
QUAIL
PERRY
Hospital
PLANK
GANSEVORT